Capital's Food Regime

Studies in Critical Social Sciences Book Series

Haymarket Books is proud to be working with Brill Academic Publishers (www.brill.nl) to republish the *Studies in Critical Social Sciences* book series in paperback editions. This peer-reviewed book series offers insights into our current reality by exploring the content and consequences of power relationships under capitalism, and by considering the spaces of opposition and resistance to these changes that have been defining our new age. Our full catalog of *SCSS* volumes can be viewed at https://www.haymarketbooks.org/series_collections/4-studies-in-critical-social-sciences.

Series Editor
David Fasenfest (York University)

New Scholarship in Political Economy Book Series

Series Editors
David Fasenfest (York University)
Alfredo Saad-Filho (Queen's University, Belfast)

Editorial Board
Kevin B. Anderson (University of California, Santa Barbara)
Tom Brass (formerly of SPS, University of Cambridge)
Raju Das (York University)
Ben Fine ((emeritus) SOAS University of London)
Jayati Ghosh (Jawaharlal Nehru University)
Elizabeth Hill (University of Sydney)
Dan Krier (Iowa State University)
Lauren Langman (Loyola University Chicago)
Valentine Moghadam (Northeastern University)
David N. Smith (University of Kansas)
Susanne Soederberg (Queen's University)
Aylin Topal (Middle East Technical University)
Fiona Tregenna (University of Johannesburg)
Matt Vidal (Loughborough University London)
Michelle Williams (University of the Witwatersrand)

Capital's Food Regime

Class Struggle, the State and Corporate Agriculture in India

Jostein Jakobsen

Haymarket Books
Chicago, IL

First published in 2024 by Brill Academic Publishers, The Netherlands
© 2024 Koninklijke Brill NV, Leiden, The Netherlands

Published in paperback in 2025 by
Haymarket Books
P.O. Box 180165
Chicago, IL 60618
773-583-7884
www.haymarketbooks.org

ISBN: 979-8-88890-569-2

Distributed to the trade in the US through Consortium Book Sales and Distribution (www.cbsd.com) and internationally through Ingram Publisher Services International (www.ingramcontent.com).

This book was published with the generous support of Lannan Foundation, Wallace Action Fund, and the Marguerite Casey Foundation.

Special discounts are available for bulk purchases by organizations and institutions. Please call 773-583-7884 or email info@haymarketbooks.org for more information.

Cover design by Jamie Kerry and Ragina Johnson.

Printed in the United States.

Library of Congress Cataloging-in-Publication data is available.

Contents

Acknowledgements VII
List of Figures, Tables and Maps IX

1 **Introduction** 1
   1   Downscaling Food Regime Analysis 4
   2   Beyond Reifications 7
   3   The Structure of the Book 11

2 **The Travels and Travails of the Global Food Regime** 14
   1   The Emergence of Food Regime Analysis 15
   2   Established Food Regime Periodisation 16
   3   Debating the Third Food Regime 23
   4   Beyond the Third Food Regime? 29
   5   Steps towards the 'Concrete' 34
   6   Conclusion 40

3 **Agrarian Change in Postcolonial India** 43
   1   The 'Resurrection' of Agrarian Scholarship 44
   2   Beyond 'cul-de-sac': Agrarian Questions and Transitions 47
   3   India's Integral State 51
   4   Neoliberalising the Indian State 56
   5   Conclusion 60

4 **Crisis, Counter-Movements, Class Analysis** 62
   1   Food Regime Crisis 64
   2   Enter Polanyi 66
   3   India's Agrarian Crisis 68
   4   Towards a Peasant Counter-Movement? 75
       4.1 *The 2020–21 Farm Law Agitations in Context* 80
   5   Conclusion 83

5 **Neoliberalisation, the State and the Case of Right-to-Food** 85
   1   Challenging 'Progressive' State Action in the Global Food Regime 87
   2   The State and Neoliberalism in Food Regime Analysis 89
   3   The Contradictions of the Neoliberalising State in India 93
   4   The Right-to-Food in India 96
       4.1 *Short-term Neoliberalisation* 97

        4.2   *Longer-term Neoliberalisation*   102
    5   The 'Long' Green Revolution, Crises and Commodity Frontiers   107
    6   Conclusion   109

6 **The Hybrid Maize Frontier**   111
    1   Hybrid Maize in the Global Food Regime   113
    2   Commodity Frontiers   115
    3   Methods and Field Site   120
    4   The Hybrid Maize Frontier Seen 'from Above'   128
        4.1   *The Maize Frontier in Karnataka*   134
    5   The Hybrid Maize Frontier Seen 'from Below'   136
        5.1   *Local Markets and Dealers in Hybrid Maize*   137
        5.2   *The Making of the Boom*   141
        5.3   *The Rainfed Dystopia and Classes of Labour*   142
        5.4   *Maize Materiality*   147
        5.5   *The Multiple Use-Values of Maize*   149
    6   Conclusion   155

7 **Concluding Reflections**   158
    1   The Contributions of this Book   161

   References   167
   Index   204

Acknowledgements

Many people have contributed to this book in direct and indirect ways. To everyone I know and have known in India over many years of travels: the time we have spent together, the rich experiences we have shared, and all the things you have taught me about your country have been indispensable in shaping everything I may claim to have understood. There are so many of you that I do not even know how to start. Most immediately involved in the research project leading up to this book, I would like to thank Y. D. Imran Khan, my dear friend and collaborator. Through your help and persistence, I was fortunate enough to get to know people in the village I have called 'Mekkenur' in Karnataka. To the people in 'Mekkenur': Your generosity has been invaluable. A. R. Vasavi also unfailingly supported me and facilitated my access into the field, both opening doors for me and providing me with intellectual inspiration. Faculty, staff and PhD candidates at Institute for Social and Economic Change in Bengaluru helped me in initial phases in crucial ways, and I made many friends in the process, some of whom, including Asheesh Navneet, I continue to have regular conversation with concerning agrarian matters in India. Acknowledging my web of relations in India would not be complete, however, without also mentioning key individuals who inspired research in India many years ago – Pamela Price and Arild Engelsen Ruud deserve guru-like veneration for this.

At the Centre for Development and the Environment (SUM) at the University of Oslo, I would especially like to thank Kenneth Bo Nielsen and Desmond McNeill, whose able supervision throughout the PhD project that is the foundation for the present book has been a source of constant inspiration, creativity and (when necessary) discipline. Drafts were also presented and discussed both at "SUM Forum" receiving helpful feedback and at SUM Research School. My research was carried out as part of the "Rural Transformations" research group under the uniquely inspiring, generous leadership of Mariel Aguilar-Støen. Arve Hansen also deserves special mention for collaborating with me on our increasingly ambitious 'meatification project', insights from which have been integrated in the present book.

Outside of SUM, I have benefitted from presentations and discussions at various conferences and panels, while parts of the book are also based on papers that were published in peer reviewed journals. I am grateful to everyone who has been involved in providing constructive – sometimes ruthlessly so – feedback at various stages, fulfilling the strenuous and largely unpaid labour that academia is too full of and without which everything falls apart. Moreover, my thinking about this writing project has benefitted especially from stellar inputs and comradely discussions with Mads Barbesgaard, Jonathan Pattenden, Ola Westengen, and Alexander Dunlap.

Special thanks also go to Jens Lerche, Nikita Sud, and Kristian Stokke for extremely insightful and challenging commentary on the PhD dissertation, on the basis of which this book has been written. Your inputs were indispensable to taking the project further into a book manuscript, and for that I am enormously grateful.

Lastly, I am grateful to David Fasenfest and Brill for competent editorial guidance on this book project, something that cannot possibly be underestimated.

Without wanting to sound overly sentimental, family is everything. I would like to thank my parents, Jorunn Jakobsen and Kristian Evensen, for always believing in me. To Ingfrid, Embla and Jo – the three of you mean the world to me. Without your endless care, none of the work over the years that has gone into this book would have been possible.

Figures, Tables and Maps

Figures

1	Number of operational holdings as per different agricultural censuses	73
2	Maize area harvested, all-India (hectares)	115
3	Maize production total, all-India (tonnes)	116
4	Chicken meat production in India (tonnes)	132
5	Agro-shop in Hanur showcasing hybrid maize seeds	138
6	Cows grazing on maize straw in Mekkenur	152
7	Working in the castor 'forest'/maize field	155

Tables

1	Input use in Indian agriculture, 1971–2011	105
2	Number and area of landholding by size group, Kollegal taluk	126
3	Landholdings of respondents in Mekkenur	128
4	Major crops in Karnataka, decadal change (area in lakh hectares)	135

Maps

1	Map of Chamarajanagar district	122
2	Map of broader field area	125

CHAPTER 1

Introduction

In November 2020 and following weeks, hundreds of thousands of Indian farmers marched by foot and with tractors upon the capital New Delhi. The majority hailing from neighboring states such as Punjab and Haryana, known as the country's key areas of intensive agricultural production, the farmers were protesting the recently announced bills directly affecting Indian agriculture. Prime Minister Narendra Modi held the bills to transform Indian agriculture – to the benefit of the country's farmers. The bills sought to liberalise key aspects of the country's agricultural legislation, providing new avenues for private capital, and the abolishment of long-established protectionist measures in pricing and marketing mechanisms. Presented as 'empowering' for farmers vis-à-vis 'middlemen' and others that feed upon their poverty, the bills were conceived of by Modi as part of his government's overall efforts towards raising the incomes and living standards of the country's farming population. However, the immediate response among farmers' organizations across the country showed massive dismay, militant opposition and fear that the proposed laws would undermine farmers' security while enabling unfettered access for corporate capital. Rapidly thereafter, farmers' organisations, trade unions, and oppositions organised a *Bharat bandh* – a national protest lockdown – and blocked national highways and railway lines. As convoys of farmers gathered upon the capital city, they were met with tear gas, water cannons and police batons. Blocking their entrance to central city space, farmers lay siege to main highways, establishing makeshift camps of tents surrounding parts of Delhi. These camps, and the protesting farmers, remained in place for over a year, in what came to be the singularly most extensive wave of protests, and social mobilisation, among the country's farmers in several decades. Met with sustained international attention as well as the state's gauntlet, the protesting farmers did not yield until late 2021, when prime minister Narendra Modi of the Hindu Nationalist Bharatiya Janata Party announced that the government would abandon the announced legislative change. Celebrated as a major victory for Indian farmers in the face of Modi's authoritarian populist regime, the farmers' protests ended – at least temporarily.

The recent wave of farmers' protests is the most overt and spectacular manifestation of agrarian struggles in contemporary India. Central is the contested liberalisation of the country's agricultural sector – its increased integration in transnational flows of capital. This book suggests that we think about this *problematique* as struggles over India's unevenly unfolding integration in the global food regime. The idea of the global food regime, or of food regime analysis as a distinct scholarly approach, has been a central concern for prominent debates in critical agrarian studies in recent years.[1] Indeed, leading agrarian scholar Henry Bernstein holds that 'it is impossible, or at least fruitless, to consider agrarian change in the world today without engaging with the issues and ideas generated by food regime analysis over the last 25 years' (2016a, 637). Offering a systemic perspective, food regime analysis takes 'food's contribution to capital accumulation' (McMichael 2013a, 41) on a world scale as its point of orientation. In a seminal paper launching the food regime approach in the late 1980s, Harriet Friedmann and Philip McMichael set out 'to explore the role of agriculture in the development of the capitalist world system, and in the trajectory of the state system' (Friedmann and McMichael 1989, 93; see also Friedmann 1987). Or, as aptly summarised by Trent Brown in a recent contribution, the food regime approach seeks to understand 'how systems for the production, distribution and consumption of food are integrated in a manner that both reflects and supports global cycles of capital accumulation' (Brown 2020, 188). Dealing with the integration of agrarian *environments* no less than societal practices, the food regime approach takes a socio-ecologically relational approach to capital's organization of nature (Moore 2015). Undoubtedly, this makes for a hugely ambitious approach to global agrarian transformation; even arguably *the* most ambitious – in its very reach and breadth – in contemporary agrarian studies and related fields.

Indeed, food regime analysis stands out in agrarian scholarship by its emphasis on the global, systemic operations of capital and its relinquishment of otherwise prevalent nationally based focus in favor of tracing world-historical patterns of accumulation. Rooted in the world-historical development of a series of distinct 'food regimes' – often seen as marked by relative stability in the structural unfolding of food relations – arising from the late 19th century onwards, the bulk of scholarship in recent years has come to focus rather on the contemporary conjuncture marked by striking corporate concentration, agro-industrial intensification, monocultural spread and, especially since the mid-2000s, land grabbing-driven dispossession of smallholders and overall de-agrarianization. Moreover, and especially after the 'convergence of crises' – finance, food, climate and energy crises – of 2007–2008, scholars

---

1 In 2016, *Journal of Peasant Studies* hosted a comprehensive debate section featuring Henry Bernstein (2016a), Philip McMichael (2016) and Harriet Friedmann (2016). See also the central position ascribed to food regime analysis in Borras' (2023a) recent overview of critical agrarian studies.

hold the current conjuncture as one where the global agro-food system is increasingly porous and volatile, as agricultural commodities become part of interchangeable and export-oriented global chains of food, feed and fuel (McMichael 2012; Borras et al. 2016). Human diets are undergoing 'meatification' where global value chains are being increasingly tied up with 'the industrial grain-oilseed-livestock complex' (Weis 2013). These complexes interweave world regions in new ways, drawing the conjuncture towards multiple poles of power in the global political economy (Borras, McMichael, and Scoones 2010; Margulis and Porter 2013; Margulis, McKeon, and Borras 2013; Hansen, Jakobsen, and Wethal 2021). In all these aspects, the current conjuncture is inextricable from ecological degradation and crisis, as nature is ravaged in the pursuit of profit (Friedmann 2005; McMichael 2013a; Clapp, Newell, and Brent 2018), with manifold, sometimes unexpected, consequences, including the emergence of zoonotic diseases threatening humanity's future (Akram-Lodhi 2021; Aguilar-Støen and Jakobsen 2023). Most influentially, McMichael has suggested that this is the 'corporate food regime' where corporate capital in the shape of transnational agribusiness companies subordinates states, consumers and producers to an extent never seen before in world history (McMichael 2005, 2013a, 2009b, 2012).

The notion of a corporate food regime marked by antagonisms between corporate capital and the global 'peasantry' has led to prolonged debate, as well as to broader engagement and influence beyond academia by offering terms of analysis that speak to activist concerns in organizations and movements such as La Vía Campesina. Most current scholarship in this field is preoccupied with assessing the defining traits and characteristics of the contemporary food regime, or even disputing whether and to what extent a contemporary food regime does exist. This book seeks to question prevailing terms of debate. '[I]t is striking', Bernstein (2016a, 631) points out, 'that there has been relatively little critique of food regime analysis'.[2] What this book offers is an immanent critique of the food regime approach in the manner of engaging from the 'inside' with internal problems in a body of thought 'in a dual process of appropriating and overcoming' (McNally 2017, 95). This approach sets the book apart from the limited engagements between food regime analysis and India in extant literature, which has rather taken the shape of an 'external' critique. In one of the most elaborate engagements to date, written over a decade ago, Jens Lerche (2013) holds McMichael's view of the corporate food

---

[2] There are, as Bernstein details, examples of influential critiques of the earlier phases of food regime analysis, such as Goodman and Watts (1994).

regime as an example of studies that forsake class analysis and speak in analytically obfuscating terms of the general destitution of undifferentiated 'peasants'. In India, Lerche (2013, 397, 400) concludes, 'the doomsday scenario of [...] McMichael's "corporate food regime" has not materialised. A general pauperization of all agrarian classes has not taken place' although it is clear that 'the agrarian system is skewed against the poorer cultivators'. This book does not contradict Lerche's view per se. Yet, I suggest that the problem at hand is not primarily or necessarily about discrepancies between empirical reality and theoretical construct; rather, we need to rethink more fundamentally the food regime approach as such.

This book offers two intertwined contributions towards such rethinking, in the spirit of immanent critique. First, the book will argue for the need to *downscale* food regime analysis beyond its hitherto prevailing fixation on the 'global', which, as I will argue shortly, fails to provide the necessary analytical tools for more fully accounting for historical-geographically specific patterns of agrarian change. This book's focus on India provides a rare, book-length attempt at precisely such downscaling. Second, and relatedly, to enable such a downscaling in a manner that simultaneously allows us to escape prevailing terms of debate that tends towards reified assessments of the defining features of 'the' global food regime writ large, this book will argue for embedding the food regime approach in a robust Marxist value-theoretical perspective. The remainder of this introductory chapter presents these two interlinked key contributions in more detail.

1 Downscaling Food Regime Analysis

The food regime analysis eschews otherwise prevalent tendencies to approach capitalist development through an emphasis on the nation-state, or dynamics therein, foregrounding instead the global scale of agro-food transformations. However, recent critique has emphasised that this focus has entailed a strong macro-oriented bias, calling for 'downscaling' the approach to open for more fine-grained empirical analysis. Gerardo Otero, for example, calls for

> a food regime analysis with suitable theoretical mediations about class structures and states; methodological sophistication with units of analysis below the world-system, including world regions and nation states; and political sensitivity toward the subordinate classes as a whole, not merely the peasantry.
>
> OTERO 2016, 303

Enquiries that take regional, national or local scales as their starting points for engaging with these debates are hitherto relatively few, and book-length contributions even rarer. Food regime analysis as a field has, overall, remained oriented towards theorising 'from above' – only in the last few years also involving more empirical and sometimes fieldwork-based orientations, yet insufficiently carried out in systematic studies so far. In dialogue with recent and ongoing attempts at 'grounding' food regime analysis in more fine-grained empirical research, while drawing on several years of researching agrarian change in India, this book seeks to contribute empirical substance to such an endeavor. India has been curiously absent from most of the debate surrounding food regime analysis, constituting an important gap covered by this book (for rare recent exceptions, which I will return to later in the book, see Brown 2020, 2018; Tirmizey 2023). India is largely omitted, it is worth stressing, despite being a key part of the so-called BRICS countries that are increasingly viewed as crucial in shifting the vector of the global food regime towards 'multipolarity' or 'polycentrism' (McMichael 2013a; McKay, Hall, and Liu 2016; Cousins et al. 2018; de LT Oliveira and McKay 2021).[3]

Drawing on Marx's famous formulation, I conceive of this endeavor as the pursuit of concrete analysis: 'The concrete', Marx (1993b, 101) writes in the famous methodological section of the *Grundrisse*, 'is concrete because it is the concentration of many determinations, hence unity of the diverse'. Speaking to this crucial dialectical point in Marx's critique of political economy, Farshad Araghi (2003) more than twenty years ago provided what I take to be a hugely important, yet still underappreciated, articulation of food regimes as 'the political face of world historical value relations' (Araghi 2003, 51). In this articulation, Araghi (2003, 49) emphasizes that 'global value relations' perceived as a dialectically 'deep' concept 'should not be hypostazised and conflated with reality', going on to say that '[p]recisely because deep concepts are not concrete, however, they must be historically concretised' to reveal the unity of the diverse. The 'descending' movement in downscaling food regime analysis through an emphasis on global value relations is thus by no means intended a localising effort, but rather one that strives towards dialectically embedding social realities in specific circumstances in the world-systemic trajectory of capital's valorization process. As such, I take the food regime approach as vital to 'the unearthing of systemic logics that underlie the workings of capitalism', which, as Mezzadra and Neilson (2019, 133) puts it, 'in the present is a crucial

---

3 'BRICS' being a group acronym for the major 'emerging economies' Brazil, Russia, India, China and South Africa, and, recently, a handful of additional new entrant countries.

task', continuing, in a wording with which I fully agree, in being 'convinced that such logics exist and that it is worthwhile not only to conceptually define them but also to empirically map the variable geometry and geographies of their steady expansion'.

Existing calls for downscaling have, however, a deficiency insofar as they rely, as arguably can be seen in Otero's formulation quoted above, on conceptualising the food regime as a 'structure' of sorts vis-à-vis empirical cases. In this book, I seek to challenge such dichotomous views by engaging with the subterranean streams of Marxism that theorizes the *value-form* and focuses on the 'modes of existence' of capital (for an overview, see e.g. Pitts 2019). This stream of thought has hitherto largely neglected within agrarian studies and associated fields, yet, as Martín Arboleda (2020a) argues in a recent trailblasing contribution, offering great potential for disruptive analysis. Relating this approach to the issue of seeing food regimes as 'structures', a more fruitful approach is to foreground *class struggle*, something I suggest can be congruent with Araghi's conceptualisation above emphasising value relations. 'The problematic issue of the relation between structure and struggle is the central question', writes Werner Bonefeld, 'for any attempt to understand capitalism'. On this basis, Bonefeld continues, 'structures should be seen as a mode of existence of class antagonism and hence a result and premise of class struggle' (Bonefeld 1992, 93). So, in 'grounding' the food regime in fine-grained empirical analysis, the approach of this book simultaneously seeks to break the 'structuralist' bent of food regime scholarship in favor of the dynamics of class struggle, drawing on an underlying 'commitment to an empirical method of inquiry – albeit, importantly, not an empiricist one – in which purportedly explanatory statements in the end have to be concretised, historically, as descriptions of the actions of "real, living individuals"' (Sayer 1987, 147).

This suggested emphasis on class struggle ties up with another important aspect of recent debates surrounding food regime analysis. Whereas McMichael's influential account focuses on the potential for the 'peasantry' to confront the global food regime through organizations and movements such as Vía Campesina, other scholars, prominently Bernstein, have critiqued the lack of class analysis found in this approach. Bernstein thus counters the notion of the peasantry with that of 'classes of labour' to recognise the differentiated class and labour dynamics of people subjugated to capital in today's world of farming and beyond, marked by combinations of livelihoods (Bernstein 2016a; see also Bernstein 2014, 2015). This book leans towards Bernstein's position, and takes class struggle as the central issue for understanding not only 'sociological classes' but the capitalist class relation as such (Gunn 1987), something I will discuss at length in terms of struggles over the Indian state, taking the state as one such central mode of existence of capital, or, more precisely, of the capital relation – which is to say of class struggle (Holloway and Picciotto 1977). It is among the peculiarities of the capitalist state that it assumes the form of 'the only social power that appears able to constitute the unity of society and to realise the democratic aspirations of the working class by bringing social production under democratic control [is the state]' (Clarke 1988, 135). Central to social struggles, the state, in turn, responds to working class assertions 'within the limits of its form as a particular kind of state', as Marx put it (quoted in Clarke ibid.). This involves both repression and concession (Clarke 1988, 141), which in food regime terms has been mostly focused on repression in the prevalent focus on accumulation by dispossession, whereas my focus in this book is mostly on concession.

Much writing in the food regime vein – and beyond it in critical scholarship on agri-food – tends to formulate an implicitly dualist worldview comprised of exploitation and degradation on the one hand and hopeful mobilisation surrounding unifying movements of food sovereignty or similar on the other. The class struggle approach taken in this book presumes no such unifying tendency – neither in actuality nor in potentiality. Under the capitalist mode of production, writes Marx, '*unity* appears as accidental, *separation* as normal' (Marx 1963, 409). The normalcy of separation comes forcefully across among the differentiated classes of labour in the Indian countryside, posing serious problems for them to unite in struggles against capital, problems that cannot be solved, in my view, a priori by imposing a hopeful category such as 'food sovereignty' or similar, but must be struggled through and through by proletarians in their own lives. If there is to be a 'real movement which abolishes the present state of things' (Marx and Engels 1974), whereby '[t]he expropriators are expropriated' (Marx 1976, 929), it has to arise from such struggles – without guarantees.

2   Beyond Reifications

Food regime scholarship, I argue, is currently at an impasse, in which its emphasis on specific traits – is 'the' food regime 'neoliberal'? Is it corporate'? – risks reifying its subject of study at the level of surface level phenomena. Instead of a reified notion of 'the' food regime, what I seek to do in this book, as already indicated, is suggest an alternative approach rooted in thinking about the value-form. Ambitious and potentially of wide-ranging implications, what this book can offer is not much more than providing some initial stepping-stones towards the development of such an alternative approach to food regime analysis.

Crucially, such a theoretical turn towards the value-form may enable an approach that both takes the properly *global* content of capital seriously while at the same time approaching capital in the *forms* it takes. Drawing on Marx's emphasis on the 'modes of existence' constituting capital as the antagonistic class relation, this approach foregrounds how 'something or other exists only in and through the form(s) it takes' (Bonefeld, Gunn, and Psychopedis 1992, XV). In taking this direction, however, the book seeks to steer clear of the tendency that is arguably found in the value-form tradition of analysis of foregrounding capital-logic to the detriment of grappling with the messy realities of actually existing *politics*. Even such a pathbreaking book as Arboleda's *Planetary Mine: Territories of Extraction under Late Capitalism* (2020a), which pioneers the integration of value-form thinking into questions at the heart of studies of agrarian transformation in the 21st century, remains puzzlingly thin on situated political dynamics in particular places. Capital is squarely not 'some mystical external force' (Harvey 2006, 81) apart from social reality, as the class struggle focused perspective also reiterates.[4] The sustained attention to socio-political and historical specificity in the Indian case in this book seeks to overcome such a limitation. In so doing, the book seeks disaggregation of central aspects of the capital relation, including, that is, specific *capitals*, thus departing from the hitherto prevailing food regime emphasis on 'Capital in general'. Towards this end, the book mobilises conceptual insights in the tradition of Antonio Gramsci, stressing the unfinished, processual nature of hegemonies and the political struggles surrounding these. Relatedly, the book draws on a conjunctural approach to analysis, striving to capture 'the concrete' in an open-ended yet rigorous way.

To reconceptualise food regimes, with Araghi, as the political face of global value relations, we need to question what I find to be a rather sterile and inadequate periodising thrust of much current debate. I suggest it is unfortunate that food regime analysis has come to operate with a relatively idiosyncratic sequence of distinct regimes that lack proper coordination with the overall systemic character of global capitalism.[5] Especially, in debating the current

---

4 Elaborating on these tensions between a sort of transcendent abstraction of capital's agency and the insistence on the centrality of class struggle in parts of these writings is beyond the purview of this book, potentially even contra-productive for the purpose of more empirically oriented research than the relatively philosophically derived value-form writings. For interesting reflections on these tensions, see Bonefeld (2004).
5 I am grateful to Jens Lerche for having pushed me towards this line of thinking at a crucial moment.

food regime, and the search for stabilising or dominant traits defining the associated period, largely missing from the conversation is the overall character of global capitalism in the period since the early 1970s. This links to an important point, already hinted at above, in the sequence of relative 'stability' (regime) and 'instability' (crisis) portrayed in the food regime literature. As I will return to later in the book, the dominant periodization portrayed in the literature, in brief terms, sweeps from the first food regime between 1870 and 1914 that was characterised by the hegemony of the British Empire; to the second food regime between 1945 and 1973 characterised by US hegemony; and onwards, from the 1980s, to a third, corporate food regime that scholars see as more or less incipient, more or less consolidated at present. As food regime analysis, in its early iterations, was drawing explicitly on the regulation school approach to 'regimes of accumulation' and their institutional scaffolding (Friedmann 2009a), the periodising device shares many of the problems of the regulation school. Although McMichael has distanced himself from the initial regulation school influence, and other authors within the food regime approach rarely draw explicitly on this 'heritage', there are still problems that linger.

It is worth recapitulating in some detail Araghi's critique of food regime analysis to bring out more fully what I am driving at here (Araghi 2003; see also Araghi 2012). Araghi criticizes food regime writings in holding that '[t]he problem with Friedmann and McMichael's account of the food regime is that their excellent world historical analysis of the relationship between food and imperialism and of food regimes as *political* regimes of global value relations are juxtaposed with theoretical concepts borrowed from the regulation school' (Araghi 2003, 50). This juxtaposition, Araghi further argues, had, among other things, as the rather unfortunate effect that it contributed towards blurring key distinctions between what Araghi calls 'food regimes of capital' and 'the postwar food order'. In Araghi's alternative conceptualisation, there is no postwar 'second' food regime, as the 1945–1973 phase should rather be seen as an exceptional phase in the history of the capitalist mode of production marked by anomalous degrees of national regulation, holding capital's food regime at bay. Food regimes of capital, moreover, came in first liberal and then neoliberal forms. This is, I think, a useful way of approach that incorporates the approach more deeply within the broader purview of global capitalism and not a more idiosyncratic periodization – and that, this book will demonstrate, applies well to uneven agrarian change in postcolonial India.

To put the argument in even sharper terms, I would be inclined to suggest that the food regime scholarship's emphasis on periodization risks rendering it unable to properly grasp the trajectory of global capitalism since the end of the exceptional phase ending in the early 1970s. While largely unacknowledged in the food regime literature, the exceptional phase was the period of what Robert Brenner (2006) calls the 'long boom' of global capitalism, driven significantly by profitability in manufacturing. Since the late 1960s, and unambiguously so since 1973, Brenner argues, the long boom was followed by the 'long downturn' of falling profitability in manufacturing, leading to prolonged stagnation across capitalist sectors. Starting in the advanced capitalist economies in the West, this process of stagnation and deindustrialisation has come to characterize global capitalism as a whole, including eventually, in recent years, so-called emerging economies such as China and India (Benanav 2020). Since 2011 in particular, economic slowdown and stagnation has characterised the Indian economy, across agrarian and non-agrarian sectors (Kothakapa and Sirohi 2023). While Modi's rhetorical emphasis on private sector growth and his propaganda of economic growth through the imagery of 'Make in India' has attracted public attention worldwide, in reality economic deceleration has proceeded apace, leading to severe crisis-conditions even before the disastrous handling of the COVID-19 pandemic (Nilsen 2022), although simultaneously seeing accelerating corporate concentration through intimate capital-state relations (Jakobsen and Nielsen 2024).

During the long downturn of deindustrialisation, the demand for labour, as Aaron Benanav (2020) argues, has drastically decreased. World agriculture has in no way has been able to meet such demand, leading to the accumulation of vast 'relative surplus populations' (Marx 1976). The latter's mode of subsistence across much of the world has ended up being partly integrated in slum archipelagos (Davis 2006), yet often, as we will see in India, far from decoupled from agrarian production. Since the onset of the long downturn, then, there has in fact not occurred anything resembling the earlier phase when it comes to mechanisms driving capital accumulation. Falling rates of profit are the order of the day.

Under these conditions, expectations of a new food regime of relative stability in the 1980s to present period – which, in a word, is the premise of most debate surrounding the status of the contemporary food regime – are misleading. What we rather need is to confront the conditions of crisis and stagnation in the global political economy. No doubt a challenging and ambitious research agenda, potentially disrupting existing disciplinary 'silos' such as that surrounding agrarian research, this book only offers initial and modest steps in such a direction. The alternative approach offered in this book thus dispenses with the view of food regimes as 'stable' interrupted by periods of crisis, instead foregrounding, with Simon Clarke, 'not the functional integration but the profoundly contradictory character of the capitalist mode of production' (Clarke 1988, 15). Crisis is internal to the capitalist mode of production; 'it is a part of the normal pattern of capitalist accumulation, the pattern of over-accumulation and crisis that underlies the permanence of the class struggle' (Clarke 1993, 233). 'Crisis', as Werner Bonefeld puts it, 'is a necessary form of capitalist social reproduction' (Bonefeld 2014, 155). Capital's food regime, then, *is always beset with crisis*. Indeed, rather than expecting the current conjuncture to be about the introduction of new forms of stability derived from 'corporate' hegemony, or suchlike, what capital's food regime is centrally about, is the demolition and dismantling of remaining structures and mechanisms from the exceptional post-1945 period keeping capital's rein at bay. In India this dismantling is currently going on at full force under Modi's rule, as the recent farmers' agitations plainly reveal. The dynamics of such dismantling and the possibilities for renewed patterns of capital accumulation amidst crisis will be central to the discussion in this book.

3   The Structure of the Book

The book proceeds as follows. Chapter 2 provides a broad overview of food regime analysis, outlining key analytical lineages and positions, with a particular emphasis on ongoing debates surrounding the contemporary – variously termed 'third', 'corporate' and 'neoliberal' – food regime. In so doing, the chapter points to ways that India has figured in food regime history, pointing also to the increased centrality of BRICS countries within emergent dynamics towards 'multipolarity' at the current conjuncture. The chapter thereby also contributes with an overview of recent debate in food regime literature that significantly updates existing surveys (Bernstein 2016a; Magnan 2012) which were written before the recent proliferation of writings covered in this chapter.[6] After such outline of food regime writings, the chapter proceeds to present some analytical steps towards 'the concrete' that will be pursued further in the ensuing chapters. Taking up in greater detail aspects of the approach that has been suggested in this introductory chapter, these steps include scrutiny of what 'downscaling' implies, moving on to questions of hegemony, the capitalist state and labour, all of which will be important conceptual issues in later chapters.

Chapter 3 then offers an overview of key aspects of agrarian change in postcolonial India, emphasising the 'neoliberal' period since around 1990. This

---

6   There are also more recent surveys such as that of McMichael (2021) that mainly reiterates a specific position rather than cover the variety of writings on the subject.

overview provides necessary context for ensuing discussion in the remainder of the book, especially so for non-specialists on India. It simultaneously covers relevant South Asian Studies scholarship that is relevant to, but has remained disconnected from, the food regime literature, providing something of an avenue for dialogue between these bodies of scholarship. Moreover, in terms of Marx's methodology of moving towards the 'concrete', the historical-geographical specification that is provided in this chapter can be viewed as an empirically informed charting of the subject matter that was covered in overarching terms of greater conceptual abstraction in the previous chapter. Crucially, this includes providing an empirically informed understanding of the actual shape of the trajectory of class struggle and the role of the state therein in the broad history of postcolonial India, in other words a closer examination of the key dynamic of the capitalist class relation is central to the country's integration in capital's food regime that is at the heart of this book.

In Chapter 4, empirical discussion moves further along the project of downscaling towards greater specificity and empirical detail by interrogating India's ongoing agrarian crisis to discuss prevailing views of the dynamics between 'crisis' and 'counter-movements' in food regime analysis. Arguing for the necessity of fine-grained Marxist class-analysis instead of prevailing Polanyian tendencies that fails to differentiate progressive mobilisations from others, and that unhelpfully portrays 'society' in organicist terms, the chapter outlines key fault-lines in agrarian mobilising among India's classes of labour. The analysis moves across the postcolonial period from the initiation of the so-called Green Revolution to the recent farmers' agitations invoked at the opening of the present chapter, offering a distinct food regime analysis of the country's agrarian crisis that locates the latter within geographically broader and temporally longer patterns of accumulation taken as socioecological ensembles of relations. These patterns involve both decline and exhaustion, thus crisis, and the attempted initiation of new rounds of accumulation – in other words, commodity frontier dynamics, that will be revisited in the following two chapters.

Subsequently, Chapter 5 takes up another key conceptual thread in food regime writings that may benefit from scrutiny, namely 'neoliberalism', which the chapter argues has tended to be approached in a relatively one-sided manner. This tendency, the chapter argues, invites more empirically fine-grained and dialectically oriented immanent critique. Taking globally prominent right-to-food legislation in India in the 2010s to the present as its empirical focus, the chapter shows how neoliberalisation can function in contexts seemingly marked by 'progressive' state action, revealing instead some of the mechanisms whereby transnational and national capital seeks to rework spaces of accumulation, to the detriment of classes of labour. Drawing on the conceptualisation of the state, hegemony and class struggle offered in the previous chapters, neoliberalisation, the chapter argues, is centrally concerned with political negotiations over the integration of agro-food sectors in India into capital's food regime. Such negotiations, it is further argued, are intrinsic, not extrinsic to neoliberalisation.

While Chapters 3–5 thus offer analyses largely at the national scale, with exemplifications at sub-national regional scales, Chapter 6 continues the downscaling efforts even further to the ground through a fieldwork-based approach. The chapter focuses on an important, yet hitherto neglected by scholars of agrarian India, commodity frontier for capital accumulation in an otherwise stagnating agrarian economy, namely surrounding hybrid maize cultivation, drawing on empirical research in a remote, and similarly understudied, corner of the southern Indian state of Karnataka. Rather than presuming that such commodity frontier dynamics are shaped 'from above' by the agencies of the global food regime, which is the approach taken in much existent food regime literature, this chapter works towards a more dialectical understanding of the driving mechanisms of food regimes, as it looks in-depth at the class composition, livelihood options and historical trajectory of a specific rural region's turn to hybrid maize cultivation, understood as a form of integration in capital's food regime. In doing so, the chapter operationalises further the suggested emphasis on labour invoked in Chapter 2. Scrutinising, simultaneously, the relational-material qualities of the maize crop and its ramifications vis-à-vis patterns of labouring, the chapter offers a novel approach to what Araghi, as we have seen above, conceptualises as an interpretation of capital's food regime in terms of global value relations.

Lastly, Chapter 7 returns briefly to the recent farmers' agitations to point towards some crucial challenges for counter-hegemonic mobilisation under Modi's authoritarian populist regime. The chapter then offers concluding reflections, summarising the main contributions of the book and seeks to take stock of what this book's immanent critique of food regime analysis can contribute to wider scholarship on agrarian change in India and beyond.

CHAPTER 2

The Travels and Travails of the Global Food Regime

As Philip McMichael puts it, '[t]he "food regime" concept was a product of its time: of declining national regulation and rising "globalisation"' (McMichael 2013a, 1). Yet, since the late 1980s, the concept has indeed 'travelled' near and far, as social science concepts (when successful) tend to do. In his famous discussion of 'travelling theory', Edward Said points to common problems inherent to the expansion and movement of a theory, as 'it risks becoming a theoretical overstatement, a theoretical parody of the situation it was formulated originally to remedy or overcome' (Said 1983: 239 cited in Morton 2010, 330). How, then, can theory travel without becoming rigid? In the words of Adam David Morton:

> The point of theory is to travel; but not in the literal sense. This is a negative mode of applying theory whereby theory loses its critical power and insurrectionary force. An alternative mode of "transgressive theory" offers the potential to connect actively to different locales, sites, situations without becoming over-generalising or transhistorical.
> MORTON 2010, 320

The alternative, critical form of travelling theory 'flames out, or develops away, from its original formulation to restate and reaffirm new tensions and conditions' (Morton 2013, 60). This book seeks to have food regime analysis 'travel' to India in such a spirit. What I seek to do is neither 'applying' (the negative mode in Morton's scheme) nor 'debunking' food regime analysis (the 'external' critique mentioned in Chapter 1). Rather, this book proceeds to offer an *immanent critique* of food regime analysis, which is, as Moishe Postone puts it, 'one undertaken from a standpoint that is immanent to, rather than outside, its object of investigation' (Postone 1993, 21). In this chapter, I suggest steps towards a food regime analysis that can retain its critical power by grounding it in the value-form. To do so, this chapter pays particular attention to questions of scale to pave the way for analysis that is grounded in the 'concrete'.

The first part of this chapter starts by reviewing in some detail food regime analysis' emergence, core traits and subtleties. From there, the chapter proceeds to provide an overview of established periodizations of the sequence of food regimes over world-historical time, while pointing to India-specific dynamics in the two first food regimes. As this book is not a thorough exploration of prior food regimes, but rather focuses on the dynamics of capital's food regime at the current conjuncture, these sections are necessarily brief, yet indispensable to the broader story of this book. The third section of the chapter then pays in-depth attention to controversies and debates surrounding the third food regime, which, as indicated in Chapter 1, is the subject of the main share of debate and controversy in current scholarship. Next, the chapter devotes a section to explore questions that arise from these debates pertaining to the emergence of novel traits in the food regime at present, including the possibility that a new food regime may be in the works, much of which surrounding the role of China and the BRICS in an increasingly 'multipolar' world economy. Having thus covered the main aspects of the food regime literature, the final section of the chapter moves on to argue more pointedly for steps towards the 'concrete' by emphasising the need to question the fixation with the 'global' in the literature, asserting the need for multiscalar analysis in order to grapple with more finely tuned dynamics across scales. Furthermore, this section points to a surprising lack of attention to labour – absolutely central to the approach taken in this book – in existing food regime literature.

1   The Emergence of Food Regime Analysis

First introduced in the late 1980s by Harriet Friedmann and Philip McMichael (1989) as a form of macro-historical sociology, food regime analysis offers a systemic and ambitious approach to studying 'food's contribution to capital accumulation' (McMichael 2013a, 41). Food regime analysis set out to relate changes in world agriculture to the evolution of the state system, the international division of labour, trade patterns, the powerful institutions that regulate and govern these flows of food commodities, and how all this interacts with social movements and contestation (Magnan 2012) as well as environments (Tilzey 2018). A food regime, then, is the specific crystallisation of these dynamics into a world-systemic pattern of accumulation. Relative stability has – particularly in earlier formulations of food regime analysis – been defining, such as in Friedmann's (1993, 30–31) view of a food regime as 'the rule-governed structure of production and consumption on a world scale'. This should not be seen as a rigid or stable form but rather a process that is contradictory, fraught with tensions (McMichael 2009b, 2013a).

The focus on stability is arguably attenuated in more recent articulations, yet it persists in the very periodization of sequences of regime-crisis-regime. The food regime literature portrays a succession of global food regimes from the late 19th century onwards. While conceived as sequential, food regimes do not follow each other linearly but in multi-layered patterns. As McMichael (2013a, 6) puts it: 'While each regime has its institutional profile, it is the case that elements of former regimes carry over into successor regimes, in reformulated fashion'. In terms of periodization, food regimes center on cycles of capital accumulation in combination with the formation and crumbling of legitimising rules, institutions and relationships (Friedmann and McMichael 1989; Friedmann 2005; Magnan 2012; McMichael 2013a). It is not hard to see the influence of regulation school scholarship on these formulations. Otero provides a useful summary:

> A food regime is a temporally specific dynamic in the global political economy of food. It is characterised by particular institutional structures, norms and unwritten rules around agriculture and food that are geographically and historically specific. These dynamics combine to create a qualitatively distinct 'regime' of capital-accumulation trends in agriculture and food, which finds its durability in the international linking of agrifood production and consumption relations in accordance with global capital accumulation trends more broadly. Each food regime is thus grounded in relatively stable (albeit typically unequal) international trade relations.
>
> OTERO 2012, 283

This holistic and relational lens sets the food regime approach apart from much overly production-centric research in agrarian studies, offering, as we will see later, a promising approach for 21st century transformations towards circulation as key to processes of capital accumulation in the wake of logistical transformations of natural resource industries into reorganized transnational supply chains (Arboleda 2020b; Henderson and Ziadah 2023) that are intimately tied to the flow of finance capital (Burch and Lawrence 2009). While the idea of a third food regime, ostensibly taking shape from the 1980s onwards, is contested in the food regime literature and beyond, scholars mostly agree about the classification of the prior regimes. At the risk of oversimplifying complex processes of world-historical change, I will proceed to lay out briefly some of the core features of the first two food regimes.

2 Established Food Regime Periodisation

The most common periodization in the extant literature sees a first food regime – centred on the British Empire – in existence between 1870 and 1914.

Following this, there was a 'transition period' leading to the emergence of a post-WWII second food regime – centred on the US – which then fell apart in the midst of the early 1970s global food and oil crisis (Friedmann and McMichael 1989; Friedmann 1993). The two first food regimes thus appear arranged around singular world hegemons and the structuring of capital accumulation in agriculture in the world economy through these hegemons' hold over international rules and institutions, trade and so on. In other words, central to the idea of a food regime is the 'subjection of international circuits of foodstuffs to a governing market price' (McMichael 2013a, 24). 'Markets' here are not autonomous devices but rather seen, often in a Polanyian vein, embedded in institutional, social and always already political contexts that include state policies (Polanyi 2001 [1944]; Friedmann and McMichael 1989).

The determination of such market price, food regime analysis argues, evinces world-historical patterning. Following Bill Winders et al. (2016, 74), the two first food regimes can be contrasted as follows: 'These food regimes differed regarding two fundamental aspects: the extent and quality of state intervention into the market (such as, tariffs and subsidies), and the direction of trade flows (for example, from colonies to the hegemons)'. Thus, in the first food regime, mercantilist policies of the British Empire shaped the world economy and brought flows of agricultural commodities from peripheries to the Imperial core. In the second food regime, nation states used supply management policies to protect their agricultural sectors. The US also used its dominance in the world economy to structure trade flows, now increasingly from core nations to the peripheries – in particular in grains through US food aid (Friedmann 1993).

The first international food regime emerged in the latter half of the 19th century with the establishment of a world market in agricultural commodities and a global division of labour in agriculture as key ingredients. Intrinsic here were the effects of technological innovation, particularly in forms such as the railway, enabling the unprecedent scale of transport of commodities, including, in the case of India, their transport away from famine-stricken populations (Davis 2002). There were also a whole set of other innovations such as agrochemicals, scientific advances in breeding and the internal combustion engine (Bernstein 2010, 66). Indeed, the first food regime was involved in the establishment of world-systemic chemical fertiliser industries crucial to the later spread of industrialised agriculture and non-agrarian industry more broadly (Dixon 2018).

These monumental shifts, it is widely agreed in food regime literature, centred on the hegemony of the British Empire in the capitalist world-economy. The first food regime thus 'created the first price-governed market in an essential means of life' (Friedmann 2009b, 125), firstly with wheat after the repeal of the Corn Laws in Britain in 1846 (Rioux 2018).[1] While the repeal of the Corn Laws can thus be seen as the instigation of processes eventually culminating in the first food regime, as Rioux (2018) argues, is was not until the 1870s that the international division of labour in agriculture, with its prerequisite in technological innovations in transportation and overall development of the world economy during the 'Age of Capital' (Hobsbawm 2010), gave rise to the first food regime. 'Free trade' organised according to the needs of the Empire was in other words a guiding principle. Central here was the structuring of settler-colonial regions as suppliers of temperate grains and livestock, and tropical regions as suppliers of other commodities, for the metropolitan parts of the British Empire. Organising world agricultures according to the needs of the British Empire, then, the first food regime 'provisioned the growing European proletariat with wage-foods' (Friedmann and McMichael 1989, 94) in a form of 'outsourcing' of food production underwriting wages and thus the rate of capital accumulation (McMichael 2009b).

Given its central role to the British Empire, India was an important component of the first food regime. Anthropologist Akhil Gupta's (1998) influential book *Postcolonial Developments: Agriculture in the Making of Modern India* is one of the few instances of relatively sustained engagement with food regime literature in analysing the historical trajectory of agriculture in colonial and postcolonial India. Yet, while Gupta emphasises that this trajectory cannot be understood without taking the influence of global forces on national dynamics, he largely views the food regime as a 'frame' or 'context' for localised ethnographic research. Key to the restructuring of India's agricultural systems under colonialism, Gupta acknowledges, was the transformation of cropping patterns for promoting export, taking the form of region-wise spatial specialisation on particular crops (Ludden 2005, 4044). This involved, as Utsa Patnaik (1986, 782) points out, that 'the stagnation of the domestic market for foodgrains was a logical consequence of the colonial government's subserving of Indian interests to the requirements of Empire'. This points clearly to the role of imperialism in the first food regime, something that has been recently emphasised in a contribution looking specifically at India, challenging the earlier formulations' central focus on settler-states over tropical and semi-tropical colonies (Tirmizey 2023). As Tirmizey elaborates in a stimulating recent revisionist intervention:

---

[1] The Corn Laws between 1815 and 1846 put in place tariffs and duties on food grains that restricted the import of cheap grains, protecting the British domestic market.

> The conceptualisation of the first food regime needs to include tropical colonies of conquest as a necessary component of the system. Doing so requires shifting the temporal and spatial dimensions of the first food regime away from temperate settler colonies and the emergence of a world food staples market to the expansion of export surplus from tropical colonies. Then, the emergence of the first food regime should be better seen with Britain's repeal of the Corn Laws in 1846, which was not the beginning of the region's shift towards a net importer of wheat as this began from the 1790s and accelerated from the 1830s, but was pivotal in being increasingly more reliant on worldwide agricultural production [...] Britain's increasing import dependence on food commodities, fuelled by industrialisation, was financed by appropriating surplus from its tropical colonies.
>
> TIRMIZEY 2023: 4

The flip-side of this form of colonial food provisioning was what Farshad Araghi (2003, 2016) calls 'forced under-consumption' among populations in subordinated parts of the Empire. Mike Davis (2002) documents one of the most grotesque manifestations of this way of organising world agriculture in his study of late-nineteenth century famines in India where several million died. The key role of British colonial capitalism in causing and exacerbating these famines led Davis (2002) to describe them as 'late Victorian holocausts'. The system of agricultural commodity extraction from the colony to the imperial centre continued unhindered by famine conditions, thus exerting strong causal influence on the spread of these famines: 'Grain merchants, in fact, preferred to export a record 6.4 million cwt. of wheat to Europe in 1877–78 rather than relieve starvation in India' (Davis 2002, 31–32). Under the first food regime, argues Friedmann (2005, 237), parts of India such as the wheat growing tracts of Punjab and elsewhere were converted into veritable 'export zones' for the Empire. Broad statements of this sort notwithstanding, 'Punjab's particular place in this global food regime has not been adequately studied' (Jan 2019, 232).

All of this is to say that the first food regime was involved in the industrialisation of world agriculture and the formation of the state system through international institutions of trade and commodity flows. In addition to these world-systemic features, the first food regime also involved expanded and deepened commodity relations within national agricultures as price-governed markets took their hold. In India, Jairus Banaji (1977, 1379) finds evidence from the Deccan region that 'a more tightly integrated market was in the process of emerging' in the late 19th century, involving price-convergences on agricultural commodities. With the more tightly integrated market came also extended state intervention through revenue systems. When this came to converge with the famine crises magnified by the extractive logic of the food regime, the Deccan region came to experience a striking process of proletarianisation of small producers, writes Banaji. The period saw, furthermore, the differentiation of the Deccan's 'peasantry' into more and less successfully accumulating classes. Important for our purposes, what emerged from this was new sections of 'landed classes' that were able to capitalise on the deepening of commodity relations (Banaji 1977). These 'landed classes' would later on turn out to be among the key forces in the countryside that the postcolonial Indian state would turn to for political support (Desai 2016), an issue that I will return to later in this book. More than merely embedding India in a global political economy of agriculture – as conceptualisations of the food regime as a 'structure' might indicate – the first food regime was instrumental in bringing about profound processes of agrarian change in the Indian countryside, transforming the direction of class struggle towards increasingly global value relations.

One important aspect of the first food regime that tends to go less noticed, as Araghi (2003, 52) highlights, is that the global production of value through the first food regime 'was based on the international integration of wage labour and non-wage labour'. In the first food regime, this took the form of 'family farms' being constructed in the settler-states, in particular, dependent on unpaid work. The integration of different forms of labour in the food regime concept has recently been taken up by Alvin Camba (2018) to argue for thinking of the conjuncture of the exploitation of paid work and the appropriation of unpaid work, drawing upon Moore's (2015) world-ecology. Looking at late colonial Philippines in the first food regime, Camba argues for seeing the extraction of food commodities from the Philippines as intrinsically linked to the capitalist state's ability to appropriate unpaid labour from rural producers, a conceptual issue that I will return to in Chapter 6.

The first food regime, in prevailing accounts, is seen to have collapsed around the First World War amidst cascading economic crises, initiating a period of instability, ecological crisis in the 'dust bowl' of North America and, overall, transition that eventually led to the emergence of a second food regime after the end of World War II (McMichael 2013a). As sketched out in Chapter 1, Araghi's (2003) revisionist account questions the conceptual underpinnings of the notion of a second food regime, preferring to approach this period as an exceptional phase in which the reign of capital's food regime was kept at bay. But other accounts have largely avoided engaging with Araghi's challenge on this point. In prevailing analyses, the role of the US is central to the second food regime. With the introduction of US commodity programmes – price supports, public purchases, etc. – in response to the preceding instabilities came a new model for state-supported agriculture unlike the free-trade oriented model of the first food regime. Initiated in the US, the 'new pattern of intensely national regulation' (Friedmann 1993, 32) was taken up in variegated ways across the Euro-American world (see e.g. Magnan 2016; Winders 2009). The US commodity programmes led to huge surpluses in production, to be dispersed through the crucial novel instrument of 'food aid', first to the recovering European states and later to the 'Third World'. Not only guided by US agrarian policy, food aid was part and parcel of anti-communist foreign policy (Perkins 1997; Cullather 2010). Starting in the 1950s, this new approach was encapsulated in the US Public Law 480, known to posterity simply as PL 480. This scheme 'grew rapidly into the principal mechanism of non-military aid, expanding by 1958 to more than $6 billion with the largest shipments, principally wheat and cotton, going to India' (Cullather 2010, 142).

Again, India had a key role in the establishment of central food regime regulations and mechanisms. Yet, whereas food aid brought food import dependencies in many countries in the South – constituting a key trend in the second food regime – India appears as an 'exception' to this trend in its emergent self-sufficiency in grains (Friedmann 2009a). While self-sufficiency was intimately linked to the so-called Green Revolution in the 1960s and 1970s, nation-building in independent India was from the outset centrally concerned with food and famine (Siegel 2018). The Green Revolution following PL 480 was crucial to the renewed integration of countries across the Global South in the second food regime (Patel 2013). Indeed, the package of agricultural industrialisation, focused primarily on wheat and later rice, that became known as the Green Revolution was a crucial component of the establishment of US hegemony in the second food regime (Friedmann 1992) through 'support of domestic ruling classes in the name of food security' (McMichael 2013a, 35). A complicated international process that tied Asian counties in particular to US policy, the Green Revolution

> fundamentally changed agrarian economies by: (1) introducing input- and capital-intensive farming methods; (2) replacing agricultural labor with technology, thus moving people out of agricultural sectors while simultaneously creating markets in the industrial economy; (3) institutionalising various elements of the development apparatus through international aid, research collaborations, and trade; and (4) expanding the role of the state in everyday life.
> FLACHS 2016a, 1

In the case of India, the domestic ruling classes came to see the development of high yielding wheat – and later rice – as crucial to national development (Perkins 1997). As the role of agriculture in the postcolonial nation was a question that saw sharply divergent political positions domestically, it is clear that India's compliance with the Green Revolution model – an intrinsic part of the global food regime – was shaped by complex interactions, interests and agendas across scales (Gupta 1998; Frankel 2005; Siegel 2018). As Raj Patel aptly puts it: 'The Green Revolution was itself a moment in struggles around the creation of value, altering the balance of class forces, reconfiguring relations to the means of production, and setting the processes of production and reproduction on a new trajectory' (Patel 2013, 3) While the relative merits and fallouts of these developments have been subject of never-ending debate, it appears justified to hold that agrarian scholars of India found the transformation of agriculture to be 'an attempt by the government to solve the food problem without upsetting existing land relations' (Dasgupta 1977, 373 cited in Patel 2013, 13). India certainly became integrated with transnational agribusiness circuits of capital through the high yielding technologies (Kloppenburg 1988), but agricultural restructuring in accordance with food regime dynamics was simultaneously shaped by domestic political economy and – as the next chapter will argue at some length – the integral state in India. Indeed, by upholding the interests of particular classes – upwardly mobile capitalist farmers in particular – the Green Revolution came to be hegemonic in the Indian landscape of agricultural development (Brown 2018).

Raj Patel (2013) has made an influential argument holding the green revolution as 'long' in its role in capital accumulation over time, by which this particular form of second food regime-initiated transformation of India's agro-food system involved the initiation of new socio-ecological 'cycles of accumulation' (drawing on Giovanni Arrighi). Fundamentally transforming capitalism's place in nature (Moore 2015), new cycles were focused on particular regions of alluvial, irrigated agriculture, shaping while being shaped by both inter-regional and intra-regional inequalities as larger farmers were especially apt at appropriating the new technologies (Gupta 1998, 62).

Corporate concentration at the global level consolidated during the second food regime. Integral to the furthering of industrialisation of agriculture protected by state policy was an international trade regime where the GATT excluded agriculture at US behest (McMichael 2013a, 33). Whereas the first food regime saw the nascent emergence of international agribusiness, this grew formidably and amalgamated with Euro-American agribusiness dominance with the second food regime (Friedmann and McMichael 1989). Processes of depeasantization/de-agrarianization took hold during the second food regime, with massive influxes of rural populations to urban centres across the world, something that only accelerated with the liberalisation of trade regimes from the 1980s onwards (Araghi 1995; Araghi 2000). In important ways, therefore, the contemporary food regime also represents a continuation, albeit in altered shape, of previously established dynamics (McMichael 2013a).

The second food regime is perceived to have collapsed amidst world economic turmoil and crisis in the early 1970s (Friedmann 1993), thus coinciding with the onset of the 'long downturn' in global capitalism – although the implications thereof are vastly under-explored in existing scholarship. This is so to a significant extent, as I indicated in Chapter 1, due to the overall tendency to periodizing 'crisis' and 'relative stability' in ways that disregard how crisis is in fact part and parcel of capital in its normalcy. With this critical objection in mind, we can proceed to look at what the food regime scholarship says about what comes after the second food regime. As indicated several times by now, this is a controversial question.

3   Debating the Third Food Regime[2]

It is not, however, these historical questions that have fueled much of the debate surrounding food regime analysis. What is at stake, academically and politically, in this field is rather how we are to understand the *present* – the global structuring of food and agriculture in the period since the 1980s. This is the period in which the international development of food and agriculture has taken on a new urgency publicly through struggles such as those of Vía Campesina. It is also the period in which environmental degradation has accelerated ensuing from an industrialised, mechanised and increasingly corporate-controlled mode of producing and consuming agricultural goods. The food regime approach distinguishes itself by ambitious, encompassing claims about the present. These claims are, however, disputed within the scholarship, with markedly differing views of the third, contemporary food regime, even disagreements as to whether and to what extent it actually exists. Exemplifying this, a recent contribution asserts that 'the contours of the contemporary food regime remain undefined' (Werner 2019, 1).

---

2   This section draws on Jakobsen, J. (2023). The international development of food and agriculture: global food regimes, environmental change and new configurations of power. In *Handbook on International Development and the Environment* (pp. 170–184). Edward Elgar Publishing.

As indicated, McMichael's (2005, 2009b, 2013a) 'corporate food regime' is the most influential conceptualisation. In the corporate food regime, McMichael argues, there is a worldwide 'broad dispossession of smallholders' fueled by corporate-led expansion and agro-industrial intensification amidst detrimental environmental changes (McMichael 2013a, 45). Ecological ramifications of the corporate food regime include, inter alia, the expansion of monocultures into new parts of the tropics amidst deforestation, land degradation and soil exhaustion; the substitution of genetic diversity for genetically patented seeds; the conversion of multifunctional agrarian livelihoods into elements of the "industrial grain-oilseed-livestock complex" (Weis 2013) fueling rapidly rising meat consumption and, unintentionally, causing socio-ecological ruptures unleashing zoonotic diseases (Aguilar-Støen and Jakobsen 2023; Akram-Lodhi 2021; Wallace 2016).

Driving the corporate food regime, in McMichael's view, is corporate agribusiness. There is a common perception among food regime authors that the period after the collapse of the second food regime has seen transnational corporations emerging as 'the major agents attempting to regulate agrofood conditions' (Friedmann 1993, 52). A key argument in the food regime literature has been in pointing to regulations that transcend the scale of the nation states. 'Reflecting the organizational logic of global capitalism', Bill Pritchard (2009, 305) writes, 'food regime theorists generally agree that any ultimate successor to the second food regime will arise in governance arrangements that transcend above and beyond the traditional domains of state sovereignty'. Around the turn of the millennium, food regime analysts discussed the World Trade Organization (WTO) as a potential successor (McMichael 2000). This scenario arguably never actualised, and the WTO has remained a case of 'hegemonic contestation in the world food system' (Pritchard 2009, 306). Pritchard argues that unceasing contestation around the WTO is evidence of its inability to establish a hegemonic institutional order, unlike the prior food regimes. While arguably not becoming the hegemonic institutional node of a new food regime, the WTO and its Agreements on Agriculture can be seen as signaling a shift from a regime governed by national interests and institutions towards privatization and the 'freeing' of markets; in other words, the global shift towards neoliberalism (Weis 2007).

McMichael takes a strong view of these dynamics, arguing that the corporate food regime embodies the ways that corporate capital has become hegemonic in global capitalism through the subjugation of states and with the backing of international institutions that include the WTO, the World Bank and the IMF (McMichael 2013a). While McMichael (2013a, 44–45) concedes that 'the WTO itself is by no means hegemonic', he sees it as instrumental in consolidating neoliberal principles in world agriculture and thus 'suggests a corporate hegemony insofar as neoliberal doctrine, in elevating "markets" over "states", transforms the latter into explicit servants of the former'. States, in this view, take a subordinate role as they 'accommodate transnational capital' (McMichael 2010, 612).

Meanwhile, other authors focus on the role of intellectual property rights in consolidating the third food regime. As Pechlaner (2012, 244) argues in the context of Latin America: 'The third food regime would indeed seem to be constituted by a state-supported international structure of intellectual property rights that facilitates local-level expropriationism and agricultural production based on biotechnological "packages" produced by a highly concentrated corporate sector'. The massive ongoing mega-mergers and acquisitions in the world of agribusiness, leading to the mentioned structure of pervasive corporate concentration, could not happen without this underlying structure of intellectual property rights (IPES-FOOD 2017).

Although McMichael does argue for a consolidated corporate food regime, this is not with the sense of stability as was the case with the two first food regimes. 'It [the corporate food regime] may not meet the requirements of stability from a state-centered perspective because it expresses a new conjuncture in which states have increasingly privatised' (McMichael 2013a, 45). Instead, McMichael argues for a conceptualisation that stresses fracture and crisis as being at the heart of the contemporary conjuncture. This does not, however, solve the problem introduced in Chapter 1 of crisis/stability dynamics as key to dominant periodization, as we will see below in ongoing attempts at articulating an emergent 'fourth' food regime. Rather, McMichael's emphasis on crisis is largely empirical: Emphasised in the crisis-aspect of the contemporary food regime is how global capital presently is destabilising livelihoods and environments. This involves, in McMichael's view, a 'broad dispossession of smallholders' (McMichael 2013a, 45), leading to the issue of 'peasantries'.

The food regime approach, as Luigi Russi (2013, 33–34) points out, perceives the development of world agriculture as revolving around struggles between 'peasant' agriculture centered on 'more-than-economic' relationships and their overtaking by capitalist agriculture geared exclusively towards economic goals. The sequence of food regimes signals the progressive 'encroachment' of the latter form of agriculture on a global scale, bringing increased 'fragility' for peasant agriculture (Russi 2013, 35–37). In McMichael's work, this is seen as amounting to a global agrarian crisis of dispossession and destruction of peasant livelihoods. '[C]apital's food regime has generalised an agrarian crisis of massive proportions', McMichael (2013a, 19) writes, 'registered now in a growing movement to stabilise the countryside, protect the planet, and advance food sovereignty against new assaults on farming cultures and diversity from "value chains" and land grabbing'. Like innumerable other scholars in agrarian studies, political ecology and beyond, McMichael (2005) draws heavily on David Harvey's (2003) writings in identifying 'accumulation by dispossession' as a central mechanism driving these processes. McMichael (2013a, 130) also concedes roles to states, as he holds these processes as being 'effected by a state-finance capital nexus dedicated to constructing new frontiers of accumulation'. Overall, the corporate food regime appears, in formulations such as these, largely to expand in accordance with dynamics that percolate to actually existing empirical circumstances 'from above' – a form of top-down perspective that triggers the critical calls for multi-scalar rethinking of food regime analysis animating this book.

Opposed to the ravages of global capital as the 'fundamental contradiction' (McMichael 2013a, 60) of the corporate food regime we find a 'growing movement' seen to represent the world's 'peasants', frequently identified as the transnational movement of La Vía Campesina.[3] Going beyond the identification of increasing incidence of 'food riots' across the world – especially since the convergence of crises in 2007/8 (Bush and Martiniello 2017) – we find that McMichael, in Polanyian terms, perceives Via Campesina as representing a 'counter-movement' responding to the crisis tendencies of the present conjuncture, a significant conceptual and empirical issue that I will take up in detail in Chapter 4. McMichael's analysis of agribusiness-peasant dynamics is criticised by Bernstein (2014, 2016a) as representing a form of 'binary' analysis and a problematic 'peasant turn' that universalises and homogenises rural populations and their politics and, consequently, is unhelpful to understanding actually existing agrarian change. Whereas McMichael strongly presses the need to align with movements like Via Campesina and their usage of the term 'peasants' as a counterhegemonic force, Bernstein (2016b, 83) has for a long time argued in favour of 'dispensing with the term 'peasant' itself and its applications to the contemporary worlds of capitalism'. Instead of 'peasants', Bernstein favours thinking in terms of 'petty commodity producers' or 'classes of labour':

> Classes of labour comprise "the growing numbers ... who now depend – directly *and indirectly* – on the sale of their labour power for their own daily reproduction" (Panitch and Leys 2001, IX). And the term "fragmentation"

---

3 For an introduction to La Vía Campesina – meaning 'the peasant way' – see Desmarais (2007) or Edelman and Borras (2016) for broader critical contextualisation of transnational agrarian movements.

encapsulates the effects of how classes of labour in global capitalism, and especially in the "South," pursue their reproduction, that is, through insecure and oppressive – and in many places increasingly scarce – wage employment, often *combined with* a range of likewise precarious small-scale farming and insecure "informal sector" ("survival") activity, subject to its own forms of differentiation and oppression along intersecting lines of class, gender, generation, caste, and ethnicity. In short, most have to pursue their means of livelihood/reproduction across different sites of the social division of labour: urban and rural, agricultural and non-agriculture, wage employment and self-employment.

BERNSTEIN 2006, 455

The notion of classes of labour will be central to analyses throughout this book. Drawing on important contributions by India-scholars such as Lerche (2010), Pattenden (2016b,2018a), Mezzadri and Fan (2018) and Noy (2023) there is significant evidence that dynamics of accumulation and exploitation in rural India can be made sense of in terms of classes of labour opposed to dominant classes. The labouring and farming majority in the Indian countryside engages in shifting and mixed livelihoods of great fragmentation, as has been acknowledged for quite some time. For the last 15 years – since the 2003 round of the National Sample Survey Organisation (NSSO) – we have known that smallholders have difficulties reproducing their households economically: 'The average income for farmers operating less than four hectares of land was shown by the 2003 NSSO data to be negative' (Shah and Harriss-White 2011, 15). Consequently, Shah and Harriss-White (2011, 15) wrote already more than a decade ago, '[m]ultiple livelihood options are necessary for the reproduction of rural households'. Complex employment patterns follow from this: daily wage agricultural labour, farming on one's own land, rural-based small-scale manufacturing and myriad other agrarian practices all intermix with rising levels of labour migration (see Shah et al. 2018). Circular labour migration is endemic, providing employment, at least during parts of the year, to as much as 100 million people according to a recent government estimate (India 2017, 267). The booming construction industry employs the largest share of the agricultural workforce (Srivastava 2012) while classes of labour also engage widely in various forms of petty commodity production, which is, as Harriss-White (2012, 117) argues, 'the most common form of production' in contemporary India.

This disaggregation of rural producers into classes of labour should, however, be accompanied by an equally rigorous disaggregation of *classes of capital*. As agrarian political economists Bernstein (2010), Campling (2021) and Baglioni (2015) have argued, the notion of 'classes of capital' may be fruitful for exploring the differentiated agencies and positioning of various capitalist actors and fractions. Bernstein (2010, 112) introduces this notion to distinguish and disaggregate 'the interests and strategies of capital in particular activities and sectors and scale from local to regional, national to transnational'. Such an approach, I would argue, can prove a powerful antidote to the reigning tendency in food regime analysis to think of 'Capital in general', illustrated for example in the quite strikingly aggregate notion of 'corporations' at the heart of the 'corporate food regime'. 'Capital in general', as Marx articulates powerfully in *Grundrisse,* remains an analytically limited category insofar as it, seen in isolation from the differentiated modes of existence of capital, it hides from view that '[c]apital exists and can only exist as many capitals, and its self-determination therefore appears as their reciprocal interaction with one another' (Marx 1993b, 414). The need for disaggregation of intra-capital relations and actors within food regime analysis has been taken up to only limited extent so far. The above-mentioned debate surrounding 'peasantry' has been far more prominent in recent scholarship – perhaps, to venture into some speculation, due to its more explicitly political appeal. In the few writings that seek to explode 'Capital in general' to expose differentiations in capitalist strategies and outcomes for capital-capital relations, Joseph Baines (2015) incisively dissects the US ethanol boom to reveal how certain classes of capital benefit on the behalf of others. Such an analytical approach is indispensable to any endeavor at disaggregating the global food regime.

Another line of debate surrounding the contemporary food regime, which this book will return to in more detail over the course of the following chapters, is that of the state. While McMichael's line of argument, as we have seen, largely sidesteps the question of the state, there has been recent debate on how to go further in conceptualising the role of the state in the structuring of the current conjuncture, which this book seeks to contribute to. As later chapters will discuss at length, a number of contributions have discussed the role of the state in processes of neoliberalisation (Pritchard et al. 2016; Werner 2019; Pechlaner and Otero 2010), with others arguing that novel patterns of renewed state action in the current conjuncture signal a break with the corporate food regime (Belesky and Lawrence 2018) with potentially transformative world-systemic implications. Such 'novel patterns' points to perhaps the most recent addition to food regime debate, namely as to whether recent tendencies towards 'multipolarity' – featuring India and other BRICS countries – point to the emergence of a new food regime, possibly centered on China.

4 Beyond the Third Food Regime?

Recent work has sought to interrogate new axes of power in the global agro-food system, departing from the spatiality of the North/South axis defining most of the earlier world within the food regime approach. McMichael writes:

> So far food regime analysis has focused on time and space coordinates associated with Anglo-American temporal and spatial relations – arguably because these coordinates have shaped recent world orders and/or how we think about such ordering. These coordinates are losing their salience in today's multi-polar world, and, accordingly, the original food regime conception is undergoing a transformation as we experience transition and massive global uncertainty.
> MCMICHAEL 2013a, 7

Several contributions to food regime scholarship in the last decade or so speak of 'multipolar' or 'polycentric' tendencies. Scholars note that ongoing global economic restructuring since the 'convergence of crises' of 2007/8 involves increasing integration of agro-food with feed, fuel and finance in an emergent unsustainable socio-environmental complex where countries in the Global South assume increasingly more central positions to reconfigured patterns of capital accumulation and global agrarian transformation (McMichael 2012; Borras et al. 2016; Cousins et al. 2018). North/South binaries thus need reconceptualising in food regime terms (Borras, McMichael, and Scoones 2010; McMichael 2010; Weis 2013, 2007). 'Current trends', Borras et al. (2012, 862) write, 'suggest multiple centres of power, and a more diverse range of key international actors within the governance structure of the food-energy complex, both sectorally and geopolitically'.

In terms of geopolitical dynamics, these authors as well as others (McKay, Hall, and Liu 2016; Cousins et al. 2018) argue, we need more attention to emerging processes and tensions revolving around the rise of 'BRICS' countries (Brazil, Russia, India, China and South Africa) as well as numerous MICS – and the relations between all of these. Reworking key international institutions such as the WTO through novel coalitions, the BRICS certainly contribute to the tearing apart of previously dominant North/South axes of power (Hopewell 2016), although not necessarily by way of 'Southern solidarity' but possibly rather by advancing their own interests (Hopewell 2021) in ways that may compound rather than challenge existing disparities not only in the realm of food and agriculture (Bond 2015).

With an eye for dynamics of multipolarity and concomitant 'regionalising' processes in the global food regime (McMichael 2013a; Wang 2018; Wang and Buck 2024), Jakobsen and Hansen (2020) for example analyse the emergence of an Asia-centered 'meat complex' where India and China both figure in key roles, including in terms of agribusiness capital. Precisely agribusiness capital emanating from outside of the erstwhile Western heartlands of the corporate food regime has been emphasised by others as well, such as Dixon (2014) dealing with Egypt, and Henderson (2021) on Gulf capital. Henderson even claims that 'new capitals in the current system remain understudied', with a prevailing emphasis on the BRICS hiding from view other, smaller capitals (Henderson 2021, 1).

Based on these tendencies, what do terms like 'multipolarity' and 'polycentrism' imply for the reconfiguration of hegemony? Some authors argue that, while the tendency towards multipolarity is a real empirical process, it does not in fact entail that new powers have taken on hegemonic positions. Rather, what we find evidence of in emergent agro-capitals outside of the capitalist core is a continuation of Northern hegemony with the new agro-capitals, such as those in the Gulf region, as a 'sub-imperium' (Tilzey 2018; Henderson 2021). Others take more of an agnostic view on the issue of hegemonic shift, such as in the more descriptive view of an 'Asian meat complex' actualising polycentric tendencies (Jakobsen and Hansen 2020). Escher (2021) explores the current conjuncture as one of capitalist 'diversity' for a more nuanced understanding of the role of BRICS, arguing that:

> capitalist diversity stems largely from the historically embedded legacy of the agrarian question in the institutional foundations and class relations of each country that the dynamics of the agrifood systems influence their development trajectories in decisive ways and that the BRIC(S)-driven polycentric shifts in the contemporary food regime are crucial to the destiny of global capitalism.
> ESCHER 2021, 47

McMichael, meanwhile, seems more convinced that hegemonic shifts are unfolding. 'Evidently', he wrote already a decade ago, 'northern states are losing their centrality in organizing and dominating the food/fuel regime' (McMichael 2013a, 129). This is where the 're-emergence' of China in the global political economy, and its role in challenging Euro-American hegemony, is especially central to current debate, where the following arguments have been made:

> First, China has adopted a neomercantilist foreign policy that aims to secure access to agro-food imports for domestic consumption. Second, the Chinese state has channeled sovereign wealth funds into state-owned and private enterprises to expand the international influence of its agribusiness industry and challenge transnational corporations' control over agro-food production, processing, and distribution. Third, China has both entrenched, and reconfigured, the dominant relations of neoliberal market rule for its own strategic purposes.
>
> GREEN, 2021: 4

The role of the Chinese state is key. Belesky and Lawrence (2018) argue – albeit based on rather limited evidence – that the global political economy as such is characterised by 'varieties of capitalism', demanding new analytical approaches to comprehend the roles of 'rising powers' in an increasingly multipolar agro-food order. On this basis, they argue that the strong involvement of the Chinese state – ostensibly concerned with issues of food security – in the recent rise of new agro-food and chemical companies from/in China substantially challenges the organizing principles of the corporate food regime. These developments, Belesky and Lawrence argue, point to another modality of capitalism than the neoliberal and corporate dominated prevalent modality – likely a form of 'state capitalism' and/or 'neo-mercantilism'. Drawing on an earlier paper by McMichael (2013b), 'neomercantilism' involves the overriding of global trade arrangements such as the WTO for the purpose of national self-sufficiency, organised through the extensive operations of state-owned enterprises (Lin 2023), thus potentially marking something of a rupture with dominant development governance arrangements.

Speaking skeptically to this discussion, however, Henderson (2021) interjects that new agribusiness capitals arising in the Gulf region with heavy state involvement do not in fact show much evidence of a departure from the profit-motive driving Western agribusiness, although imbricated in state strategies of 'corporate food security'. Even more recently, Henderson and Ziadah argue that these state strategies need to be seen together with the shift towards logistics and distribution in global capitalism (Henderson and Ziadah 2023), in turn pointing towards the increased centrality of circulation amidst the 'long downturn' of global capitalism since the early 1970s that I have alluded to above. With a focus on the Chinese state owned enterprise COFCO, Fares argues that

> COFCO has pushed forward a finance-driven accumulation strategy by taking advantage of open capital markets overseas to attract foreign investors and raise shareholder value. COFCO's case demonstrates that

> neomercantilism narratives do not correspond to China's role in the current food regime. Those narratives often fall into commercial reductionism, turning a blind eye to the diversity of China's going-out strategies. Instead, neomercantilism fits into easy accusations from Western media and governments that stigmatize Chinese policies as self-centred economic protectionism.
>
> FARES 2023, 478

Similar assessments have also recently been made of Chinese state-owned enterprises in other sectors (Jones 2020), inviting careful assessments of the actual degree to which 'multipolarity' of this kind breaks with patterns of action among more 'established' actors in the capitalist world economy (see also Hung 2015).

Characteristically, the most striking formulations about China's role in the global food regime writ large come from McMichael. In a recent much-discussed paper, he puts forward a purposely speculative analysis of the possible emergence of a *new*, i.e. fourth, food regime transitioning away from the corporate food regime (while also reliant on aspects of the neoliberal trade order), now to be centered on China (McMichael 2020). China's Belt & Road Initiative (BRI) is viewed as evidence of China's new food regime strategy, reliant on neomercantilist logics crucially concerned with issues of food security through strategies of direct land access and the overruling of WTO trade rules, e.g. in the context of feed grain trade for China's sprawling industrial meat complex. A recent contribution takes this approach with its focus on neomercantilism further empirically by scrutinizing the activities of Chinese investments in Latin-America through the major company COFCO (Wesz Junior, Escher, and Fares 2021). Through a more grounded empirical approach to 'an emerging Chinese food regime', Green looks at concomitant processes of agrarian transition in Cambodia (Green 2021). Green's approach resonates strongly with the perspective offered in this book, as he argues that 'understanding China as an agent of intensified agricultural development in countries like Cambodia is limited if theoretical analysis is confined to food regime relations at the global scale', pointing to the need for analyzing 'multiscalar market relations, political negotiations, and agricultural practices' (Green 2021, 1250).

Largely missing from these contributions centered on neomercantilism (and on multipolarity, to a certain extent), however, is the question of imperialism. Critical agro-food scholarship on relations between China and Latin America has pointed to the emergence of new commodity complexes – with soy being a prominent example – intertwining the two regions in and through exploitative and uneven relations of resource control and dependency, leading some scholars to draw upon the notion of a 'new imperialism' (M. McKay et al. 2016). Simultaneously, recent research has warned against exaggerated views of Chinese land grabs in Latin America and pointed to the similarities between Chinese companies' actual practices and those of Western counterparts (Oliveira 2018).

Based on this recent debate, I suggest critical scrutiny as to whether the broad characterization of 'China' – as a relatively unitary actor – hides from view more than it reveals for our understanding of key patterns of change in the world of food and agriculture. Engaging with McMichael's postulation of an emergent Chinese food regime, Yan Hairong criticizes the very notion of neomercantilism based on research among Chinese agro-investers in Africa, finding that profit-motives among investors that largely serve host-countries' domestic rather than Chinese markets blatantly contradicts the 'neomercantilist thesis'. So, in this view, the conceptualisation of an unfolding food regime reorientation along a 'Chinese' pathway risks ignoring the ways that the deployment of capital and labour by actually existing firms is driven by the pursuit of profit, pitting them in competition with each other and in frequently uneasy relationship to the agency of the Chinese state. In short, ground realities reveal complicated state-capital relationships that may be clouded by aggregated concepts of 'China's role' in the singular.[4] Similarly, recent scholarship on China's recent 'rise' in the global political economy has stressed its 'fractured' character: rather than a monolithic actor with a 'grand strategy' seeking geopolitical aims (ala the mentioned focus on the BRI), we find a multiplicity of contending profit-seeking capitalist actors pursuing their own interests amidst perhaps surprisingly permissive and fragmented state apparatuses (Jones and Hameiri 2021). All of this calls for disaggregating the notion of a 'Chinese state-led strategy' to reveal variegation and constitutive capital-state-labour relations (Oliveira, McKay, and Liu 2021). It also arguably calls for caution in assessing claims about the extent to which China's role in emergent food regime dynamics involve rupture and transformative change more broadly.

---

4   Transnational Institute (2021) "Global Food Regimes and China: Agrarian Conversations Episode 2" available at Global food regimes and China: Agrarian Conversations episode 2 – YouTube.

5 Steps towards the 'Concrete'[5]

With this outline of recent strands of debate in food regime analysis in place, I turn in this section to argue more assertively for the necessity of questioning the 'global' fixation in the literature as well as of bringing the state into the conversation in a way that resonates with the theoretical stance laid out in Chapter 1, emphasising the value-form and class struggle. Arguing for the need for a multiscalar approach, this section suggests steps towards a revised food regime analysis that is more thoroughly attendant to the 'concrete'. In so doing, I situated the book among a relatively small, yet important stream of recent writings engaging with food regimes and the question of downscaling.

Food regime analysis, as we have seen, was 'global' in scope from the beginning. Theoretically, it 'combined two strands of macro-sociological theory' (Magnan 2012, 3), namely French regulation school theory and world-systems theory. The approach grew out of a recognition that food and agriculture had been accorded a relatively marginal position in 'world systems and other approaches to history of global capital and shifts in inter-state power' as well as in broader studies of class power in global capitalism (Friedmann, Daviron, and Allaire 2016). In doing so, the food regime approach placed itself within streams of scholarship seeking to interweave insights from the traditions of Marx and Polanyi, as both the regulation and world-systems theory are located at the confluence of Marxian and Polanyian thought (Dale 2010, 5).[6]

The influence from regulation theory, as pointed to in Araghi's (2003) critical reading in Chapter 1, is evident in the emphasis on distinct accumulation regimes pivoting on configurations of 'institutional forms', where the latter 'make possible or problematic an accumulation regime, but they result from a very complex process combining social struggles, political deliberation and law enforcement' (Boyer 2007).[7] Unlike regulation scholarship, however, food regime analysis does not proceed by incorporating econometrics but remains instead rooted in qualitative methods. Moreover, food regime analysis arguably emerged in the late 1980s as a variety of then-prevalent 'end-of-Fordism

---

[5] This section draws on Jakobsen, J. (2021). New food regime geographies: scale, state, labor. *World Development*, 145, 105523.

[6] The confluence of Marx and Polanyi is clearly found in Giovanni Arrighi's work (2010), a strong influence on food regime analysis (for Arrighi, Marx and Polanyi, see Dale 2010, 222–226).

[7] As a recent review of French regulation theory's engagement with agriculture shows, it forms a scholarly tradition that only briefly and tangentially enters into dialogue with food regime analysis (Touzard and Labarthe 2016).

theory' (Bonanno and Constance 2008, 34). Yet, as Friedmann explains, food regime analysis does not use terms such as 'Fordism', in order to avoid becoming entangled in dynamics internal to specific (Western) economies, aiming rather to study a globally emergent system (Friedmann, Daviron, and Allaire 2016). As I argued in Chapter 1, the periodization and 'regime-crisis-regime' dynamics driving food regime writings does not accord well with an integrated understanding of patterns of change in global capitalism in the period since the early 1970s, which I have suggested we approach in terms of a sustained 'long downturn' (Brenner 2006) that has increasingly come to incorporate countries across the world including allegedly 'emerging economies' such as India.

While it is warranted to hold the regulation school influence as largely displaced to the sideline of food regime writings at present, world-systemic thinking is still present. This is seen in the emphasis on 'global' dynamics before nation-states as well as the fundamental interest in holding world-historical patterns of change as grounded in contradictory processes that imply the possibility of rupture.[8] Food regime analysis's close affiliation to world-systems theorising also has methodological implications. As a recent summary of Wallerstein's approach holds, 'his key assumption was that local and global processes partake of the same causalities and are determined not by the contingencies of the local, but by the imperatives of the global' (Makki 2015, 478).[9]

The orientation towards the global scale has triggered recent criticism – which provides a key stimulus for the analytical stance taken in this book – of food regime analysis for relying on a 'broad brush' that 'remains at the level of the world economy' (Otero 2012, 283), limiting the level of precision and empirical depth to be found in many (or most) of its extant studies. This arguably relates to a tendency in food regime writings to locate key concepts at a level of generality that is 'too vague and abstract' (Otero, Pechlaner, and Gürcan 2013, 271). The macro-orientation, critics point out, 'confines us to looking at "capital" as a whole, in general, without properly disaggregating different fractions of capital, including possible contradictions between them' (Otero and Lapegna 2016, 4; see also Tilzey 2019), something that points to the analytical need for coupling classes of labour with the concept of classes of capital, as noted above.

---

8   For an introduction to world-systems theory, see Wallerstein (2004).
9   In Marxian studies of capitalism, we are reminded of the divide between 'internalist' explanations of capitalism in terms of 'paths of transition' under specific circumstances versus 'externalist' explanations of capitalism as world-systemic (Bernstein 2010, Chapter 2; Anievas and Nisancioglu 2015, 7).

In his elaborate critique of food regime analysis, Bernstein suggests that a fruitful way to deal with these challenges can be found in paying more sustained attention to multiple determinations with distinct loci – 'internal to the countryside, internal to "national" economies and "external" emanating from the world economy' (Bernstein 2016a, 642; see also Bernstein 2015). Specifically, Bernstein argues that the food regime approach so far has leaned too heavily towards the third locus of determination, thus constraining the ability to incorporate elements of varied temporal and spatial scope necessary.

Food regime scholars increasingly recognise these concerns, leading to arguments for downscaling to the scale of regions and nation-states or even further to local scales (Otero 2012; McMichael 2013a, 96; Otero, Pechlaner, and Gürcan 2013; Otero 2016; Green 2021; Wang 2018). There is an emerging, yet still limited, body of publications that take regional, national or, to some degree, local scales as their focus. Included in this literature are studies, inter alia, of the transformation of the Spanish livestock system in the second and third food regime (Ríos-Núñez and Coq-Huelva 2015); the dynamics of accumulation in the colonial food regime in the Philippines (Camba 2018); the workings of scientific institutions in the second food regime in Asia (Wang and Buck 2024); as well as cases exploring the contemporary food regime through corporate agricultural expansion in the deserts of Egypt (Dixon 2014); transgenic soybeans in Argentine (Torrado 2016); and oil palm expansion in Guatemala (Pietilainen and Otero 2018). This book seeks to contribute to this nascent stream of scholarship.

Departing from formulations that imply that the 'global' is where food regime analysis primarily operates, we find McMichael (2013a, 108) arguing that the approach 'can be deployed in a variety of ways to illuminate local, national, regional and global processes'. Empirical tendencies are triggering this move beyond 'the global', including the rising importance of 'multipolarity', as discussed above. Such empirical trends have been triggering an increased interest among food regime scholars in 'regionalising' the approach. Yet, it may still be the case, as Otero (2016) argues, that the acknowledgment of regional scales has only been utilised to a limited extent in actual analyses. For example, while the corporate food regime is perceived as revolving around struggles – as the focus on Vía Campesina attests – the relevance of struggles to food regime dynamics are located almost exclusively at the global level. Struggles at other scales are thereby largely effaced (Otero 2016), a neglect that is addressed especially in Chapters 4–5 in this book, dealing with struggles over India's ongoing agrarian crisis and right to food legislation.

While formulations such as the above may seem to imply a relatively atheoretical take on scale, we also find recent contributions to food regime scholarship that go further in scrutinizing scale conceptually. In a recent contribution to these debates, Rioux (2018) argues for a renewed focus on scale and spatiotemporality, scrutinising the 'relative scalar fixity of the food regime concept'. He emphasizes the limitations in food regime literature ensuing from its close to exclusive focus on the international scale:

> While the influence of the world-systems perspective informs the food regime concept's ability to problematise the international dimension of social change, too strong an emphasis on the same dimension has tended to conceal the importance of sub-national processes as key to the effective deployment and stabilisation of agri-food orders.
> RIOUX 2018, p. 715

In another recent contribution focusing on food regime 'regionalisation' and scale in the context of East Asia, Wang argues that 'any analysis of food regimes should incorporate the global, regional, national, sub-national, local and so forth as different spaces through which the reach of food regimes is territorialised, regulated and contested' (Wang 2017, 6). Going further than some of the contributions above, Wang suggests that we think of such 'regionalisation' in terms of geographer Johan Allen's notion of 'spatial topology' to understand 'the power of food regimes across space' (Ibid.). Similarly, Lapegna and Perelmuter (2020) have pointed to an abiding 'methodological nationalism' within much food regime scholarship that 'understands countries as units' and argue instead for opening up for regional variation within nation states, involving variegated and multiscalar forms of spaces, actors and overall food regime dynamics. Lapegna and Perelmuter's point is important, and may be rethought from the value-form perspective suggested in this book to point towards Arboleda's (2020a) argument that methodological nationalism in understanding capitalism does not suffice for understanding the global content of capital. Simultaneously, as Arboleda argues, we cannot but study the specific modes of existence of capital, that includes centrally that of the nation-state as a political form. Speaking to the concerns of this book, rescaling and challenging methodological nationalism can be compatible with an emphasis on specific dynamics within singular nation-states – in our case, India – through the analytics of food regime analysis and its emphasis on global value relations. An emphasis on the state will be central to my efforts at reaching towards the 'concrete' and will be revisited repeatedly throughout the book.

The question of rescaling to account for novel regionalised dynamics in the global food regime brings us to the notion of hegemony. As Perry Anderson (2017, 107) argues, notions of hegemony have tended to be formulated either in terms of international power relations *or* in terms of power relations between classes. McMichael (2013a) holds that the food regime concept comprises a notion of hegemony that conjoins these two. Yet, as is arguably the case with Giovanni Arrighi (2010) whose pioneering conjoined notion of hegemony along these lines has been an enduring influence on food regime scholars (Friedmann, Daviron, and Allaire 2016), McMichael's hegemony is oriented towards the world-system, leaving the construction of hegemony among class forces internal to states relatively underexplored (Anderson 2017, 115; Brown 2019, 6).

Counter to an either/or perspective, Adam David Morton argues that Gramsci's concept of hegemony encompasses both national and international scales and their interrelations (Morton 2007). Gramscian perspectives on hegemony, I suggest, can help advance the food regime approach into the domain of conjunctural analysis that can redress limitations of scalar fixation. Crucially to the critique of 'stability' in prevailing food regime conceptualisation, the notion of hegemony in Gramscian terms remains fragile, subject to negotiations (Hall 2011, 727–728), which opens for discussions of hegemonic contestations over the contemporary food regime as involving struggles around 'unstable equilibria' (Gramsci 1971; see also Nielsen and Nilsen 2015) between dominant and dominated classes, as Chapter 5 suggests. Poulantzas, similarly, expresses the notion that hegemonic processes revolve around class compromises mediated by the state as follows:

> The State organizes and reproduces class hegemony by establishing a variable field of compromises between the dominant and dominated classes; quite frequently, this will even involve the imposition of certain short-term material sacrifices on the dominant classes, in order that their long-term domination may be reproduced.
>
> POULANTZAS 1978, 184

Unlike Poulantzas' approach to the 'relative autonomy' of the state, however, the value-form informed stance suggested in this book asserts that the state is the political form of capital, or, as Bonefeld puts it, 'the form of the state needs to be seen as a mode of existence of the class relation which constitutes and suffuses the circuit of capital' (Bonefeld 1992, 122). Holding, in this perspective, labour as intrinsic to the class relation and thus to the value-form, it is somewhat puzzling to find a relative neglect of labour in food regime writings, constituting another area in which our movement towards concrete analysis demands rethinking. Put differently, to proceed with the multiscalar conceptualisation of food regime geographies, renewed attention to labor is the next necessary step. That labour has been given little analytical attention in food regime analysis was recently pointed out by McMichael in a lengthy list of 'more analytical dimensions to include in the repertoire' (McMichael 2016, 650). Labour should not, however, be seen merely as an 'analytical dimension'. Doing so points, at worst, at an impoverished conceptualisation of the capitalist mode of production.

The lack of sustained engagement with labor has been noted by some scholars. Otero (2016) argues that there is a tendency in food regime analysis to perceive capital as something that is held by agribusiness, and not as a social relation, consequently downplaying workers and work. Pye (2019) also points to a surprising disconnect from labor, stressing that food regime scholarship has tended to neglect the agrarian proletariat, focusing close to exclusively on farmers, smallholders and, especially, the so-called peasantry. Based on extensive fieldwork in Indonesian palm oil plantations, Pye argues that the rapidly growing palm oil proletariat needs to be recognised to the operations of the global food regime as well as the potential for working class emancipatory struggle against the food regime. As later parts of this book will explore in more depth in the context of notions of 'commodity frontiers', labour is not only central due to the exploitation of wage labor on farms and plantations, but also by the ways that the global food regime articulates with unpaid work.

Furthermore, Rioux (2018) suggests a labour-centered approach to food regime analysis stressing that cheap labour has been foundational to all three food regimes, as he locates the first food regime within processes of agrarian change in mid-19th century Britain. Food regime analysis, writes Rioux – drawing on Araghi's (2003) theoretical intervention, that has also been key to the approach suggested in this book – centrally concerns how '[g]lobal value relations are key to understanding the uneven geographical development and integration of agrarian spaces of production as constitutive of both capital-expanded reproduction and global wage-labor' (Rioux 2018, p. 715). We need, then, to scrutinise how such 'integration of agrarian spaces' happens and, thus, the role of labour in channeling agricultural commodities into global value relations.

Multiscalarity, again, is key. As a final aspect thereof, I suggest that steps towards concrete analysis may fruitfully involve attention to the materiality of these commodities that channel into global value relations. As part of the mentioned recent debate between leading food regime scholars in the pages of the *Journal of Peasant Studies,* Friedmann (2016) criticizes the notion of the corporate food regime for its monolithic tendencies, tending to rule out the role of specific commodities to shaping global patterns of accumulation, and the crucial nuanced questions about 'specific crops, regions and types of farmers' as well as the forms of states. Chapter 6 will return to this as I present an extensive argument for taking heed of commodity-specific dynamics, focusing on hybrid maize. Such commodity-specificity should, moreover, not be viewed in isolation from its place in the broader technological system, recognizing the especially formative influence of agricultural biotechnology – with its key interest groups at different scales – to the shape and trajectory of the contemporary food regime, and the resultant shifts in cropping patterns towards transgenic crops (Pechlaner and Otero 2008).

Reaching towards concrete analysis, not only commodities are diverse, but so are the shapes of organizing labour. As Ben White and colleagues (2012) argue, global agrarian change can be studied using what they term a nested hierarchy of 'umbrella' concepts. Moving from the global food regime, through global commodity chains or – in Araghi's terms – global value relations, we arrive at agrarian labour regimes, which have been defined by Bernstein as 'specific methods of mobilising labour and organising it in production, and their particular social, economic and political conditions' (Bernstein 1988, p. 31–2, quoted in White et al. 2012, p. 622). These are crucial dynamics for a 'grounded' food regime analysis that have been insufficiently addressed to date and that will be particularly important to the analysis offered in Chapter 6 on south India's hybrid maize commodity frontier and its constitutive labour dynamics.

6 Conclusion

This chapter has presented an in-depth overview of writings in the food regime literature. In so doing, I have included discussion of recent writings from the last few years that have not been covered in earlier overviews – writings that, in sum, illustrate a resurgence of sorts of interest in examining the food regime approach from different angles. This book thus contributes to an already lively and stimulating literature. However, as I already indicated in Chapter 1, I am hesitant of the continued tendency to debate 'the' food regime and 'its' characteristics – whether these are neoliberal, corporate or, as this chapter has also shown, leading towards a 'new' food regime centred on China. This tendency, I suggest, risks reifying phenomena at the surface level, leading, at worst, to a stale form of debate. Rethinking is, in my view, needed.

The alternative articulation of food regimes as 'the political face of world historical value relations' (Araghi 2003, 51) that I draw on in this book points towards a more dynamic approach, and one that more thoroughly embeds the global food regime in the overall patterns of accumulation in global capitalism – rather, that is, than seeking to define a 'distinct' and potentially overly idiosyncratic periodization for agro-food. This chapter has shown how established literature tends towards consensus on the first two food regimes, yet Araghi's dissenting view holds the second food regime (1945–1973) rather as an exception in the history of global capitalism in which capital's food regime receded and was kept at bay. The period from the early 1970s onwards, which Brenner (2006) terms the 'long downturn', thus marks the re-emergence of capital's food regime. Viewing crisis as internal to the capital relation, we should not be surprised that capital's food regime is marked by numerous tensions and contradictions in a period in which the capitalist mode of production writ large faces longstanding stagnation. Seeking spaces for capital accumulation, the integration of new spaces in the workings of the food regime can but be seen to involve, in no small part, the dismantling of remnants of the post-World War II exception. As later chapters will show in detail, struggles over agrarian change in contemporary India can be interpreted in this light.

Having outlined existing debates in the literature, this chapter moreover offered conceptual suggestions towards a multiscalar analysis that breaks with prevailing fixation with the global scale, seeking concrete analysis in which, as Marx famously put it, '[t]he concrete is concrete because it is the concentration of many determinations, hence unity of the diverse' (Marx 1993b, 101). In taking this approach, however, this book offers is decidedly not a 'localist' approach – mirroring the sadly prevalent tendency in political economy to refuse to acknowledge global capitalism as a coherent whole (Altun et al. 2023).

Drawing together the streams of multiscalar analysis suggested in this chapter – including attention to the state, to hegemony, to class struggle and labour – what I suggest in this book can rather be conceived of as a conjunctural approach. Bringing together multiple forces and elements – operating according to different logics, at different scales – in a condensed moment, helps avoiding reifying 'global' or other scales, as if these operate as 'structures' rather than mutually shaped through class struggle, as scholars in the Open Marxism tradition point out (Bonefeld 2014). In Gramscian conjunctural analysis, attention is directed at exploring 'how multiple forces come together in practice to produce particular dynamics or trajectories' (Hart 2004, 97). The conjuncture, in this approach, is 'composed of a set of elements that have varied spatial and temporal scope' (Li 2014, 19). Conjunctural analysis is thus about following Marx's invitation to study 'concrete' social reality as the 'differentiated unity' of 'many determinations' (Hall 2003). As agrarian scholar Ben White comments, however, '[i]t would be a pity if 'conjuncture' became an attractive but too easy way out [...] if complex phenomena and processes that need to be explained get explained away, as conjunctures all the way down' (White 2015, 1398). Food regime analysis prevents such backsliding; in its emphasis on constitutively *global* value relations, the food regime approach insists on structuring processes inherent to the universal movement of the valorization of capital that cannot be whisked away. In order to 'break into' (Hall 2007, 277) what I perceive as key determinations of varied spatial and temporal scope, which I would argue as being a crucial part of making food regime 'travel' to India with its critical power unbroken, we need to engage with how general (world-systemic) processes of capital accumulation are interwoven with the embedded, historical-geographical specificities of agrarian change in India. This is the subject of the next chapter.

CHAPTER 3

Agrarian Change in Postcolonial India

When writing about agrarian change 'in India', the problem of diversity immediately flies in one's face. How to claim speaking of a country of bewildering diversity – in terms, *inter alia,* of agrarian structures, agro-climatic regions or sociopolitical historical trajectories – without glossing over the differences that make a difference? This problem vastly complicates notions of 'regionalising' or 'rescaling' food regime analysis in the context of India, and needs to be taken seriously. Meanwhile, South Asian studies has for long excelled in problematizing the construct of 'India' (e.g. Inden 1990), leading to an attitude of resistance to generalised analysis at the level of the nation-state.[1] Although this attitude is not undisputed – as recent calls for 'scaling up' analysis to the all-India level show (Sinha 2015) – it is still broadly agreed that 'one of the most fundamental truths about India is that it is, in a manner of speaking, unlike itself. Its capacity for confounding generalisations is infinite' (Kaviraj 2017, 57). The notion of 'region' internally in India is also complex. Most commonly, 'region' is taken to refer to administrative-political units in the Indian nation-state, a problematic notion for studying agrarian change insofar as the 'spatial patterns of Indian capitalism' arguably follow distinct logics (Harriss-White 2017, 45). It is therefore, as Lerche (2014) points out, rather the case that India houses a mosaic of regionally constituted patterns of agrarian capitalism. These regional patterns have been described in different ways by scholars, such as in David Ludden's agrarian historical geography showing how South Asia has for centuries been criss-crossed by agrarian regions that do not overlap with official administrative demarcations of territory (Ludden 1999). Or, for contemporary India, in A. R. Vasavi's argument that 'we can identify at least eight distinct types of ruralities in India' (Vasavi 2012, 44) shaping actually existing agrarian capitalism. 'India' is thus a problematic unit of analysis, possibly one that hides from view the unevenness by which capitalism in the country operates on the ground (see e.g. Basile, Harriss-White, and Lutringer 2015; Harriss-White and Heyer 2015).

With these concerns and pitfalls plainly in view, this chapter presents a synoptic and necessarily partial overview of processes of agrarian change, the

---

1   The notion of 'South Asia' comprising the object of study for South Asianists is no less problematic in its polysemy – although this is perhaps less commonly debated than what is the case with the notion of 'India' (Mohammad-Arif 2014).

state and capitalism in postcolonial India. Attempting to 'ground' food regime analysis in concrete analysis is futile, I would argue, without a comprehensive view of such dynamics in *any* historical-geographical circumstances. The chapter starts by outlining debates in the regional scholarship that are relevant to, but so far rather disconnected from, food regime literature. This involves a renewed interest in agrarian change in India-specific scholarship. The chapter then outlines the trajectory of the integral state in postcolonial India. While these discussions focus on the regional scholarship, I will also show that insights and analytical angles offered therein can, and perhaps should, bear directly upon food regime analysis, including by contributing to 'deepening', with empirical content, the multiscalar analytics suggested in Chapter 2. For food regime analysis to 'travel' with unbroken critical potential, then, insights from the regional scholarship provides fruitful tensions and frictions to build further upon in the remainder of this book.

Barring the few examples already mentioned, such as Lerche's (2013) rather negative and 'external' criticism of the corporate food regime conceptualisation for missing the target in Indian circumstances and Brown's (2020) more recent synoptic account of how hegemony plays out in how agrarian India articulates within a food regime frame, very little work has to date been done that puts India into dialogue with food regime analysis. It one of the ambitions of this book that a more extensive, systematic and multiscalar food regime approach to understanding agrarian transformation in India offers novelty hitherto largely underexplored in existing scholarship.

1 The 'Resurrection' of Agrarian Scholarship

This book seeks to contribute to Shah and Harriss-White's (2011) by-now over a decade old call for 'resurrecting scholarship on agrarian transformations' in India. This call came as a response to a significant shortage in scholarly attention since the 1990s that warrants some explanation. During the heyday of ethnographic ad socioeconomic 'village studies' in the 1950s and 1960s, sustained interest was shown in agrarian matters in the country.[2] Relevant to my purposes, the tradition of village studies revealed the manifold ways that local power relations worked (and, although in morphed and reconfigured ways, still may work) in rural India – and therefore the actually existing basis for

---

2 The 'village studies' tradition, including its limitations, has been recounted and summarised in several publications later on, see e.g. Jodhka (1998).

agrarian political economies. Rich village studies from various parts of India – such as the work of Srinivas (1976) in the village of Rampura in Karnataka, Beteille's (1965) work in Sripuram in Tamil Nadu and many others – generated crucial insights about the relations between power, dominance and accumulation, and land, caste and class, including how these intersect and intertwine. These insights, I would argue, provide an underlying – or, in terms of regional scholarship, even paradigmatic – scepticism to statements about undifferentiated notions of 'the peasantry' of the sort found in parts of the food regime literature.

The scholarly interest in things agrarian continued into the 1970s with strong emphasis on analysing the expansion of capitalism in Indian agriculture. Notably, Marxian scholars engaged in the legendary and somewhat infamous 'mode of production debate' (see Patnaik 1990).[3] While much of this debate is commonly considered to have ended up in counterproductive forms of debate (Mohanty 2016b) where scholars would seemingly endlessly debate whether Indian agriculture qualifies as 'capitalist', 'semi-feudal' or 'feudal', it also brought about empirically rich, grounded studies of agrarian change at the village level (e.g. Harriss 1982).[4] The mode of production debate, as one recent recapitulation puts it, 'explored the configuration of the principal rural classes and class relations, and the main contradictions in rural society and in society at large' (Lerche, Shah, and Harriss-White 2013, 338). As such, it generated important insights of relevance to any analysis that seeks to grapple with the multiple determinations of agrarian change across scales. The somewhat older notion of the landlord 'depressor' (Thorner 1956), as I will turn to below, can be seen as a product of precisely such village studies of class configurations and contradictions.

India studies since the early 1990s have subsequently experienced changing priorities away from rural affairs, partly due to the broader transformations in society towards new forms of dynamics in 'emerging' India (Jodhka 2017). This entailed, as Shah and Harriss-White aptly summarize, that 'with the rise of the critique of village studies, the problems of categorising "modes of production", and the push for scholarship to move to urban studies and address the urgent problems of liberalisation, in-depth research and reflection on the agrarian economy declined' (Shah and Harriss-White 2011, 13). In parallel, in

---

3   For an overview of the mode of production debate more broadly, see e.g. Foster-Carter (1978) or, for specific application to agrarian studies, Byres (1985).
4   While largely left behind as a scholarly concern, interestingly the mode of production debate is still very much alive in the revolutionary strategies and tactics of Maoist guerrillas in central-eastern India (Shah 2019).

the real world, India has witnessed transformative socioeconomic changes where mobility and betterment of life conditions have increasingly come to be identified with urban areas and where the village, in the eyes of large sections of the Indian population, is decidedly *not* 'where the bright lights are' (Gupta 2005, 752).

While there are presently numerous scholars responding to the call for 'resurrecting' interest in agrarian change, the rather long hiatus has implications. 'There is a dearth of detailed studies', writes Richa Kumar (2016b, 21), 'that analyse the transformations taking place in rural India by focusing on how longer-term processes and the broader socioeconomic, political, historical, cultural, ecological, and technological context influence the nature of outcomes'. Moreover, as I will get back to, there is a dearth of work placing India's experience in the realm of food and agriculture explicitly in view of 'global' theorisation. On a speculative note, this dearth may perhaps, in part, be a 'fallout' of the mode of production debate and, in part, a tendency in regional scholarship to foreground 'Indian exceptionalism', implicated in scholarly priorities such as the decline of class analysis in view of the ostensible 'uniqueness' of caste (Herring and Agarwala 2008). For example, an authoritative overview argues in strong terms that 'India has undoubtedly followed a very original path in the field of food and agriculture' (Dorin and Landy 2009, 20).

There have been recent attempts at 'reinvigorating' anthropological studies in/of villages in India (Mines and Yazgi 2010), as well as initiatives towards 'revisiting' the sites of the classical village studies (Simpson 2016; Jodhka 2017), yet these emerging bodies of literature do not seem to speak much to the critical agrarian studies debates animating this book. Closer to the pertinent sort of 'global' debates we find a stream of publications dealing with land dispossession, often engaging with broader debates in critical geography, agrarian studies and political ecology about 'land grabbing' and 'accumulation by dispossession', while simultaneously embedding these in empirically nuanced local realities (Adnan 2016; Andreas et al. 2020; Levien 2018; Nielsen 2018; Vijayabaskar and Menon 2018; Oskarsson, Lahiri-Dutt, and Wennström 2019; Whitehead 2013).[5] Agrarian distress and crisis – discussed at length in Chapter 4 – has also triggered recent work that brings agrarian issues in India into broad debates about the neoliberalisation of agriculture and capitalist transformation (Münster 2015; Flachs 2016b; Vasavi 2012) and the contradictions of sustainable agriculture initiatives (Brown 2018). Other work scrutinises

---

5   While there are also examples of work that interrogates India's role internationally in land grabbing, these do not involve empirical realities in India (Gill 2016; Michael and Baumann 2016; Hules and Singh 2017).

experimentation with agricultural technologies frequently promoted as offering 'global solutions', stressing instead the context-specificity of their articulation in agrarian India (Taylor and Bhasme 2018, 2021). Others yet have explored the agrarian dynamics – including processes of dispossession -- accompanying so-called energy transitions in Indian solar and wind energy initiatives (Stock and Birkenholtz 2021; Stock 2023; Singh 2022; Yenneti, Day, and Golubchikov 2016). Yet, apart from such noteworthy instances of engagement with interlinked 'global' debates, the predominant frame in the Indian context for critical agrarian scholars interested in global terms of debate has recently been rejuvenated interest in 'agrarian questions' or 'transitions'. As this literature is extensive and poses relevant questions to food regime literature, it merits closer consideration.

2 Beyond 'cul-de-sac': Agrarian Questions and Transitions

While we can, as the above indicates, identify emerging interest in agrarian issues, it is still relatively limited, triggering a recent assessment to hold that '[n]ot only in the old nineteenth-century debate but also in recent global debate, India was rarely a case in point despite the recent phenomenal changes in its agrarian economy and society' (Mohanty and Lenka 2016, 168).[6] Implied here in 'recent phenomenal changes' is the impact of the opening of the Indian state and economy to global capital and related processes of neoliberalisation since around 1990 – processes that are central to analysis in this book. It is widely agreed that politico-economic restructuring 'set in motion a process of agrarian change in India on an unprecedented scale and pace' (Mohanty 2016a, 20), although, as we can expect from any historical-geographical context, this did and does take place unevenly and in varying ways locally (Münster and Strümpell 2014). In sum, this accelerating integration in global capitalism under neoliberalisation has been triggering renewed scholarly interest.

An emerging literature seeks to relate India's overall national trajectory of agricultural change to agrarian questions (Lerche 2011, 2013; Lerche, Shah, and Harriss-White 2013; Ramachandran 2011; Mohanty 2016b). In some instances, moreover, agrarian questions are explored through village scale research (Shah 2013; Sudheesh 2023), including by tracing urban ramifications (Cowan 2018;

---

6 Qualifying this statement, the role of India and its alleged 'despotism' in the global expansion of capitalism was a significant topic in Marx as well as ensuing debate. Recent work that questions the extent to which Marx was blinded by Eurocentrism undermines blanket statements about the neglect of India (Anderson 2010; Musto 2020; see also Shanin 1983).

Gidwani and Ramamurthy 2018). This literature contains tendencies at intermixing of 'agrarian questions' and 'capitalist transitions' to denote the role of agricultural surplus to capitalist development in the country.[7] Bernstein has made an influential intervention – echoed among several scholars of agrarian India – by arguing that the agrarian question in its classical meaning has been 'bypassed' (Bernstein 2006; Lerche 2013). Given the lack of capitalist expansion in agriculture, the classical transition, where agrarian accumulation feeds into national industrial development (Byres 1986), will not happen even though the transition from 'noncapitalist' forms into capitalist agriculture is 'essentially complete' (D'Costa and Chakraborty 2017b, 20). Some scholars have consequently recently argued for seeing India's particular experience as a 'blocked transition' (Sinha 2017) or as evidence of 'compressed capitalism' (D'Costa 2014). Moreover, Sanyal (2007) and Chatterjee (2008) go even further in holding the contemporary Indian political economy as 'dual', encompassing both a 'need economy' (including agrarian and informal economies) and an 'accumulation economy'. In such a scenario, the question of transition is off the table.

Along these lines, numerous scholars point to strong evidence of stagnation, distress and crisis in Indian agriculture, revealing that 'there is little capitalist expansionary dynamic in Indian agriculture' (D'Costa and Chakraborty 2017b, 26). Tendencies towards stagnation are commonly assembled in what forms quite a scholarly consensus (Lerche 2011), the content of which I look more thoroughly into in Chapter 4. Among the commonly listed tendencies is the declining share of agriculture to national GDP, dropping from more than 50 percent in 1950–51 to somewhere well below of 20 percent in 2010–11, indicative of a fundamental shift in India's macroeconomic composition during the period of rapid economic growth since the onset of neoliberal reform. Nevertheless, agriculture is still the main occupation of more than half of the county's workforce, signalling a situation of agrarian distress (D'Costa and Chakraborty 2017b, 25). This points, moreover, to lacking or deficient integration between agrarian and industrial sectors of the economy (Bardhan 2010; Corbridge, Harriss, and Jeffrey 2012). Adding to this, agricultural landholdings in the country have undergone a gradual fragmentation along sharply divided class and caste lines, with small and marginal sizes of holdings (below 2 hectares) in the latest census (2015–16) comprising 86,21 % of total landholdings (Editorial 2018; Krishnan 2018). Landlessness – 'effectively' so for those owning below 1 acre of land – is concomitantly rising (Basole and Basu 2011). Rural

---

7 This intermixing can be seen, for example, in two recent edited volumes: *The Land Question in India: State, Dispossession, and Capitalist Transition* (D'Costa and Chakraborty 2017a) and *Critical Perspectives on Agrarian Transition: India in the Global Debate* (Mohanty 2016b).

poverty rates and levels of indebtedness – structured along lines of class and caste – are high, and so are the much-noted farmer suicide rates, commonly taken as proof of agrarian crisis in the country (Walker 2008; Narasimha Reddy and Mishra 2009a; Münster 2012). Indebtedness and agrarian distress are implicated in the political ecology of environmental degradation, notably in the form of groundwater depletion (Taylor 2013). In this scenario, agricultural stagnation is seen as part of the broader predicament of rural India where 'the lives of the marginalised and the disadvantaged have become fragile and untenable' (Vasavi 2012, 32). Meanwhile, the dominant sections of the agrarian economy have shifted, in part or in whole, their economic interests out of agricultural production to other sectors where accumulation finds place (see e.g. Damodaran 2008; Harriss-White 2008b; Aga 2018).

Some adherents to versions of this position hold that Marxian debate about 'the agrarian question' or 'transition' in India has reached a 'cul-de-sac' (D'Costa and Chakraborty 2017b, 17). This debate may, then, potentially end up paralleling the mode of production debate. The food regime approach goes beyond, while complementing, prevailing terms of debate. At this point it is worth noting that Araghi – whose dissident interpretations of food regime analysis have inspired this book – holds a healthy scepticism when it comes to framing contemporary capitalist transformation in terms of 'agrarian questions', as an angle of inquiry that originated at the late 19th century, in other words under specific historical circumstances. Taking a food regime approach (in Araghi's case, to the question of global dispossession of peasantries), Araghi argues that 'by situating my argument within a specified world-historical context, I do not ahistorically transfer research questions from one historical and social complex to another, as is done in much current study of the agrarian question' (Araghi 2012, 120). While taking stock of this critical remark, which to my knowledge has been left rather uncommented in subsequent literature, remains beyond the ambition of this chapter, I do find it interesting to bringing out the distinctiveness of the food regime approach among other approaches to understanding the nexus between capitalism and agriculture at a world scale.

By virtue of its holistic and relational perspective, moreover, food regime analysis is able to interweave phenomena that are left out of the 'cul-de-sac' debate, which focuses quite narrowly on agriculture or – as in the tradition of agrarian studies more broadly – dynamics surrounding 'the farm' and the point of production as the analytical crux (Walker 2004, 6). Food regime analysis, at least in the reformulated version that I have put forwards in the previous chapters, takes questions of food and agriculture in a broader sense that encompasses production, circulation and consumption as a differentiated unity, in keeping with Marx's processual understanding of capital, especially as articulated in the second volume of *Capital* (Marx 1992; Arboleda 2020b). While the prevailing India-specific debate tends to focus on production, intrinsic to the food regime concept is the integrated analysis of both production and 'circulation relations' (McMichael 2016, 651). This is not to say that the approach recapitulates some of the older, and problematic, notions of disconnect between 'production' and 'circulation' – with the latter pointing to so-called 'merchant capital' (Jan 2019). The main point is more straightforward: food regime analysis interrogates a broader canvas of relations in the overall circuit of capital than what the 'cul-de-sac' debate tends to do. The more narrowly defined focus of the 'stagnation thesis' leaves out important ways that capital's food regime emerges in contemporary India, the subject matter of much of this book.

In Chapters 4–6 I will proceed to analyse some of the ways that unfolding processes of agrarian change enable corporate capital to expand in the countryside through the 'industrial grain-oilseed-livestock complex' where hybrid maize is a key component (Weis 2013). Changing dietary patterns, especially among India's middle classes (see e.g. Bruckert 2015), drive the restructuring of agrarian production along the requirements of an expanding meat industry. This links India to broader Asian patterns of change in production and consumption, where the global food regime is acknowledged as centring increasingly on 'meatification' where the expansion of the industrial grain-oilseed-livestock complex is key (McMichael 2013a; Weis 2013; Neo and Emel 2017; Jakobsen and Hansen 2020). Sustained accumulation may well not happen at the level of the farm in much of India. Yet, the transnational food industry and the 'Asian meat complex' – the endpoint of circulating commodities – is a dynamic vector of corporate accumulation. Although there are scholars such as Lerche (2014) and Sinha (2020a) arguing that accumulation does in fact take place in some places and among certain (dominant) groups in agrarian India, such caveats to the 'stagnation thesis' largely refrain from looking at the broader food industry, which may more readily be 'seen' through the food regime lens.

In a seminal review of agrarian questions literature, Akram-Lodhi and Kay (2010, 264) argue for disaggregating ongoing debates to 'identify seven different and at times competing approaches to framing the contemporary agrarian question'. One of these approaches they identify as 'the corporate food regime agrarian question' which implies that 'for McMichael the agrarian question is now about the terms and conditions by which peasant households and rural labour are reproduced when increasingly excluded from the global food regime' (Akram-Lodhi and Kay 2010, 268). The co-existence of widespread agrarian stagnation at the farm level with striking corporate accumulation within the food industry is less surprising when approached in these terms. Nevertheless, this co-existence is about more than exclusion and dispossession; rather, it is incumbent that we ask how – under what circumstances and by what mechanisms – regions, crops and classes of labour are incorporated in the food regime, the latter approached, as this book suggests, in terms of global value relations and their political forms.

The above indicates that the current conjuncture is one where capital's food regime emerges unevenly and partially in India. How and why this happens relates closely to the agency of the integral state. It is to this I turn next.

3   India's Integral State

Notwithstanding recent debates about the 'neoliberal' nature of the contemporary food regime, existing deliberations on the role of the state are insufficiently developed, something I return to in Chapter 5. This issue arguably connects to a broader tendency in critical agrarian studies to underplay the state conceptually, as Vergara-Camus and Kay highlight:

> The recent literature on agrarian transitions and questions, land grabbing, green grabbing, and the rise of agribusiness have all highlighted the central role that the state plays in processes of agrarian change. However, very few studies have attempted to re-examine the ways in which we understand the state or have scrutinised the underlying assumptions about the nature of the state that agrarian scholars reproduce. Even fewer studies are dedicated to theorizing the current nature of the state within the countryside or in respect to agriculture.
>
> VERGARA-CAMUS AND KAY 2017, 242

As indicated in the previous chapter, the notion of the integral state, drawing on Gramsci, may be fruitfully complement the literature on this point. In the integral state, 'political society' (the public institutions of the state) and 'civil society' (which otherwise may appear 'apart' from the state) are brought together in 'dialectical unity' (Thomas 2009, 69). This enlarged or expanded notion of the state – which Thomas holds to have a 'legitimate claim to be Gramsci's novel contribution to Marxist political theory' (Thomas 2009, 137) – brings within its fold 'the entire complex of practical and theoretical activities through which the ruling class not only justifies and maintains its dominance, but manages to win the active consent of those over whom it rules' (Gramsci 1971, 244). Power, in Gramsci's integral state, is 'diffused through civil society as well as being embodied in the coercive apparatuses of the state' (Simon 2015, 74). Counterpoised to this view, we find that in much of the prevailing debate in food regime analysis, 'the state' appears conceptualised as a distinct 'element' separate from others such as 'capital' or 'class'. Gramsci's notion of the integral state instead invites us to think of these as *internally related* (Bieler and Morton 2018; Ollman 2003), resonating with the Open Marxist and value-form theoretical conception of the state as the 'political form of capital' (Bonefeld 2010). In this approach, class struggle forms part of the state, and the state is consequently 'the form of a particular condensation of class forces as well as the terrain within which and through which these social forces struggle to achieve hegemony' (Bieler and Morton 2018, 124). This approach also entails going beyond the opposition between 'state' and 'classes' as seemingly separate elements (Clarke 1991) – or, as is more common in McMichael's vocabulary, 'state' and 'social movements', 'peasants' or 'counter-movements'. Instead, what is required in view of an enlarged concept of the state is, always, 'an analysis of the historic bases that constitute this state' (Buci-Glucksmann 1980, 99).

Returning to the challenge of studying multiplicity invoked at the beginning of this chapter, it comes into play again in conceptualising the state in India. In a sense, this challenge appears especially pressing in studies of neoliberal India, as the period has seen increased agency for the sub-national states and concomitant competition between these in pursuit of economic spoils (Jenkins 1999; Corbridge, Harriss, and Jeffrey 2012). Sub-national states arguably have their own 'political regimes' of class/caste power (Harriss 1999; see also Sinha 2005). And, as Nikita Sud argues, the sub-national level is becoming increasingly central to policy-making as regional states actively 'rescale' policy (Sud 2017; see also Kennedy 2014). The integral state, in other words, is a multi-scalar phenomenon of massive complexity and not a monolithic central government-driven entity. The integral state in India is an analytical abstraction; it both discloses and encloses.

The scale of the nation-state can be problematic in another way as well, in that it threatens to hide from view the broader spatial frame of the 'international' or 'transnational' where food regime analytics has been most commonly placed, and where the dynamics of the world market shape capital accumulation as a constitutively global process (Arboleda 2020a). The persistent tendency towards 'methodological nationalism' (Goswami 2004) found in much area studies literature (and social science more broadly) comes with 'the tendency to assume the existence of "the nation" as the privileged spatial frame rather than to explain its production in a dynamic relation with various global fields' (Sinha 2008, 58). The approach that I draw on in this book can more appropriately be described with Bonefeld's words:

> The 'national' and the 'global' are not externally related things. Of course, the national and the global are not identical but neither are they related to each other as mere external entities that happen to collide with one another from time to time. The global and the national are different-in-unity: they are movements of the social relations of production, which constitute their distinct forms of existence, suffuse their interrelation and contradict their differentiations. The global dimension of the capital relation, its aspatial character, is thus not without 'space'. The aspatial exists contradictorily through nationally divided spaces of political sovereignty.
>
> BONEFELD 2014, 159

The area-studies tradition of Gramscian analysis provides a strong foothold for analyzing dynamics *within* the nation-state in the postcolonial period.[8] Recounted in more detail elsewhere (e.g. Brown 2018), the construction of the postcolonial integral state, in this perspective, emerged in and through a 'passive revolution' where the pursuit of national independence was sought through alliances and compromise both with the prior institutional settings and with dominant classes in the country (Arnold 1984; Chatterjee 1986; Kaviraj 1988). Continuities with the colonial period were clear, where power had likewise been 'critically dependent on the collaboration of the propertied classes' (Guha 1997, 32). The dominant classes were not confronted head-on but, rather, nationalist leaders' focus was, as Partha Chatterjee (1997, 288) puts it, to 'limit their former power, neutralise them where necessary, attack them only selectively, and in general bring them round to a position of subsidiary allies within a reformed state structure'. The relative weakness of the Congress leadership – comprised of an urban bourgeoisie with feeble hold over the countryside – necessitated such compromise with dominant interests (Kohli 1987, 52–61). The story of the making of India's integral state is thus intertwined with the broader story of democratic India. While the broader story of democracy is beyond the purview of the present overview (see e.g. Jakobsen et al. 2018), in what follows I will merely focus on outlining salient aspects of the class composition of the integral state and its reconfiguration under neoliberalisation.

---

8 According to Perry Anderson – quite an authority in Gramscian scholarship – Ranajit Guha's (1997) *Dominance without Hegemony* is 'perhaps the single most striking work ever inspired by Gramsci' (Anderson 2017, 102). The India studies tradition of Gramscian analysis has a rich body of literature and a trajectory worth more than passing comment, recently perhaps most visible in the form of polemics surrounding Vivek Chibber's (2013) ferocious criticism of Subaltern Studies (see also Nilsen 2017).

Based on the nationalist struggle during which the Congress established its upper-class and upper-caste character (Frankel 2005), the integral state at Independence saw the bureaucratic-political elite in the Congress entering into an internally conflictual coalition. This coalition consisted of what Pranab Bardhan (1998, 54) calls 'the dominant proprietary classes' comprising 'the industrial capitalist class, the rich farmers and the professionals in the public sector'. The Nehruvian state's ambitions of developing the country thus faced challenges to its implementation, and the upper class segments of the ruling coalition disrupted attempts at land reform (Herring 1983; Varsney 1995). This ruling coalition was continuously changing, however, and by the 1960s there was a politically influential segment of emergent capitalist farmers – 'bullock capitalists' (Rudolph and Rudolph 1987, 50) or 'kulaks' (Omvedt 1981) – that pressed for commercialising agriculture, a demand that came to fruition with the Green Revolution. As Trent Brown (2020) argues in one of the few articles that explicitly link India to food regimes, the hegemony of the second food regime-model of agriculture in India must therefore be seen at the interface of localised power structures and global forces (see also Patel 2013).

The hegemonic constellation of powers, however, was not unitary. There were internal conflicts, some of which came to the fore with the 'new farmers movements' emergent in the late 1970s and onwards, where dominant farmers mobilised in relation to accumulation strategies pursued by the other fractions of capital (Brass 1995b). Moreover, as a caveat, this view of the dominant power bloc in the integral state may leave relatively downplayed the role of 'the intermediate classes' of smaller scale capital throughout the country (Harriss-White 2002, 43). Relatedly, an influential early view of the functioning of the Indian state after Independence was that it was premised on the 'Congress system' where the ruling party brought into coordination a vast network of factions where local political leaders were in competition (Kothari 1964).[9] Key to the functioning of this 'system' was, as classics in village studies show, the workings of 'brokers' from dominant sections of society (Bailey 1963). Indeed, the local or 'everyday' state in India has taken on highly personalised forms (Fuller and Benei 2001; Price and Ruud 2010). In more general terms, a view for the dominant classes comprising the integral state shows that 'local power relations have been central to the workings of modern India, as both colonial and postcolonial regimes have had to realise in practice' (Chari 2004, 40). This fact has entailed that successive regimes have established their rule through

---

9   The scholarly assumption that 'factionalism' was fundamental to the Indian polity was most influential during the 1960s and 1970s, later on receding from view in India studies (Nielsen 2011).

intricate negotiations with powerful intermediaries at different levels throughout India (Bardhan 1998; Corbridge and Harriss 2000).

Relating these insights to questions of agrarian transition, Radhika Desai (2016) presents a persuasive argument that transition has been fundamentally shaped 'from below' in ways that have led to the continuation of localised power, although rearranged, into contemporary Indian agrarian capitalism. Rather than being effaced by the expansion of capitalism in rural India, then, difference has instead been entrenched and crucial to enabling such expansion. In a recent contribution, Shah et al. argue for the notion of 'conjugated oppression' as a complement to classes of labour 'to express how multiple axes of oppression – such as caste, tribe, gender and region […] are constitutive of and shape class relations, inseparable from each other in capitalist accumulation' (Shah et al. 2018, 24). Class formation and class struggle are thus *internal to* capitalist expansion and *internal to* the social relations of production in Indian agriculture (Chari 2004, 44).

In the tradition of village studies and, later, drawn into the modes of production debate, Daniel Thorner's (1956) concept of the 'built-in depressor' points to the role of landlords – as important fractions of the integral state and social relations of power – in obstructing capitalist accumulation in agrarian India. Driven by localised rentierism and the profits derived from this rather than the search for increased productivity, the 'depressor' would not perceive the expansion of corporate agriculture as beneficial to its claim to power (Patnaik 1986). In reviewing our knowledge about landlordism in India, John Harriss (2013) argues for seeing the decline of landlordism in the course of the last couple of decades as intrinsically related to broader patterns of agrarian change and capitalist transformation including the patterns of livelihood and work mobility evidenced by the country's growing classes of labour. While the 'depressor' may thus have been instrumental in obstructing the integration of Indian agriculture in broader circuits of capital during the second food regime – that, is in Araghi's (2003) terms, the period of exceptional state involvement during the first decades of postcolonial India's existence – the rearrangement of local power relations involved in the undoing of the depressor may likewise be seen as an enabling condition for heightened integration in capital's food regime. Apart from that, neoliberalisation has reconfigured the integral state in other and no less profound ways, something that warrants closer inspection.

4   Neoliberalising the Indian State

Neoliberalisation is especially central to the arguments made in Chapters 4–5 and will only be introduced here in an overarching and contextual manner for readers less familiar with India's political-economic history. The onset of neoliberal reforms in India was – and still is – far from straightforward but rather uneven, gradual (i.e. carried out phase-wise) and incomplete. Regional scholarship agrees that the ruling coalition – i.e. the dominant social forces comprising the integral state – between the 1950s and the emblematic reforms of 1991 onwards, was marked by proprietary groups having such strong and diverse interests that any comprehensive reform could be blocked or undermined (Corbridge, Harriss, and Jeffrey 2012, 124–125). The dismantling of the 'License Raj' – the intricate set of licensing, siphoning of funds and regulated distribution of resources that characterised the Nehruvian developmental state – thus happened in and through contradictory class interests. Vivek Chibber (2003, 252) comments that the dismantling of the Licence Raj should be seen as importantly revolving around a combination of the 'spiraling disillusionment among policy elites and experts' combined with 'pressure from segments of the Indian capitalist class'. The latter found the regulatory regime to be working increasingly against their class interests, complicating strategies of accumulation. Broad sections of the capitalist classes were (at least up to the early 2000s) most concerned about internal controls, remaining 'guarded', as Chibber (2003, 253) puts it, on issues of external liberalisation. It is thus important to bear in mind that significant parts of the dominant fractions in the integral state have a distinctly complicated outlook on opening to global capital circuits. Not only was and is the integral state internally differentiated and contradictory, it also changes over time, as we find that 'different fractions of capital have had different relationships with the state' (Das Gupta 2016, 6).

What emerges in the 1990s and consolidating further in the 2000s is a new dominant class configuration, where corporate capital is gaining ground vis-à-vis small-scale industrialists, dominant farmers and others (Chatterjee 2008; Gupta and Sivaramakrishnan 2011). In Corbridge and Harriss' (2000) influential analysis, this represents an 'elite revolt' against the workings of the postcolonial integral state that had previously worked to elites' benefit but that now gradually came to be seen by corporate capital as detrimental to their interests (in economic liberalisation). 'Revolt' may however give the impression of rupture, whereas what happened was more of a 'limited stop-go process' (Corbridge, Harriss and Jeffrey 2012, 130). This restrained process lasted for several years (up to the mid-2000s, at least) largely restricted to select sectors of the economy and carried out by 'stealth' (Jenkins 1999). The elite revolt, it is moreover worth mentioning, was underpinned by shifting composition of the policymaking apparatus, which already by the early 1980s started being dominated by pro-business 'technocrats' (Hasan 2012, 48).

Dominant farmers' position in the reconfigured power constellation is at least partly due to their changing role in the period of neoliberalisation; that is, their diversification into new economic domains with accompanying loss of interest in mobilisation for agrarian issues. This implies new configurations of power in agrarian settings that go beyond the 'classic view' of dominance recounted above in the making of the postcolonial integral state (Gupta and Thakur 2017). Desai (2016, 40) argues for seeing aspects of this transformation as marking the emergence of a 'seamless capitalist class – stretching from the village and district towns to the larger cities and abroad'. In such a perspective, it is not quite precise to say that corporate capital is 'gaining ground' at the expense of other fractions, or classes, of capital. Following such trends, the class composition of the integral state is in a way becoming more narrow and the state is taking on an increasingly unambiguous pro-business stance (Kohli 2012). In line with Kohli's take on the growing business-friendliness of the Indian state, Sud (2009, 663) argues for seeing 'the evolving state as a business-friendly operator that ideationally, institutionally and politically legitimates, buffers, negotiates and facilitates a contested and complex liberalising landscape'. Indeed, while the onset of neoliberal reforms certainly saw the state 'retreat' through deregulation of the economy in various ways, it also involved 'relocation' of state action such as relations of patronage vis-à-vis the private sector (Chandra 2015).

This contradictory outlook of the Indian state came visibly to the fore under the United Progressive Alliance coalition headed by the Congress Party that was in power in India in two consecutive rounds from 2004 to 2014. During this period, the central government launched a series of (world-historically) ambitious programs in social protection dubbed a 'new rights agenda' (Ruparelia 2013), including the much celebrated and debated National Rural Employment Guarantee Act. These programs, importantly, signalled a contradictory process of neoliberalisation – as discussed in the context of right-to-food legislation in Chapter 5 – where the changed class alignment of the Indian state nevertheless coexisted with social democratic agendas (Nilsen and Nielsen 2016). While the extended Congress-governed period, in key respects, amounted to a form of 'roll-out' neoliberalism, the last few years has seen authoritarian right-wing Hindu nationalists pushing for altered forms of governance (Chacko 2018), something that has only accelerated aggressively under Modi's regime in the last few years (Jakobsen and Nielsen 2024).

Whereas 'unstable equilibria' were negotiated through social protection measures under the Congress Party (see Chapter 5), the emerging class realignment away from the former composition of the integral state is most strikingly visible under the present government. Prime Minister Narendra Modi's National Democratic Alliance (NDA) – now in its second period, at the time of writing just having secured electoral victory and thus set to assume a third consecutive period in power – came to power in 2014 promising the capitalist class what Desai (2016, 26) calls an 'expedited neoliberalism', which seems bound to cause rising unrest as the narrow class interest of such an orientation clashes with broad sections of the population. One could easily think of this as illustrative of the BJP's tradition as a predominantly upper caste party; yet, the BJP has by now expanded its constituency to incorporate also lower castes – in particular parts of the 'Other Backward Classes' (Jaffrelot 2015). In the 2019 elections, the lower caste constituency of the BJP markedly deepened (Nilsen 2021). While the broader story of the transformations of India's political economy under Modi's authoritarian populism is beyond the purview of this book (Jaffrelot 2021), important reasons for the broadening of BJP's appeal are found in its 'business friendly' stance that promises private sector, market oriented economic growth, projected as benefiting broader sections of the 'neo-middle classes', while simultaneously pursuing a forceful drive towards 'hinduizing' state and society in India (Jaffrelot 2017b). Here, the NDA differs markedly from the preceding Congress-led United Progressive Alliance government with its social democratic ideology and policies aimed at 'inclusive growth' (Chacko 2018). Standing for a change of direction that implies the 'empowerment of capital at the expense of labour' (Ruparelia 2015, 775), it thus appears that the Modi-led trajectory that India is presently seeing is one where the government may consider itself less bound to negotiate the conditions of dispossession and disenfranchisement that pro-business politics generates.

Indications of an unprecedented will to 'cut through' an expedited neoliberalism – even in the midst of 'unstable equilibria' with popular demands – can be seen in the BJP's recent and ongoing attempts at dismantling the food security apparatus in the country (see Chapter 5). While the Modi government thus appears set to 'expedite' further incorporation in capital's food regime, promises and realities have been very different, and the last decade has, as Chapter 1 indicated, seen stagnating growth rates and industrial slow-down. India thus more and more clearly falls within the 'long downturn' characterizing contemporary global capitalism (Kothakapa and Sirohi 2023).[10] However, within

---

10   See also Suwandi (2019, 153–161) for a relevant discussion that questions widely held accounts of 'growth miracles' in the Global South more broadly over the last decades.

this context, the period of Modi's authoritarian populist regime has seen staggering acceleration of corporate concentration in various parts of the Indian economy, signaling that certain classes of capital – especially those with close ties to the Modi regime, many of which of the consolidated, corporate type – have come to assume a position of increasing opportunity for seeking out new spaces for accumulation. Recent assessments by political economists indeed point to the outright unprecedented opportunities for dominant fractions of capital under Modi (Banaji 2022; Sircar 2022; Damodaran 2020; Chatterjee 2023). While the next chapter shall show that crucial class dynamics in the Indian countryside and in the agrarian sectors of the integral state have been diverging from any neatly linear directionality towards consolidation such as has been witnessed in other parts of the economy, these are nevertheless central transformations in the country's political economy more broadly that are significant to this book. As indicated in the first chapter, I believe it is crucial that food regime analysis work towards integrating its understanding of agro-food change in broader understandings of the overall shape of the capitalist mode of production.

The above does not, however, imply that I follow Chatterjee's (2008) influential argument that corporate capital has become hegemonic in India's 'civil society', whereas non-corporate capital remains ruling in 'political society'. Chatterjee's argument, critics have pointed out, relies on binary conceptions of 'civil' and 'political' society that not only misrepresents empirical reality in India (Nilsen 2012) but also misreads Gramsci's take on the integral state. 'Political society, civil society and the state', writes Judith Whitehead (2015, 671), 'do not represent pre-given bounded moral universes, as in Chatterjee's analysis, but rather knots of tangled power relations which, depending on the context, can be disentangled into different assemblages'.[11] The restructuring that has been going on with particular force in the class composition of the Indian state during the period of neoliberalisation enables new forms of accumulation. While favouring capital's food regime, these dynamics should not be assumed to centre primarily on the imposition of external ('global') circuits of capital into India. The remainder of this book rather suggests an important role for classes of domestic Indian capital – certainly tied to international circuits but rooted in the country's differentiated classes of capital. Disentangling these to gain a better understanding of their variegated agencies and strategies is crucially needed, not the least to grasp possibilities for classes of labour to

---

11   For further criticism of Chatterjee's argument, see also Baviskar and Sundar (2008).

engage in progressive counter-mobilisation, which is explored further in the next chapter.

5   Conclusion

This chapter has surveyed relevant streams of India-specific scholarship pertaining to agrarian change in the postcolonial period. I started by looking at the relative neglect of agrarian issues in scholarship over the last decades, and the subsequent more recent calls for reasserting agrarian scholarship seeking to address, not the least, India's dramatic incorporation in global capitalism since the onset of neoliberal reforms. Thereafter, the chapter scrutinised scholarship most closely tied to the interests of food regime analysis, including that of agrarian questions and transitions, noting a gap in efforts at integrating India in 'global' debates on agrarian transformation that is only gradually being addressed in recent years. In surveying this field, the research gap this book seeks to fill has been made more evident. Having done so, the chapter proceeded to laying out a more historically informed and empirically oriented – via, that is, a conceptual foray into Gramscian theory – story of India's integral state since Independence and its subsequent experience with neoliberalisation.

These are topics that will be revisited later in the book. In the present chapter, these have been introduced as a foundational context for readers unfamiliar with postcolonial India. Simultaneously, the chapter has pointed to aspects of postcolonial India's uneven capitalist development that provide partial explanations for later food regime dynamics. In particular, I have pointed to the role of specific articulations of class relations that emerged in the period of the second food regime – or, alternatively, in Araghi's terms, the exceptional post-Second World War period in which capital's food regime was kept at bay – that we will encounter in later chapter, then as aspects of the remnants of the prior phase which capital's food regime seeks to demolish. The story of the struggle over such demolishing, and the possibilities for new avenues – frontiers – for capital accumulation will be central to the chapters that follow.

Furthermore, as I have argued, any food regime analysis that seeks to grapple with the 'concrete' and thus supersede existing limitations in 'global' fixation needs careful attention to historical-geographical specificities. This chapter's discussion of the trajectory of India's integral state is thus a direct response to the call, in Chapter 2, for multiscalar analytics that speak to the state and class struggle in a conjunctural idiom. Taking the global value relations of food regimes as intrinsically comprised of the 'shape' of the capital relation, as Chapter 1 argued drawing on Open Marxism, there is no other way of determining such 'shape' than through empirically (yet not empiricist) oriented historization. This chapter has thus offered a level of detail needed for looking at food regimes as the 'political face' of global value relations, as incisively formulated by Araghi (2003) that is frequently missing in the value-form oriented scholarship that I have been inspired by in this book. Arboleda's groundbreaking book *Planetary Mine,* as a prominent rare example of mobilising a value-form approach within the broader field of agrarian studies, is surprisingly thin on the nitty gritty of situated *politics*, including empirical discussions of the politics of the state in his case of Chilean mineral extraction. The Gramscian analytics that have been introduced in some detail in this chapter – and that have, as shown, played a significant part in shaping influential scholarship on postcolonial India's encounters with capitalist transformation – offer fruitful tools for precisely such political analysis. Seeking to further the value-form informed line of thinking in and through empirical research, the 'grounding' in India-specific scholarship offered in this chapter provides an important basis for the following investigations in the remainder of this book.

CHAPTER 4

Crisis, Counter-Movements, Class Analysis

The previous chapter situated the transformations of the Indian state amidst processes of neoliberalisation and a stagnating agrarian economy as key areas of inquiry worth investigating for grounding food regime analysis in concrete studies. What this chapter seeks to do, is bringing this outline to bear upon a central point raised earlier in the book, namely, that of how food regime analysis has articulated crisis and relative stability as central yet increasingly problematic and often theoretically under-developed conceptual focal points for its periodization.[1] I have already indicated my sceptical stance towards the analytics of the crisis-stability couplet, grounded in the dissident view of value-form Marxism that perceives crisis as intrinsic to capital, not extrinsic or merely periodic, as may otherwise appear to be the case. Yet in this chapter I seek to take discussion further towards the concrete by taking India's ongoing agrarian crisis as my *empirical* point of departure for questioning *conceptually* how food regime analysis articulates dynamics of resistance – often put in Polanyian terms as 'counter-movements' – against the ravages of capital's food regime. Key to ongoing struggles in the 'corporate food regime' in McMichael's influential rendering are the broad and escalating forms of accumulation by dispossession driving smallholders out of their livelihoods. These deleterious sides of the food regime, argues McMichael, amount to a *global* agrarian crisis: 'capital's food regime has generalised an agrarian crisis of massive proportions, registered now in a growing movement to stabilise the countryside, protect the planet, and advance food sovereignty' (McMichael 2013a, 19). The Polanyian counter-movement, in McMichael's rendering, is showing the way forward – even beyond the contemporary food regime – to a more just future. Paradigmatically represented by the transnational movement Vía Campesina ('the peasant way'), the ongoing resistance against the food regime appears fighting for peasant subsistence farming in the name of food sovereignty. In this rendering, the corporate food regime is thus counter-poised to the mobilisation of the world's 'peasants'.

Following such a view of global food regime dynamics, we should expect sizeable counter-movements, rallying for their right to smallholding farming,

---

1 This chapter is a revised version of Jostein Jakobsen (2018) Towards a Gramscian food regime analysis of India's agrarian crisis: Counter-movements, petrofarming and Cheap Nature. *Geoforum*, 90, 1–10.

gathering forces in places where agrarian crisis takes its toll. India is one such place. In fact, it is a striking one. Since the early 1990s the country has registered a situation of deteriorating livelihoods for smallholders – epitomised in the globally prominent spates of farmers' suicides often described as 'epidemic' – which presently routinely is seen as an agrarian crisis, as indicated in Chapter 3. Given all of this, what can India's actually existing agrarian crisis teach us about resistance to the food regime?

Existing criticism of food regime analysis, as recounted in Chapter 2, has already questioned the role ascribed by McMichael to the global food sovereignty counter-movement. Whereas Bernstein's (2016a) penetrating reading criticizes McMichael's reliance on Chayanovian organicist understandings of the 'peasantry', I seek to take the discussion in another direction by focusing on the part played by readings of Polanyi in food regime theorization. This chapter seeks to demonstrate that the empirical case of India's agrarian crisis helps us see some limitations to the prevailing Polanyi-derived focus on relations between the market and society – smallholders, in this case – as a counter-hegemonic force. While undoubtedly fruitful and incisive in many contexts, this analytic disregards Gramsci's complementary focus on relations between the state and society, taking the latter to be intrinsic to the formation of capitalist hegemony in an expanded notion of the state (Burawoy 2003). Drawing on this points, I shall argue that India's agrarian crisis constitutes a conjuncture where some of the limitations in prevailing Polanyian renderings can be made visible. In particular, I seek to challenge the notion of a 'counter-movement', which I find to be analytically obfuscating and politically unhelpful. What we rather need, is a class-analytical approach that dispenses with the agrarian populism embedded in the Polanyian language. Contributing to grounding food regime analysis in the 'concrete', this chapter thus offers more substantial analysis of the actual 'shape' of class struggle.

The following section is devoted to spelling out how food regime literature conceptualises crisis as a socioecological phenomenon, leading to a discussion of the Polanyian influence in food regime analysis – and the benefits of a Gramscian response in its stead. Thereafter, the chapter offers a broad outline of India's ongoing agrarian crisis, picking up the mantle where Chapter 3 left us in its brief introduction of stagnation in the country's rural economy in the neoliberal period. As a distinct form of food regime approach to India's agrarian crisis, this section focuses on accumulation patterns as these have shifted over the postcolonial trajectory, always relating accumulation patterns to the shifting dynamics of class struggle. It thus becomes clear that, seen through a food regime lens, India's agrarian crisis articulates the downward slope of accumulation in the wake of the post-second world war phase, in which capital's food regime struggles to rejuvenate accumulation. The last section of the chapter then returns to confront the question of counter-movements in light of the concrete dynamics of the country's agrarian crisis.

1   Food Regime Crisis

Despite the crucial theoretical importance ascribed to crisis in food regime writings, the literature has largely refrained from taking head-on 'actually existing crises'. To the extent that actually existing crises have been invoked, it has primarily been in the relatively overarching – that is, global scale – context of the 'world food crises' of 1972–3 (Friedmann 1993) and 2007–8 (Holt Giménez and Shattuck 2011; McMichael 2009a, c). Agrarian crisis, which figures centrally in McMichael's most recent formulations of the 'fundamental contradiction' of the corporate food regime (McMichael 2013a, 60), has in other words been largely left empirically undescribed – although articulated conceptually at some length. In his recent discussion of crisis formation, McMichael perceives the global food crisis as involving a 'layering of spatio-temporal relations' (McMichael 2013a, 110) in the contemporary food regime: 'The current crisis of accumulation combines a long-term structural feature of capitalism (under-reproduction) with a conjunctural form (financialisation)' (McMichael 2013a, 114), while pointing out 'the food sovereignty movement is the most direct symptom of this socio-ecological crisis' (McMichael 2005, 298). Here, McMichael aligns his perspective closely with Jason W. Moore's influential work on the 'capitalist world-ecology' (McMichael 2013a, 113–117). The world-ecological approach to accumulation borrows from Arrighi (2010) and Annales School style *longue durée* analysis in seeing cycles of accumulation as going through systemic sequences of boom and bust (Patel 2022). As we will encounter aspects of this argument throughout the following chapters, a brief first introduction is warranted.

Moore frames his argument through what he suggests as a reconceptualisation of Marx's general law of underproduction as involving the dialectics of 'accumulation by capitalisation' and 'accumulation by appropriation'. Appropriation are those processes 'through which capital gains access to minimally or non-commodified natures for free, or as close to free as it can get' (Moore 2015, 95). What Moore calls 'Cheap Nature', here, is the 'work/energy' of both human and extra-human natures (for more on the notion of cheapness, see also Patel and Moore 2017). Through appropriation of Cheap Nature in 'an endless frontier process' (Moore 2015, 107), in short, capital seeks to expand accumulation while minimizing the rising costs of production and overproduction. In these processes, as Parenti has argued, the state operates as the crucial apparatus that mediates capital's ability to appropriate cheap nature and channel it into cycles of accumulation (Parenti 2015). 'Capitalism thrives', Moore writes, 'when islands of commodity production and exchange can appropriate oceans of potentially Cheap Natures – outside the circuit of capital but essential to its operation' (Moore 2017, 6). As accumulation cycles proceed, the ways of organizing human and extra-human nature that once brought windfalls of surplus value tend to 'progressively exhaust the relations of reproduction' (Moore 2017, 10). This conceptualisation of the world-historical trajectory of capitalism in the web of life, it bears noticing, borders on the apocalyptic. As Kohei Saito (2023, 125–129) recently interjects, Moore's view of 'exhaustion' of the ecological foundations for capital arguably underplays the 'elasticity of capital' with its astounding tendencies and abilities to rebound and profit off from crises, something I will return to shortly. How commodity frontiers work within a food regime framework is the subject of Chapter 6.

Although slightly awkwardly situated alongside such apocalyptic imagery of capitalism's demise, both Moore and McMichael do consider historical capitalism to manage crises of accumulation through reshuffling the crisis tendencies spatiotemporally; in other words, in accordance with David Harvey's notion of the 'spatial fix', referring to 'capitalism's insatiable drive to resolve its inner crisis tendencies by geographical expansion and geographical restructuring' (Harvey 2001, 25; see also Harvey 1982). Referring primarily to the uneven geographical development of the built environment, Harvey's concept can be made more germane to agrarian contexts as a 'socioecological fix' (Ekers and Prudham 2015, 2017a, b; McCarthy 2015; Palmer 2021). Socioecological fixes are also and simultaneously sociopolitical processes responding to struggles over legitimacy, which 'pushes us to consider how a socioecological fix doubles as a hegemonic project' (Ekers and Prudham 2017b, 11). In a related stream of eco-Marxism, James O'Connor long ago argued that deterioration in the 'conditions of production' (including land and labour) can bring about legitimation crises for the state in particular (O'Connor 1998, 150).

This points to the abiding interest in food regime analysis for seeing crisis as revolving around the normative, legitimizing function of regimes, which tends to be implicit in times of relative stability and made explicit in crisis:

> even at their most stable, food regimes unfold through internal tensions that eventually lead to crisis, that is, to an inability of the key relationships and practices to continue to function as before. At this point, many

of the rules which had been implicit become named and contested. This is what *crisis* looks like.

FRIEDMANN 2005, 229

As an example of how 'naming' catches on, Friedmann uses the example of how international transfers of agro-commodities went from being called 'aid' to 'dumping' (Friedmann 2005, 232–233). Social movements are seen as among the main actors shaping the trajectory of food regime transitions in naming and contesting crises (Magnan 2012).

2 Enter Polanyi

This brings us to the Polanyian influence in food regime analysis. Polanyi is an omnipresent reference point in the literature, embedded in early formulations of the food regime approach, as Chapter 2 showed, although only rarely articulated in more explicit terms (sometimes explicit, see e.g. McMichael 2006). Yet Polanyi's lasting influence on conceptualising 'society' in particular in food regime analysis has hitherto avoided critical scrutiny. Taking stock of his Polanyian analytics, McMichael recently argues for the continued relevance of the 'double movement' lens to make sense of world-historical patterns of agrarian change and mobilisation at the current conjuncture, marked by the confrontation between neoliberal reforms and aggressively expanding agribusiness and the global 'peasant' counter-movement Via Campesina rallying for the land and for food sovereignty, while recognizing the significantly altered conditions separating our times from the context of Polanyi's analysis (McMichael 2023). In this overview, McMichael clearly acknowledges the multifarious character of such counter-movements rather than subsuming them all within a single 'global' dynamic. In other articulations of Polanyian analytics of 'society', we find McMichael arguing that food regimes can be seen a 'constituted through state/market relations' (McMichael 2013a, 7) and leaves it at that. Or elsewhere, McMichael asserts that 'Polanyi was singularly focused on containing market override' (McMichael 2023, 2131).

A central concern I have with these wordings and associated underlying analytical presuppositions is that they point to a problematic notion of 'state' and 'market', where these appear 'as two distinct modes of social organization' (Bonefeld 2010, 16), something a value-form informed approach would warn against. McMichael's reading of Polanyi and the notion of 'double movements' underpinning the alleged global reactions to the corporate food regime rests, I suggest, on a debatable organicist notion of 'society'. Explicitly rejecting what he perceives as 'orthodox Marxist' fixation with class-analysis as a rather obvious line of criticism of the counter-movement analytic, McMichael holds that Polanyi's 'concern was ultimately for an institutional re-embedding of the market, eliminating market *rule* – thereby focusing on multi-class mobilisations championing a broader conception of social obligation and responsibility' (McMichael 2023, 2131, emphasis in original).

While Polanyi's analysis of state-society relations arguably is more nuanced in certain readings,[2] what I want to bring out is the incommensurability of Polanyi's view of 'society' and a Marxist class-analytic. This is incisively revealed in Burawoy's interrogation of differences between Polanyi and Gramsci (Burawoy 2003). Where Polanyi talks about society having a certain 'autonomy of its own' (Burawoy 2003, 206), Gramsci takes the 'integral state' to *include* civil society (Gramsci 1971, 263). As we also saw in Chapter 3, it is through the integral state that hegemony arises, where ideas and practices of dominant social classes are spread more widely and assume legitimacy, taking on the guise of representing society as a whole. The Polanyian perspective foregrounds relations between markets and society, emphasizing the latter's potential as a counter-hegemonic force. Polanyi's notion of society, Burawoy argues, at least in part fails to analyse class domination: 'For Polanyi, *any* class can represent its interests as the general or societal interest *within* capitalism' (Burawoy 2003, 229 emphasis in original). The Gramscian perspective differs in focusing instead on state-society relations and the ways by which society enfolds in the state to bring about capitalist hegemony: 'For Polanyi, society counters the market, while for Gramsci, it is an extension of the state' (Burawoy 2003, 214). Where Polanyi's notion of society is one of commonality of interests, Gramsci's is one of 'antagonistic class interests' (Burawoy 2003, 229). It arguably follows that whereas the Polanyian perspective allows for defining as counter-hegemonic movements housing anything from fascism to socialism, the Gramscian perspective would not allow as a counter-hegemonic anything that is less than politically *progressive* (see Carroll 2010).

Put differently, the Polanyian perspective is seemingly unfit for differentiating between 'movements from below' and 'movements from above', where the latter are fronted by dominant groups and 'aims at the maintenance or modification of a dominant structure of entrenched needs and capacities in ways that reproduce and/or extend the power of those groups and its hegemonic position within a given social formation' (Nilsen 2009, 115). We have seen how

---

2   For readings of Polanyi's double movement analytics which arguably are more attentive to nuance, see for example Block (2008) and Dale (2012).

Gramscian state-society conceptualisations have a strong scholarly tradition in South Asian studies. Drawing on stormy debates, first over Subaltern Studies and its distinctions between 'subalterns' and 'elites', and second over Partha Chatterjee's (2004) influential reconceptualisation in terms of 'political society' and 'civil society', Gramscian scholars have come to criticize both for their binary divisions. Understanding hegemonic processes should arguably rather be seen as involving the dialectical interweaving of the 'knots of tangled power relations' (Whitehead 2015, 671) of subaltern and dominant groups – or, in the terms of this book, between classes of labour and dominant classes – through the integral state (Nielsen and Nilsen 2015). Drawing on these points, I would argue that the idea of counter-movements in a distinct realm of society makes for a limited theory, not only of reactions to crisis and restructuring but of resistance to the contemporary food regime.

3   India's Agrarian Crisis

With these conceptual issues covered, I turn to sketching out key dynamics of India's agrarian crisis more empirically, set within a specifically food regime lens on its spatiotemporal unfolding.[3] Central to much recent scholarship on India's political economy since liberalisation, the country's agrarian crisis is frequently narrated starting from the onset of neoliberal reform, and is thus well-established in scholarly accounts (e.g. Narasimha Reddy and Mishra 2009a; Swaminathan and Baksi 2017). Challenging such methodological nationalism, Raj Patel (2013) offers a revisionist account the 'long' Green Revolution moving from the early state-directed stage of the 1960s and 1970s to presently being incorporated in globalised financialisation. Drawing on food regime analysis and world-ecology, Patel's account embeds agrarian crisis in much longer trajectories of global capital, imperialism and (cold) war rivalries, in which the early stage of the long revolution gives way, first to a gradual declining rate of profit in capitalist agriculture, and then to socioecological exhaustion.

While an account of agrarian crisis that operates at this relatively overarching scale is necessarily somehow synoptic of a hugely diverse agrarian landscape (see Chapter 3), it does not seek to imply uniformity. There are various rural classes – fractions of the dominant classes, that is, of various landholdings and crop specialisations – that certainly do accumulate in specific

---

3   What this section offers is a synthetizing account of empirical descriptions, to be precise. To reach towards the 'concrete' in even greater level of specificity, the account provided in this section would have to be revisited from a field-research based angle.

sectors of the agro-industrial economy, as witnessed from different parts of the country by scholars such as Lerche (2014), Münster (2015) and Sinha (2020a). Nevertheless, I suggest that crisis in Indian agriculture does constitute an 'organic crisis' in Gramsci's (1971) sense. Organic crisis, in Gramsci, entails that 'the structures and practices that constitute and reproduce a hegemonic order fall into chronic and visible disrepair, creating a new terrain of political and cultural contention, and the possibility (but only the possibility) of social transformation' (Carroll 2010, 170–171).

What the Green Revolution did was to put Indian agriculture on a particular path of agro-industrialisation. Whereas much food regime scholarship tends to emphasise corporate dominance around large-scale agribusiness, Indian agro-industrialisation has been noteworthy different, at least up to recently, in taking a predominantly decentralised form, driven largely by agrarian capitalists in cohort with the state. As already indicated in the previous chapter, the recently expedited neoliberalism under Modi's authoritarian populism with its accelerating tendencies of corporate concentration and consolidation must be seen in this specific context of agro-capitalist patterning. The early stage of Green Revolution farming was heavily state-reliant, as Patel notes, with elaborate systems of protectionist measures established from the late 1960s onwards. These systems, comprising the Public Distribution System, Minimum Support Prices and other forms of subsidies and protectionist measures, became in effect the lifeline of agrarian capitalism in India (e.g. Dorin and Landy 2009), something the next chapter will return to in more depth.

Conversely, capitalist farmers, whose political power had grown with commercialisation in the late 19th century (Desai 2016), became the lifeline of the developmental state by providing vital political support. The country's bourgeois elites in the Congress Party were, as Chapter 3 recounted, relatively feeble in their hold over the countryside, necessitating class coalitions with dominant capitalist farmers (Bardhan 1998). The latter comprised not only the richest strata of rural society but also, importantly, the 'bullock capitalists' of 'small to medium-sized self-employed independent agricultural producers' (Rudolph and Rudolph 1987, 50). In Gramscian terms, this is the integral state at work. It follows that the farming blocs of the integral state later came to focus on these protectionist measures in mobilising for their class interests. Unlike Latin-American countries, which have arguably been disproportionately influential on key thinking in food regime analysis, especially for the contemporary juncture, the agrarian structure in India is thus not characterised by an opposition between smallholding and massive agribusiness. Instead, agribusiness has been 'dominated by small-scale, informal firms' (Frödin 2013, 230; see also Harriss-White 2002). This has been acknowledged by international capital, which is significant in terms of how dominant actors in the contemporary food regime perceive the country. A report from the US Department of Agriculture report, for example, noted in the early 2000s: 'Even though India has one of the world's largest agricultural economies, Indian agribusiness is characterised by a multitude of small-scale, nonintegrated processing and marketing firms that use mostly outdated technology and are uncompetitive in global markets' (Landes 2008, 111).

This dynamic has, however, changed over the last decade or so, at least in certain parts of the agrarian economy. In recent years, parts of the agro-industry have undergone restructuring triggering both the Indian government under Modi's regime and international capital to assess rapidly 'upgrading' processing facilities, for example, as 'sunrise' sectors of marked growth potential. Such processing facilities, it bears noticing, are largely in the hands of upper class interests and relatively consolidated forms of capital that depart significantly in character from the more traditional agrarian capital ascendant with the Green Revolution.[4] In other words, this shift entails an intra-capitalist change, seemingly redirecting profits and avenues for expanded accumulation towards new classes of capital. Yet, to reiterate, until recently, the pattern of decentralised agrarian capitalism has been characteristic. And, moreover, as the dynamics of stagnation in the Indian economy writ large signals, claims about economic growth surrounding the Modi regime should be treated with scepticism, as rhetoric departs from a reality of meagre and declining investments across sectors of the economy (Mody 2023).

The agro-industrial path – or accumulation pattern – that Indian agrarian capitalism has pursued through the 'long' green revolution falls under what Richard Walker (Walker 2004) aptly calls 'petrofarming', based on the progressive 'override' of biophysical contradictions (Weis 2010). As the next chapter will explore further, crisis-conditions of levelling and falling yields and exhaustion of key resources has been documented to follow over decades of petrofarming in the heartland of the Green Revolution. Kicking off in fertile alluvial valleys with irrigation facilities, particularly in Northwest India (Punjab, Haryana, Western Uttar Pradesh), petrofarming then expanded from being confined to regions that were water rich to include semi-arid regions in the course of the

---

4 See Jakobsen and Nielsen (2024) for evidence and discussion of these processes of upgrading and corporate consolidation in the context of the country's bovine sector. In the bovine political economy, we find evidence of noteworthy shifts away from the predominant pattern of small-scale, informal trade in livestock among classes of capital in rural and peri-urban parts of the country towards a rapid rise of corporate trading houses and abattoirs that are largely in the hands of dominant class interests.

following decades (Gulati and Kelley 1999). This can be exemplified with the expansion of soybeans in semi-arid Central India from the late 1970s onwards. Richa Kumar's ethnographic study of soybean cultivation in Madhya Pradesh shows that expansion 'developed largely as a result of replicating the green revolution package strategy' (Kumar 2016b, 154). The result, Kumar argues, is a 'constancy of crisis' for livelihoods and environments where the agricultural model has 'pushed farmers onto a technological treadmill' where farmers 'find themselves in a position where their long-term reproduction – the need to be able to farm in the future – is increasingly under threat' (Kumar 2016b, 155). As socio-ecological fixes, or, in Moore's terms, the expanded appropriation of 'Cheap Nature', crop expansions such as this clearly rested on tenuous grounds, paving the way for the generalisation of crisis-tendencies in Indian agriculture.

Ensuing negative ramifications for water resources have been well documented. Irrigation through boreholes spread into semi-arid parts of the country unsuited for such intensive extraction of water. This also entailed dependency on electricity, and agitation among farmers consequently revolving around the politics of electricity access, leading in some cases (e.g. Andhra Pradesh, Telangana and Punjab) to heavy subsidisation by state governments (Price 2011). The sadly predictable result has been rapid exhaustion of groundwater reserves: 'Between 1980 and 1998 [...] almost 30 percent of Indian districts saw the level of their groundwater reserves drop by at least 4 m' (Dorin and Landy 2009, 177). As Marcus Taylor shows through field-research based political ecological enquiries, these processes have entailed a devastating 'race to the bottom' involving debt relations for borewell investments, structured by, and unevenly ramifying across, relations of dominance in terms of class and caste (Taylor 2013, 2014).

As the next chapter will proceed to examine in more depth, the downwards spiraling trajectory of petrofarming was further aggravated and locked in as neoliberalisation kicked in during the late 1980s, but only accelerated properly into the 2000s. Prabhat Patnaik provides a concise summary of the consequences for India's agrarian crisis:

> a reduction of input subsidies; a gradual winding down of institutional credit to agriculture, forcing the peasantry to turn to private moneylenders as in colonial times; a dismantling of the insulation between world market and domestic agricultural prices; a whittling down of publicly funded research for improving agricultural practices; a decimation of the public extension network that had been set up earlier; and a retreat from the commitment to a universal public distribution system [...] This withdrawal of support by the state makes agriculture an economically

> unviable occupation for large segments of the peasantry, much larger than ever before in the post-colonial period.
>
> PATNAIK 2014, 11

While Patnaik's somewhat McMichael'esque blanket-statements regarding agrarian India tout court may need tempering in view of the mentioned differentiated tendencies to accumulation among certain fractions of the dominant classes, the claim regarding the economic unviability of agriculture for larger sections of the rural population is borne out in numerous recent statistics. Although the percentage of agriculture's share of GDP has been contested, it is clear that it has shrunk significantly in the post-1990 period, with recent reports reveal a decrease from about 35 percent in 1990/91 to an estimated share of only 15 percent.[5] Other evidence of economic unviability include declining welfare indicators for agriculturalists; widespread unemployment and precarious underemployment, and, as reported widely in global news, alarmingly high suicide rates in many agricultural regions (e.g. Vakulabharanam and Motiram 2011; Swaminathan and Baksi 2017; Kennedy and King 2014). Suicide rates have been broadly acknowledged as closely tied to pervasive indebtedness, which, in rural India, is socially structured along lines of class and caste (Kandikuppa 2022). These negative indicators converge with the miniaturization of landholdings in the context of an expanding rural workforce that is, overall, lacking employment opportunities (Dorin 2017, 11) and simultaneously undergoing 'feminization' involving unevenly distributed distress along gendered divisions of labour (Pattnaik et al. 2018; Naidu and Ossome 2016; Das, Mohapatra, and Patnaik 2021). Landholdings classified in censuses as 'marginal' (less than one hectare) are now strikingly predominant across the Indian countryside: more than 70 % of landholdings are marginal (see Figure 1 below).

In this context, it is not altogether surprising to find that agricultural land increasingly finds new usages and value through financialisation. As Nikita Sud shows, 'since 1990–1991, over 5 million hectares have been transferred to non-agricultural uses such as industry and infrastructure' (Sud 2017, 80). This fits into the neoliberal pattern of redistributing assets to the upper classes by 'transferring landed wealth and resources upwards' (Oskarsson and Nielsen 2017, 8; cf. Harvey 2005). Any cursory visitor to peri-urban parts of India will quickly observe real estate developments usurping previously agricultural land – raising numerous questions of the political economy at work that has

---

5 According to Dorin and Aubron (2016), writing in 2016 based on numbers that are by now already a few years old, the share was in reality closer to 14 %.

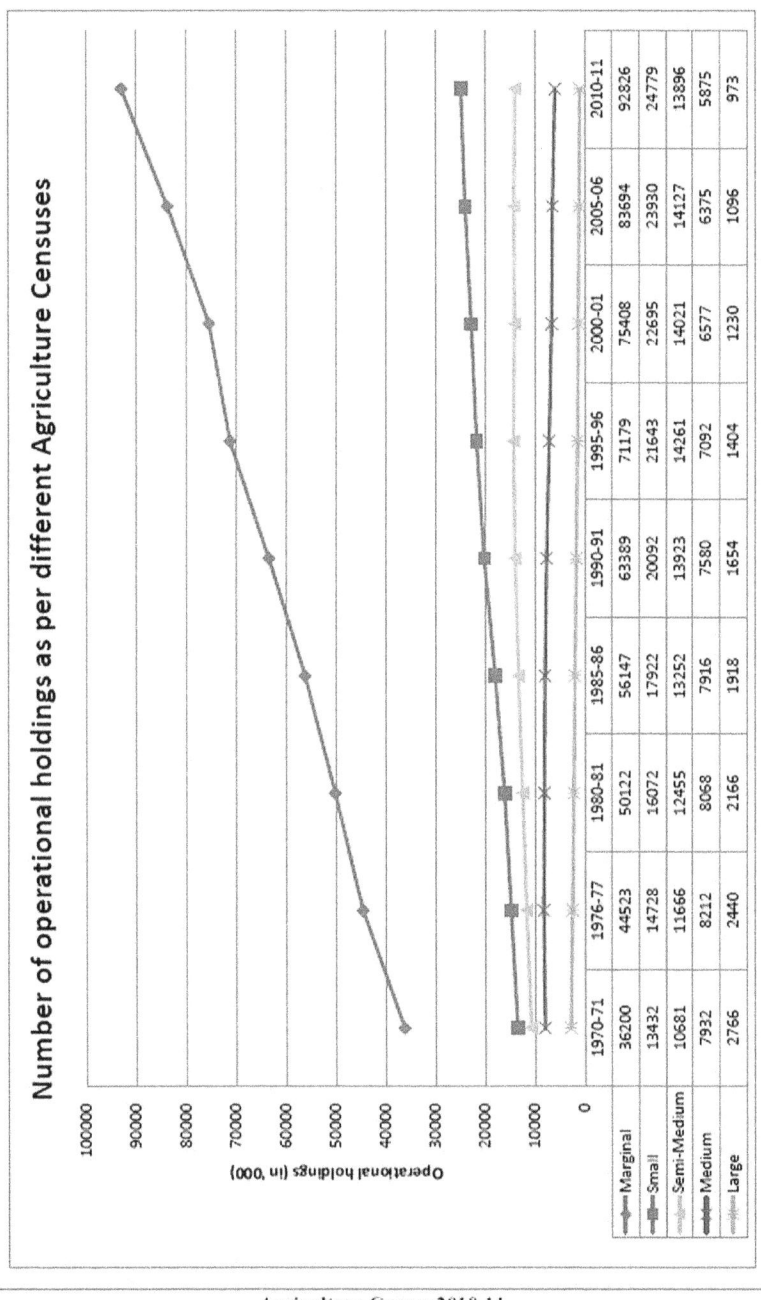

FIGURE 1 Number of operational holdings as per different agricultural censuses
SOURCE: GOVERNMENT OF INDIA (2011)

been subject of recent scholarly attention (Searle 2019; Levien 2018; D'Costa and Chakraborty 2017a).

While we have seen that organisational structures underpinning petro-farming were based on forms of state interventionism favoring dominant groups in the integral state, the neoliberal period in India has witnessed significant reordering where the formerly dominant class coalitions changed as the Indian state became increasingly dominated by corporate capital (Gupta and Sivaramakrishnan 2011; Kohli 2012). With the opening up of the economy came increasing exposure to international markets for agricultural commodities with their boom-and-bust fluctuations.[6] Moreover, with commodification through petrofarming came also skyrocketing reliance on credit – and thus skyrocketing loan rates – to maintain input expenditure and wage labour (Suri 2006; Narasimha Reddy and Mishra 2009b; Ramprasad 2019). As public banks drastically reduced their rural presence, agro-loans were increasingly reliant on private moneylenders with interest rates steered by greed, all of which shaped, again, structures of class, caste and, not the least, gender (Reboul, Guérin, and Nordman 2021). Farmers' suicide among smallholders cultivating crops predominantly for markets governed by international price fluctuations arises within this context (Kennedy and King 2014; Vasavi 2012). The trajectory of India's petrofarming thus glaringly illustrates Marx's insight that

> all progress in capitalist agriculture is a progress in the art, not only of robbing the worker, but of robbing the soil; all progress in increasing the fertility of the soil for a given time is a progress towards ruining the more long-lasting sources of that fertility [...] Capitalist production, therefore, only develops the techniques and the degree of combination of the social process of production by simultaneously undermining the original sources of all wealth – the soil and the worker.
>
> MARX 1976, 638

Bearing in mind the pitfalls of 'apocalyptic' tendencies under-acknowledging the 'plasticity of capital' (Saito 2023) in Moore's (and hence McMichael's) notion of 'exhaustion', the following two chapters will examine ongoing attempts by state and capital at 'exiting' from this crisis-ridden agro-system through socio-ecological fixes and commodity frontiers. Before doing so,

---

6 As John Harriss' (1982, 110) classic study from Tamil Nadu shows, Green Revolution technologies were, from the start, designed such that local economies became dependent on external resources – seeds, fertilisers, electricity, etc. – but these dependencies only heightened with the removal, from liberalisation onwards, of barriers to international price fluctuations.

however, what is needed is looking carefully at whether and how India's agrarian crisis has been spawning a counter-movement. Having outlined India's agrarian crisis in empirical terms, it is, in other words, time that we return to food regime analysis' Polanyian bias.

4   Towards a Peasant Counter-Movement?

Even a cursory observer of India's political scene may find it obvious that the country is indeed experiencing an upswing in farmers' agitations – something that easily can be perceived as precisely a counter-movement seeking to re-embed agriculture within forms of protection hitherto provided by the state. Indeed, McMichael (2023) gives attention to the recent farmers' protests in his recent 'update' of Polanyi's double-movement analytic for contemporary critical agrarian studies. 'PM Modi's attempt to unleash corporate power across the agri-food sector instigated a territorial-based countermovement', McMichael (2023: 2136) writes, as he recognizes the broad social base of the farmers' protests: 'Somewhere in this complex groundswell lurks Polanyi's "discovery [*or expression*] of society"'(ibid.). Nevertheless, what I seek to argue in this section is that the broader trajectory of farmers' mobilisations in which recent agitations is located has not in fact been one seeking food-sovereignty or otherwise 'protection' to allow the pursuit of a smallholder – 'peasant' – way of life. Rather, a strong and persistent tendency has been the attempt at 'exiting' from smallholding altogether, something that makes sense in view of the broader arc of accumulation in agrarian India since Independence, as discussed above. It is not even 'farming' or being 'farmers' as such that holds together the different fractions of classes of labour in recent mobilisations, but their class position of being subordinated to capital, pointing to the need for food regime analysis to integrate the 'agrarian' with the 'non-agrarian' under contemporary conditions of capitalist crisis, distress and stagnation.

While India's farmers' agitations in 2021 onwards may have appeared somewhat out of the blue to the global public unfamiliar with protesting farmers occupying streets in the capital city, years prior had also seen a surge of agitations surrounding the plight of the country's farmers and its crisis-ridden agrarian sector. As Jens Lerche summarised back in 2011: 'The Indian government, academics and farmers all agree: Indian agriculture is in crisis' (Lerche 2011, 104). During the spring months of 2017, in a noteworthy upswing of contestation, India witnessed a series of protests spearheaded by farmers, where issues related to agrarian crisis were emphasised, or 'named' in Friedmann's sense: debt traps, drought, suicides, degraded livelihoods and environments.

Agitations across several states saw farmers demanding loan waivers and higher minimum support prices from the government. In some cases, protests turned violent, resulting in police forces killing several farmers in Maharashtra. Moreover, dramatic increase in 'agrarian riots' have been reported. Some scholars quickly termed the protests erupting in 2017 'the return of *kisan* [farmer] politics' (Jaffrelot 2017a). Although the 2017 juncture did not bring any significant momentum to claims being made, and were at the time characterised by ad hoc initiatives rather than sustained mobilization, later developments reveal that kisan politics has made something of a reappearance indeed, invoking famous earlier iterations such as the farmers' rally that New Delhi witnessed in late 1978, when somewhere around half a million farmers mobilised to 'ventilate their grievances', as their leader Charan Singh expressed it (Chawla 1979). What has reappeared, however, is as we shall see substantially different from the earlier phase of kisan politics.

The time of Charan Singh was the period, in the 1970s and 1980s, of what came to be known as the 'new' farmers' movements in several parts of the country (Brass 1995b). Among the most important of these were, inter alia, the Shetkari Sanghatana based in Maharashtra, the Bharatiya Kisan Union in various parts of North India, the Bharatiya Kisan Sangh in Gujarat and the Karnataka Rajya Ryota Sangha in Karnataka (Brass 1995a, 3). Some of these still exist, although now in reduced strength. How 'new' they actually were, moreover, is contested. It is widely acknowledged that these movements relied on long-held patterns of power in agrarian social structures. Their newness rather consisted in their ability to bring farmers' interests to national attention. What, then, did such 'interests' consist of? These movements were often of a distinct class character, in stark contradiction to their often professed ideologies of 'an undifferentiated rural universe' (Byres 1995, 2). Class interests revolved around that of farmers who had become integrated in capitalist markets with the Green Revolution, for whom the search for more, better and cheaper inputs and support from the state proved to be a main axis of contestation (Brass 1995a).

The South Indian civil rights activist and prolific thinker K. Balagopal incisively held the 'provincial propertied classes' (PPCs) as the main class force behind these farmers' movements. Writing in 1987 – amid these movements – Balagopal described the PPCs as follows:

> A typical family of this provincial propertied class has a landholding in its native village, cultivated by hired labour, bataidars, tenants or farm-servants and supervised by the father or one son; business of various descriptions in towns – trade, finance, hotels, cinemas and contracts – managed

by other sons; and perhaps a young and bright child who is a doctor or engineer or maybe even a professor at one of the small town universities that have sprouted all over the country during the last two decades.
BALAGOPAL 1987, 1545

The PPCs are in other words not by far exclusively 'farmers' (cf. Upadhya 1988). These classes 'used their prosperity to straddle both the rural and urban sectors and have diversified their sources of income (e.g. real estate, trading, etc.). Despite the reduced profitability in agriculture, they have managed to protect themselves' (Vakulabharanam and Motiram 2011, 118–119), although they have to a significant extent *remained* provincial in their accumulation patterns (Kalaiyarasan and Vijayabaskar 2021). Less prosperous lower-middle sections of farmers experienced neoliberal reforms more threatening. Yet by the 1990s, aspirations for middle class lifestyles had become the new norm in rural areas, with smallholding agriculture increasingly seen not as the future but as the past (Jeffrey 2010). The least resourceful petrofarmers that are presently suffering under crisis thus appear as the sections that have not been able to diversify out of agriculture and are now left in a 'shadow space' where widespread disenchantment with agriculture combines with a neoliberal 'political economy of uncaring' (Vasavi 2012).

Consequently, the reserve army of labour in India is expanding. Among classes of labour in the Indian countryside the last decades has seen an immense rise in search for employment outside of agriculture with widespread labour migration – counting at least 50 million people, according to estimates by Jan Breman back in 2010 (2010, 7). This means that 'agriculture is no longer the primary basis of material reproduction of rural-based labouring class households' (Pattenden 2016a, 216). In India's 'jobless growth' trajectory (see e.g. D'Costa 2016), individuals having 'exited' agriculture do not, however, face any easy transition into wage labour, and to a significant extent pass from being a reserve army of labour into what Marx (1976) called 'surplus populations' toiling under a form of 'wageless life' (Denning 2010). As such, the Indian trajectory can be seen as tied up in a broader processes of structural change in the global capitalist economy, whereby deagrarianization has been intertwined with under- and unemployment, stagnation and misery (Benanav 2014). Although unfolding at a later stage than in the advanced capitalist economies, India's trajectory in such regard arguably needs to be seen in view of the 'long downturn' of global capitalism since the 1970s (Brenner 2006).

Radhika Desai argues that India's turn to neoliberalism should be seen, not as a state-initiated venture from the late 1980s, but rather as a 'slow-motion counterrevolution' where landed agrarian elites and dominant middle-caste farmers worked against the developmental state's attempts at progressive reform in agriculture after Independence. Breaking apart state planned land reform, these dominant farmers 'organised an agrarian transition of their own devising, on their own terms' (Desai 2016, 28), whereby Indian neoliberalism was shaped to their interests – rather than to large corporate capital, as in many other parts of the world. The turn to capitalist agriculture with the Green Revolution was thus shaped to these farmers' interests, remaking them into 'agricultural bourgeoisies' (Desai 2016, 38). However, as the green revolution initiated accumulation pattern saw sinking profitability within the next decade, agricultural bourgeoisies diversified out of farming and 'turned to industrial and agricultural investments' (Desai 2016, 39; Bardhan 1998, 64). While these dominant farmers used farmers' movements in the 1970s in order to push their demands from the state, diversification led this to change and 'by the 1980s, farmers' movements proved too narrow as platforms for the widening interests of the dominant castes' (Desai 2016, 42). The dominant class driven farmers' mobilisations thus ran out of steam. To the extent that dominant farmers are mobilising as blocs – such as we have seen in the 2010s with protests among Jats in Haryana and Patels in Gujarat – this is not for the cause of farming per se but rather for reservation quotas to gain access to education and government posts.[7] The provincial propertied classes are not uniformly successful in their diversification strategies. Groups that fall behind – also facing poverty – largely do not perceive farming as the future.

One of the most prominent 'new' farmers' movements is the KRRS, still active in parts of Karnataka. KRRS gained particular fame internationally in the early 1990s for its aggressive stand, direct action strategies against multinational companies and important role in Vía Campesina. The fame led Raj Patel (2012), in his activist writings, to perceive KRRS as at the forefront of promising struggles for farmers' dignity. Yet, KRRS was in many ways *not* a progressive organization. Through ethnographic research among KRRS activists and in villages where KRRS enjoys support, Jonathan Pattenden (2005) shows a stark contrast between rhetorical emphasis on anti-capitalist mobilisation and lived experience of domination. KRRS supporters, it turns out, are primarily upper caste/class farmers engaged in capitalist agriculture, while relying on exploitative labour relations and patriarchal as well as casteist power structures. Pattenden (2016a, 224–226) argues that, since the mid-1990s, rising diversification in the economic bases of capitalist farmers as well as the incorporation of

---

7 Both Jats and Patels – being dominant castes in their respective regions – have been agitating for classification as 'Other Backward Classes' and the quota rights this classification brings (see e.g. Hindu 2016; Iyengar 2015).

these farmers in the local state played an important role in the decline of the KRRS over time. Recently, prominent scholars of Vía Campesina have taken heed of the less than progressive stand and upper class nature of the KRRS (Edelman and Borras 2016, 46–47).

While it is thus highly problematic to argue for the 'smallholder' character of India's established farmers' movements, there are more recent tendencies that may appear to point in a different and more promising direction as far as outright resistance against the contemporary food regime goes. For example, focusing on the smallholder oriented agroecological movement known as Zero Budget Natural farming based in Kerala, Münster (2016) argues that this movement constitutes precisely a Polanyian counter-movement to socioecological crisis. Responding to the agrarian crisis, ZBNF seeks, in this analysis, to repair the metabolic rift of capitalist agriculture. Centered on charismatic leader Subhash Palekar, ZBNF promotes an alternative agronomy where the minimizing of market and capital dependency is central. ZBNF has spread in South India in the last decade or so, presently constituting what Khadse et al. (2017, 3) characterize as a 'massive grassroots social movement'. Numbers are however hard to ascertain. Münster rather uncritically quotes Palekar in holding – wholly unbelievably – that there are '30 million practitioners in South India', while in the same instance saying that there are 80–100 organised in his own field site in Kerala (Münster 2016, 234). Khadse et al. hold that 'a rough estimation for just Karnataka puts the figure there at around 100,000' (Khadse et al. 2017, 3). While these estimates are seemingly based on self-presentation by ZBNF leaders and cannot be taken at face value, ZBNF has garnered enough attention to be highlighted by McMichael (2023) as well in his recent 'update' of Polanyian analytics.

Although fascinating, recent engagements with ZBNF reveal some of the pitfalls of the Polanyian lens. Münster acknowledges that ZBNF consists of 'former' capitalist farmers turned down by the agrarian crisis of spiraling debt and labour costs, in particular. These farmers profess beliefs in the sanctity of the Indian cow that puts them into 'ideological proximity' to Hindu nationalist chauvinism, with its clear upper caste bias (Münster 2016, 235). As these points entail that ZBNF 'is not an easy partner for transformative politics in India' (Münster 2016, 239), holding that ZBNF is indeed a 'counter-movement' amounts to being willing to define, as Polanyi himself, counter-movements regardless of political ideologies. As we have seen, a Marxist class analytical approach would object strongly to such a wide net, unable as it is to differentiate the politically progressive from the reactionary. A more rigorous class analysis would likely enable even further insights into the agrarian elite position of the ZBNF practitioners. Khadse and colleagues do also point out that in nearby Karnataka, ZBNF has evolved in close connection to the KRRS, with ZBNF practitioners primarily from KRRS support groups, namely propertied and upper/middle castes (Khadse et al. 2017, 7–8). ZBNF has therefore only to a very limited extent taken hold among lower class group. In class analytical terms it should be seen, rather than an allegedly Polanyian double movement, as the working of distressed PPCs who find debt traps and labour costs unmanageable in the context of an exhausted accumulation cycle.[8] Brown's (2018) work on sustainable agriculture initiatives, similarly, finds empirical realities in India to differ significantly from prevailing notions of 'food sovereignty' as a counter-hegemonic force resisting the corporate food regime.[9]

4.1 The 2020–21 Farm Law Agitations in Context

The 2020–21 agitations against proposed new farm laws witnessed significantly different class dynamics.[10] Critical views of earlier movements, and of ZBNF, would not be immediately appropriate for the recent agitations. To understand the unfolding dynamics, a short recapitulation of the farm law struggle is in place. The proposed new laws were The Farmers' Produce Trade and Commerce (Promotion and Facilitation) Bill, 2020; The Farmers (Empowerment and Protection) Agreement of Price Assurance and Farm Services Bill, 2020; and The Essential Commodities (Amendment) Bill, 2020. Strongly pressed by the Modi government, the ostensible rationale behind the laws were to attain Modi's ambitious plans of doubling farmers' income in the country, as a piece of his overall populism (see Jakobsen and Nielsen 2024). However, despite pro-poor rhetoric, these laws were clearly of a neoliberal nature, allowing for the furtherance of dominant class interest in the country's agro-food sector – dominant class here understood as the class interests behind consolidated agribusiness, not provincial propertied class (Singh, Singh, and Dhanda 2021).

---

8 Research from another 'natural farming' initiative in Haryana similarly shows that distressed PPCs are the main elements involved apart from middle-class activists – all in all restricted to a 'niche position' (Brown 2013, 242). Apart from distress, health concerns also matter. It is interesting to note that there is a tendency for farmers to convert only parts of their land for agroecological methods for own consumption, while keeping remaining land under agrochemicals for sale (Brown 2013, 238–239). Based on fieldwork in Kerala in 2015 looking at state-initiated systems of organic farming, I have indications that similar dynamics are found among ZBNF practitioners.

9 Brown's (2018) book is an important contribution that attempts relating Indian realities to food regime analysis, although the book considers food regimes mainly as a 'frame' for empirical investigations. See my review of the book in Jakobsen (2019b).

10 This section draws on Jakobsen and Nielsen (2024) and Nielsen and Jakobsen (forthcoming).

Centrally about privatizing and restructuring the entire agro-food system from production to retail, the proposed laws would, centrally but not exclusively, have benefited major Indian conglomerate capitals such as Reliance and Adani that have moved into the fresh food supply chains, and whose ascendancy in the Indian political economy writ large has been closely tied to Modi's regime, leading Elizabeth Chatterjee to speculate recently about the emergence of an 'oligarchic state capitalism' (Chatterjee 2023).

The immediate critique, and ensuing protests, against the farm laws clearly recognised that the laws would instigate new accumulation patterns in agriculture. However, rather than the strength of the protests being about seeking to secure the farming way of life, their scope and broad class basis were rather about the recognition that the laws would undermine broader livelihood strategies among classes of labour in the countryside, not confined to agriculture. In Gramscian terms, this points to a recognised 'organic crisis' of the Indian political economy writ large. While the 'exit' from agriculture that we saw above for the provincial propertied classes was at least partially successful, this has not been the case for classes of labour. For them, livelihoods have remained a mixture of land-based agriculturally derived streams of income and various forms of shifting, often precarious wage labour, with the continued link to land being an important security. Rural classes of labour thus at a large scale comprise part of what Marx (1976) called 'latent' surplus populations, lingering in family farms due to lack of work in India's 'jobless growth' economy, yet they nevertheless, as pointed out by Bernards in the context of Senegal, 'remain embedded in capitalist circuits of accumulation' (Bernards 2021). There are, I would assert, no 'peasants' in contemporary India. The search for a non-capitalist way of life as an 'Other' vis-à-vis capital's food regime remains a chimera.

These forms of livelihood characterising classes of labour significantly shape the class interests at play during the farm law movement (Baviskar and Levien 2021; Kumar 2022; Lerche 2011). Lerche (2021, 1383) argues that 'the different classes of farmers and farmer-labourers have different class interests in many respects, but when it comes to the farm laws, they are united by the fact that they all stand to lose'. Similarly, as summarised by Baviskar and Levien in one of the collections of scholarship looking at the farm law movement:

> One thing that is thus new about the current protests over the farm laws is that they are not just about agriculture. Rather, they must be located in the totality of India's post-liberalisation political economy, and specifically the way exclusionary growth driven by financialisation, real estate speculation, and high-end services has afforded few and precarious life boats from the sinking (deliberately sabotaged?) ship of agriculture. If it

was possible to locate the early movements of the 1980s in the dynamics of post-Green Revolution agriculture, it is necessary to locate the current protests in the multi-pronged squeeze on the social reproduction of increasingly diversified households whose livelihoods cross the urban-rural divide.

BAVISKAR AND LEVIEN 2021: 1345

Experiencing a 'multipronged squeeze' along agrarian and non-agrarian parts of their livelihoods, classes of labour are by no means first and foremost concerned with their agricultural base, and the protests need to be seen as evidence of precisely the commonly experienced sense of losing out of the country's political economy in general. Assessments of the farm law movement acknowledges its complex class composition, with significant cross-caste elements and participation of women, Dalits as well as wage-labourers (Pattenden and Bansal 2021). Left-wing unions have herein worked across the interests of farmers and landless labourers (Singh, Singh and Dhanda 2021). While relatively unprecedented in its class composition, the prospects for enduring mobilisation are less than certain (see Lerche 2021; Singh 2022). Yet, the movement does point to the possibility that a broader alliance of classes of labour may emerge at a moment of distress in India, although, as always, confronting what Borras (2023b, 458) calls '[t]he operational challenge' in 'how to translate amorphous notions of class alliances into something tangible and workable in politico-organisational terms'. Echoing Bernstein's (2016a) sustained critique of food regime analysis, it would be misleading to think of this as a potential for 'farmers', 'peasant' or 'smallholders' resisting capital, and no less misleading to think of it as a reaction by 'society' in a Polanyian idiom.[11]

What the discussion above invites, I would rather suggest, is the both analytically and politically pressing need for centring the capital-labour relation in analyses of crisis/resistance dynamics within a food regime approach. The capital-labour relation, variegated as it is, remains *the* fundamental structuring force in which all stand to lose. Bringing this into focus, rather than fixating on 'farming' as some imaginary autonomous domain, may bring analysis more firmly into relevance for the manifold struggles ongoing among classes of labour in the global countryside. However, in more overarching value-theoretical terms – and perhaps a bit speculatively so – the crisis explored in this chapter not only points beyond the 'agrarian' but even, possibly, bears

---

11   This is not to undervalue, however, the real grains won through sustained efforts around 'peasant' politics in transnational arenas of struggle (Claeys and Edelman 2020; Edelman 2024).

witness of a more fundamental 'crisis of the reproduction of the capital-labour relation' (Benanav and Clegg 2010). In a world of capitalist stagnation, what sort of mobilisations are needed to address, or even remedy, the plight of India's rural classes of labour? Open Marxism would have us guard against preconceived notions what 'form' such struggles would take, in the expectation that the overall direction of class struggle in specific circumstances is a better guide. Yet, theorists ought not have any illusions of a privileged vantage point somehow outside of actually existing struggles. Leaving the question of counter-hegemonic resistance to the food regime thereby open, the next chapter continues to shed new light of an issue only left implicit in this chapter, namely the question of the state and neoliberalisation.

5 Conclusion

This chapter has explored the conceptual relationship between crisis and resistance in the form of counter-mobilisation – a central, yet so far rather undescribed analytical *problematique* within food regime analysis. Given that McMichael, in particular, argues for massive resistance in the shape of a global 'counter-movement' under Vía Campesina's banner is presently forming in direct response to the ravages of the corporate food regime, clarifying how these things cohere is important. While existing critique, especially that of Bernstein (2016a), has focused on McMichael's emphasis on the 'peasantry', what I have done in this chapter is rather emphasise the notion of 'society' with its Polanyian underpinnings. I have argued that food regime analysis better dispense entirely with this Polanyian influence, placing robust Marxist class-analysis in its stead. A class-analytical approach that is embedded in the Gramscian approach to the integral state spelled out in Chapter 3 may more forcefully help us make sense of crisis/resistance dynamics.

To develop this critique, the chapter has taken further steps towards the 'concrete' in that it has paid sustained attention to the empirical shape of India's ongoing agrarian crisis in a food regime perspective. In so doing, the chapter has operationalised some of the multiscalar analytics proposed in previous chapters, including that of scrutinizing the capitalist state as the political form of capital, the directionality of class struggle around the capital relation, and the overall outline of postcolonial India's trajectory of agrarian change. What is important to reiterate at this point, however, is that the 'downscaling' directionality of these analytical steps do not, unintentionally, end up in a form of localist stance, or that of a variant of methodological nationalism. Returning to Patel's incisive angle on the 'long' green revolution, it is imperative that the 'arc' of capital accumulation initiated in the early postcolonial period and gradually degrading into a condition of crisis and stagnation be perceived in view of constitutively *global* patterns of capital accumulation – something the food regime approach provides a strong affirmation of.

The chapter has showed how an arc of accumulation initiated with the 'petrofarming' of the 'long' green revolution and its apparatus of supportive state regulation in the first decades of India's postcolonial history has gradually waned through socioecological exhaustion, accompanied by shifting class dynamics, and been supplanted, in the neoliberal period, by conditions of crisis across the country's differentiated agrarian landscapes. Objecting to the Polanyian analytics of 'counter-movements', as prominently identified with the Vía Campesina, that has been emblematic to much food regime writings, what this chapter has rather shown is class struggle over forms of 'exit' from agriculture – real, imagined and stalled exits, that is.

This, in turn, brings us to a central concern in the following chapters. What we have seen in this chapter, is that India's ongoing agrarian crisis revolves, in a food regime perspective, around the exhaustion of longer patterns of accumulation understood as socioecological processes. The food regime perspective, drawing on wider scholarship in the uneven geographical development of capitalism, points to tendencies towards 'socioecological fixes' and, moreover, the search for new 'commodity frontiers' to rejuvenate capital accumulation, and or, more precisely, initiate entirely new patterns of accumulation in new geographies. Indeed, the struggle over India's integration in capital's food regime in the neoliberal period is, crucially, about such dynamics. The following two chapters will dive further into what these dynamics of frontiers look like in contemporary India. And yet, what the food regime approach says somewhat less about – as I have argued throughout this book, in no small degree as a result of its 'global' fixation – is the *politics* involved in specific historical-geographical circumstances, including the constitutive role of the capitalist state therein. What the next chapter seeks to do, is pry open some of the intricacies of the politics of surrounding recent 'right to food' legislation in the country, which provides a fruitful entry point for understanding some of the key dynamics of neoliberalisation that have been sketched out in broader terms so far in the book.

CHAPTER 5

Neoliberalisation, the State and the Case of Right-to-Food

Over the last few years, the role of the state has gone from being a relatively neglected aspect of food regime analysis to forming a central point of contention for a by-now burgeoning stream of writings and debate.[1] To a significant degree, this shift is triggered by real-world phenomena in the realm of agro-food and beyond, whereby many observers have pointed to renewed, intensified and transformed activities carried out by states, both in the North and the South, with some scholars pointing to a 'return' of sorts of the state in governing the global agro-food system. While I would reject any imaginaries of a 'return' on the fundamental grounds of the centrality of the state to capital and the value-form (Clarke 1991), there are undoubtedly patterns of change unfolding, including prominently in major 'rising' economies in the South such as China and India, patterns in need of sustained scrutiny (Alami and Dixon 2020), not the least to advance the project of downscaling food regime analysis to account for processes 'below' the hitherto fixated global scale. The contribution of food regime analysis, however, lays in insisting – *dialectically* – on the continued, yet altered through added 'determinations', analytical significance of the global and world-historical patterning of capital accumulation. This insisting stance puts food regime analysis apart from more narrow approaches that take forms of predominant methodological nationalism as their starting point, which includes, as Chapter 3 documented, major proportions of India-specific scholarship including that which focuses on agrarian change. As Arboleda puts it in his sustained critique of methodological nationalism, 'the very concept of a national state is better understood as the concentrated expression of a process whose scale is planetary' (Arboleda 2020a, 123). While Arboleda frames his intervention in terms of mining, and natural resource extraction, the point stands sharply relevant for agro-food systems as well. Yet, and again dialectically, the project of downscaling that this book pursues would retain a certain scepticism to the 'planetary' approach taken by Arboleda insofar as it risks underemphasising – both empirically and

---

1 This chapter is a revised version of Jostein Jakobsen (2019a) Neoliberalising the food regime 'amongst its others': the right to food and the state in India, *The Journal of Peasant Studies*, 46:6, 1219–1239, DOI: 10.1080/03066150.2018.1449745

conceptually – *political* processes, including contestations over the direction of capital's movement, hence losing slightly from sight the constitutive class struggles that comprise the capital relation. With these concerns in relief, this chapter seeks to take steps in the direction of downscaling food regime analysis by scrutinizing the role of the state.

The mentioned 'real-world' changes invoked above as stirring debate include protectionist currents, but also seemingly neo-mercantelist tendencies in agro-food, as we have seen argued for in the China case lately, as well as overall increasing prominence of seemingly 'progressive' state intervention in legislation and policy realms surrounding agro-food. Focusing on recent right-to-food legislation in India, this chapter seeks to advance the conceptualisation of state action in the contemporary food regime in a way that goes beyond prevailing terms of debate, by approaching neoliberalisation as a dynamic and unstable process of political compromise. While neoliberalism is a concept that is 'increasingly promiscuous in application' (Peck 2013, 133), causing its 'perplexing mix of overreach and underspecification' (Brenner, Peck, and Theodore 2010, 183), this chapter seeks to demonstrate some of the efficiency of the concept when specified and used more parsimoniously. In doing so, the chapter seeks to advance the disaggregated approach to food regime analysis, by prying open the concept of the state and, relatedly, neoliberalism, in a novel way.

The chapter starts by presenting claims that India's right-to-food legislation amounts to a form of progressive intervention, offering a first set of conceptually based critical assessments thereof. Next, I provide an overview of the treatment of the state and neoliberalism in food regime analysis, deepening the treatment of these topics only cursorily addressed in Chapter 2 of the book. Subsequently, the chapter zooms in on looking at these same dynamics in the Indian context, exploring some of the contradictions of the neoliberal state in India, similarly extending and sharpening the earlier discussion of this topic in Chapters 3 and 4 of the book. Having done so, the rest of the chapter takes as its empirical focus the struggles over recent right-to-food legislation. In doing so, my analysis is organised as a series of shifting lenses in a stepwise periodisation: First, I approach the recent and ongoing dismantling of the right-to-food agenda since 2013. Second, I look at contemporary processes are embedded in a history of neoliberalisation in the realm of agro-food in India that started in the late 1980s but has only accelerated since, centrally involving a legitimising ideology of 'efficiency' and its alleged adversaries which has masked extensive breaking down of walls for accumulation to the benefit of dominant classes. Third, picking up the mantle from Chapter 4, I provide the even broader lens of capital accumulation in the 'long' Green Revolution (Patel 2013), to show that the persistent attempts at dismantling the edifice upon which recent right-to-food legislation rests can be interpreted as struggles over remnants of, and eventual destruction of, the second food regime – or, in Araghi's (2003: 51) terms, the 'anti-food regime' that held capital's food regime at bay – in the context of ecological degradation and shrinking avenues for renewed capital accumulation in agrarian India. The chapter thus ends by pointing towards dynamics of emergent commodity frontiers that will be more fully explored in Chapter 6.

1 Challenging 'Progressive' State Action in the Global Food Regime

Contributing to ongoing debate surrounding the role of the state in food regime analysis, Pritchard and colleagues (2016) have argued that we need to take into serious consideration recent trends of 'progressive' state action in the realm of food security, challenging McMichael's (e.g. 2013a) view – invoked in Chapter 2 – of the state in the 'corporate food regime' being 'subordinated' to neoliberal capital. Pritchard et al. assert that the state does not merely 'step back' through neoliberal reforms, but also 'moves in' through right-to-food legislation. 'Conceptualisation of the emergent global food regime needs sophisticated appreciation of the ongoing, however altered, presence of progressive state action in global food geopolitics', the authors conclude (Pritchard et al. 2016, 706). Along with South Africa, India is used by Pritchard and colleagues as a striking, globally prominent example of right-to-food legislation, culminating in its landmark 2013 National Food Security Act (NFSA). As this chapter will explore in more detail, the act is based on a 'targeted' system in relation to the national poverty line, entitling nearly 800 million people living below and just above the poverty line to protection against hunger. Concisely summarised by Pritchard and colleagues, the 2013 NFSA involves that it:

> Provides legal protection against hunger and takes a gender-sensitive life-cycle approach to tackling the issue of food insecurity in India. The major provisions in the Act include providing food and cash benefits to pregnant and lactating mothers so that they and their newborns are well cared for, nutrition benefits for children aged between 6 and 59 months, free school meals for children attending schools, and 5 kilograms of subsidised food ration per person to 67 percent of the country's population through the existing Public Distribution System.
> PRITCHARD ET AL. 2016, 702–703

Writing relatively shortly after the passing of the act, and drawing on earlier meticulous research on food security in India (Pritchard et al. 2014), Pritchard and colleagues are explicit in seeing the right-to-food agenda as having 'transformative potential' in upholding and strengthening food security in the country. This transformative potential is seen to follow from the legally binding nature of the right-to-food, which 'constrains the scope for future governments to walk away from food policy' (Pritchard et al. 2016, 703). Presently, over ten years after the NFSA, there is more evidence to assess than what Pritchard and colleagues had at their disposal. Moreover, there are conceptual issues with this reading of India's right-to-food legislation that deserve scrutiny and, more significantly, help advancing theorizing of the state in the global food regime. First, the argument about the 'progressive' character of state action in this context lacks reference to scholarship on the neoliberal state in India or to broader critical theories of neoliberalisation. Second, the view of food security legislation implicitly departs from core food regime analytics in that it does not actually focus on capital accumulation.

This chapter offers a rather different interpretation foregrounding how the right-to-food agenda in India has, perhaps counter-intuitively so, contributed to a broader neoliberalising thrust, opening spaces for capital accumulation for upper class and transnational circuits of capital, with accompanying marginalising effects on broad sections of the rural population. In contradistinction to McMichael's view of states' 'subordination' under neoliberalism and its associated, widespread imaginaries of neoliberalism being about 'weak' or 'withdrawing' states (Slobodian 2018), I draw on the Open Marxism stream's emphasis on the 'strong' state as being quintessential to neoliberalism, despite its often-held ideological claims to the contrary (Bonefeld 2010). To complement the level of analysis often at work in this line of value-theoretical Marxist scholarship, which, as I have pointed to earlier in the book, has a tendency to refrain from tackling head-on the nitty-gritty of politics and political processes in their messy reality in specific circumstances, I suggest, drawing on the initial moves in this direction taken in Chapter 3, that food regime analysis here can benefit from Gramscian approaches to neoliberalisation and hegemony as working through unstable equilibria – or class compromises (see also Nielsen and Nilsen 2015). As economic geographer Jamie Peck puts it, 'although this may be analytically inconvenient, neoliberalism can only be found amongst its others, in a state of messy coexistence' (Peck 2013, 139). Neoliberalism, then is 'not as an already known monolith but as a moving matrix of articulations, predicated on conditions of existence that necessarily involve programmatic incompleteness and contradictory cohabitation both in – and, once again, across – multiple sites, struggles, situations, and settings' (Peck and Theodore

2019, 246–247). Neoliberalisation thus happens through 'contradictory cohabitation' (Peck 2013, 140) with other (non- or even counter-neoliberal) social forms and projects, such as welfare in India.

The notion of unstable equilibria is not, however, meant to imply a binary distinction between 'elites' and 'rural subalterns' where the latter is conflated with agriculture. As earlier chapters have revealed, classes of labour in the countryside in India – as in the South more broadly (Bernstein 2010) – increasingly engage in a broad spectrum of livelihoods mixing land-based production with multiple forms of often shifting wage-labour (Pattenden 2016b). The marginalising effects I invoked above must therefore be conceived of as variegated in accordance with specificities of livelihoods and positions in agro-industrial production systems. What unites India's 'classes of labour', as Jonathan Pattenden (2016b) argues, is their position of being exploited by the dominant classes. The notion of class compromise is thus a covering term, encompassing heterogeneity, pointing to the compulsions facing neoliberalisation as a hegemonic process in the context of India's electoral democracy (Ahmed and Chatterjee 2016; Nielsen and Nilsen 2015).

2 The State and Neoliberalism in Food Regime Analysis[2]

Scholars have recently criticized food regime analysis for its relative neglect, or under-conceptualisation, of the state, despite the obvious centrality the state has been given in the overall food regime framework focused on the state system (Pritchard et al. 2016; Werner 2019; Lin 2023). Critics have pointed out that the influential view of the 'corporate' food regime relies heavily on notions of deregulation and privatisation seen as ushering in a period where states recede in importance. While McMichael (2013a, 44–45) concedes that 'the WTO itself is by no means hegemonic', he sees it as instrumental in consolidating neoliberal principles on world agriculture and thus 'suggests a corporate hegemony insofar as neoliberal doctrine, in elevating "markets" over "states", transforms the latter into explicit servants of the former'. States, in this view, take a subordinate role as they 'accommodate transnational capital' (McMichael 2010, 612). To the contrary, critics hold, the 'neoliberal' food regime is indeed marked by continuing importance of state action through forms of 'neoregulation' that enable shifts towards market-oriented rule that favors transnational corporations (Pechlaner and Otero 2008, 2010; Otero 2012). Neoregulation 'encompasses the

---

2 This section draws on Jakobsen (2021).

state's trade policies, including those regarding agricultural trade, and other policies to entice corporations to invest and expand' (Pietilainen and Otero 2018, 4). In a book-length contribution to this strand of work, Otero (2018) discusses the way state-enforced measures of neoregulation have been key to the global spread of what he terms 'the neoliberal diet'. By no means presuming that states recede in importance, Otero reveals their centrality to the operation of the 'neoliberal food regime' through specific interventions in the economy serving biotechnology and agribusiness interests. Pointing back to the discussion above of the renewed emphasis on the complexities of spatiality in food regime writings, Otero's concept of neoregulation thus allows us to pinpoint the state as a key nexus where food regimes are institutionalised within specific geographical-historical circumstances.

In their already mentioned contribution to these debates, Pritchard and colleagues (2016) argue somewhat differently for incorporating contemporary state interventions in the realm of right-to-food in terms of a dialectical move between 'stepping back and moving in'. Such a dialectic, they argue, is a more fitting analysis of the current conjuncture than McMichael's (2013a) view of the state as subjugated to corporate capital. These sort of seemingly paradoxical articulations of state regulation are also elaborated upon by Werner (2019) who argues for the concept of 'uneven regulatory development' in dialogue with critical geographical theories of neoliberalisation exploring the blending of 'neoliberal' and seemingly 'extraneoliberal' regulations. In dialogue with Otero's notion of neoregulation, Werner holds that '[t]his blending is inclusive of, but distinct from neoregulation, which presumes that the main role of the state in the global South is to facilitate corporate governance and a world-market price for agriculture' (Werner 2019, p. 5). As a form of 'institutional heterogeneity', these analytics open for a multifaceted theoretical approach to state action in food regime analysis where regulations can take more or less neoliberal forms – even differentiated based on specific crops' significance in national agro-food systems – based on interactions with supranational ('global') pressures and interests, intra-state dynamics and relations between states and civil society contestations (Werner 2019).

Taking state action as central to the formation of hegemony, Werner (2019) also draw on perspectives in the tradition of Antonio Gramsci (1971) stressing the processual and incomplete nature of hegemonies. Advancing this line of analysis in the Indian context, Brown (2020) argues that food regime analysis has tended to be overly focused on resistance, neglecting deeper analysis of the dynamics that generate acquiescence with, or consent to, food regimes; in other words, the formation of hegemony. This, Brown emphasizes, is to no small degree precisely about the relations between capital, states and societies, with the intricate class dynamics this involves. Meanwhile, Tilzey (2019) offers a more critical take on the state and class relations in food regime analysis where he revisits Friedmann and McMichael's seminal early work. While curiously largely leaving out discussion of the recent reinvigorated work in food regime analysis, Tilzey criticizes the founding texts for lacking a relational view of the state, which Tilzey suggests we can locate in the Marxist state-theoretical work of Poulantzas (1978), which can be viewed as closer to the Gramscian view of the 'integral state' than Tilzey would have it (Bieler and Morton 2018, 124).

How, then, does food regime scholarship approach neoliberalism, more specifically? McMichael tends to equate neoliberalism with market rule, which is problematic in the sense that it leaves the concept largely bereft of other inherent contradictions. I think it is warranted, moreover, to scrutinise McMichael's use of concepts such as neoliberalism and hegemony – both of which he frequently invokes in characterising the corporate food regime (McMichael 2009b, 2013a, 2016). In McMichael's view, a food regime is understood as 'embodying a historical conjuncture comprising contradictory principles' including 'an organizing principle that expresses a form of rule or hegemony' (McMichael 2013a, 18, 21–22). His conception rests on the notion that states have become increasingly subordinated to the organising principle of hegemony of international finance and corporate capital in a neoliberal world economy where states, as he puts it, 'now serve markets' (McMichael 2013a, 47). The corporate food regime, consequently, revolves around a 'fundamental contradiction' (McMichael 2013a, 60) between a global tendency of the regime to cause dispossession and obliteration of smallholders and a global peasant Polanyian counter-movement under the banner of food sovereignty (see Chapter 4). Neoliberal hegemony appears thus, in McMichael's usage, as 'corporate hegemony insofar as neoliberal doctrine, in elevating "markets" over "states", transforms the latter into explicit servants of the former' (McMichael 2013a, 45).

Hegemony appears curiously one-sided here. While acknowledging the influence of Arrighi's (2010) Gramscian study of international hegemony, McMichael thus appears to sidestep some interesting avenues for further thinking. Meanwhile, scholars working in Latin America have recently argued for the term 'neoliberal food regime' to be applied to the contemporary conjuncture. In this view 'states continue to be central to the deployment of neoliberalism' (Otero 2012, 285) through engaging in 'neoregulation' involving the facilitation of policies for agro-TNCs, particularly in biotechnology, to advance their position in Latin American markets (Otero 2012; Pechlaner and Otero 2008, 2010).

Meanwhile, critical scholarship on neoliberalism has more deeply acknowledged and conceptualised the role of the state as intrinsically active and strong, arguably due to divergent conceptualisations of the state as such. Whereas the food regime literature appears to approach the 'state' as standing in external relationship to the 'market' and 'capital', Open Marxism takes the state as a mode of existence of capital, thus intrinsic to the value-form itself, rather than extrinsic as it may appear in food regime writings. This approach, which sees the state as the political form of capital, can be taken as complementary to Araghi's view of capital's food regime as as 'the political face of world historical value relations' (Araghi 2003, 51).

In a broader set of critical geographies that recognize neoliberalisation as an uneven and variegated process, there is by now a well-established understanding that neoliberalisation does not mean wholesale 'roll-back' of the state – under the influence of global policy regimes (Peet 2007) – but rather often highly interventionist 'roll-out' state action guided by the objective of creating spaces of opportunity for accumulation for hegemonic classes and forms of capital (Harvey 2005). Seeing neoliberalism, which, among others, Harvey's (2005) influential account does, as a response by capital to rising labour militancy and profit squeeze in the late 1960s, is crucial. Food regime scholars have – unproductively, in my view – fixated on whether and to what extent neoliberalism constitutes a defining feature of the contemporary food regime, even possibly being transcended by 'progressive' state action heralding a novel configuration of the food regime as such, something I take as exemplary of the tendency in food regime writings towards fetishizing the food regime at the level of surface phenomena. Rather, the historical-geographical materialist view of the state in neoliberalism rather alerts us to neoliberal measures imposed by states across the world being responses to declining profitability and capitalist stagnation in the 'long downturn' since the early 1970s. This line of analysis has hitherto been largely curiously absent in food regime writings. Instead of approaching neoliberalism as a phenomenal 'element' in the establishment of a novel food regime, it can be perceived as a symptom of prolonged crisis, and, as Harvey (2005) also does, a weapon against labour wielded by capital. As I proceed to explore the politics of right-to-food in India as an exemplar of neoliberalisation in the remainder of this chapter, what I seek to bring out, significantly, is how the Indian state as a mode of existence of capital, and thus of capital's food regime, seeks to rework possibilities for upper class accumulation patterns while also seeking to dismantle the crumbling institutions that remain partly from the previous period of state-interventionist measures in the pre-neoliberal phase of postcolonial India's politico-economic history.

3 The Contradictions of the Neoliberalising State in India

To advance the discussion, I suggest that we have a look at what prominent debates in the scholarship of the neoliberal state in India have to offer. Broadly fitting into the global pattern of neoliberalisation of state and economy from the late 1980s onward – taking off in 1991 at the height of fiscal deficit – evidence nevertheless shows that India has been more restrained and cautious in its integration with global capitalism than has been the case for many other countries in the South (Eriksen 2017; Pedersen 2008). Or at least, as pointed to in Chapter 3, this has been the case up until recently, i.e. until the rise to power of Modi's authoritarian populist regime.

The literature on India's political economy tends to emphasise that the incomplete, uneven and piecemeal nature of neoliberalisation compared to many other countries, even under pressure from international agencies, reflects the ways by which the state in India is 'penetrated by powerful social actors' (Mukherji 2014, 2) ranging from caste groups and capitalist farmers to financial elites some of whom invariably will be found disinclined towards any given reform. Dominant class coalitions, as we have already seen earlier in this book, since Independence have been fragile, reflecting tenuous relationships between the state apparatus and the electorate. Crucial to our purposes, bourgeoisie classes have been relatively weak, relying on the support of dominant sections of capitalist farmers. The state has in its turn become dependent on protecting the latter's interests (Bardhan 1998).

A prominent strand of writings in the political economy of the Indian state turned to Gramsci's notion of 'passive revolution' to understand the ways by which the state-directed developmental reforms in the early years of postcolonial nationhood facilitated the hegemony of capital accumulation through the incorporation of 'the old dominant classes into partners in a new historical bloc and only a partial appropriation of the popular masses' (Chatterjee 1986, 30; see also Kaviraj 1988). These writings, as Chapter 3 indicated, gave birth to a long-standing and sometimes bitter debate about modern Indian state and society. Here, dominant and subaltern classes went from being conceptualised as largely autonomous to relational and dialectical – the latter view stressing subaltern groups experiencing an 'adverse incorporation into structures of power' (Nilsen 2012, 257).

Broadly consonant with such perspectives, Corbridge and Harriss (2000) argue compellingly that India's uneven and contested turn towards liberalisation should be analysed as an 'elite revolt' at the intersection of contradictory interests wielded by corporate and industrialist classes favouring liberalisation and agrarian capitalists favouring continuing protectionism. At play here was also a strongly felt need, among some elites, to get rid of elements of the developmental state which evidently 'needed to be reformed' (Corbridge and Harriss 2000, 160). The revolt has allowed corporate elites to gain steadily more solid control over the Indian state apparatus at its various levels (cf. Gupta and Sivaramakrishnan 2011). Atul Kohli argues that these transformations have implied that 'a multiclass state that used mass incorporating ideologies to legitimize power has been transformed into a much narrower ruling alliance between the state and big business'. In its turn this has necessitated the ruling classes to 'manage the excluded', arguably through 'illusions of inclusion' as broad sections of the population find themselves increasingly displeased with policy change (Kohli 2012, 77).

A related, although differently phrased and more far-reaching, argument is made by Kalyan Sanyal (2007). In his view, Independent India saw a developmental state building legitimacy on its promise to extend welfare universally. However, experience quickly turned to capitalist growth alongside, and generative of, poverty and widespread dispossession. These threats to legitimacy were assuaged by the introduction – especially from the late 1970s onwards and expanding rapidly in the neoliberal period – of anti-poverty programmes promising socioeconomic betterment across the board (Sanyal 2007, 184–188). Sanyal thus perceives Indian capitalist development as involving processes of primitive accumulation bringing deprivation to the majority, which then 'requires that a part of the capitalist surplus be transferred from the domain of capital for implementing anti-poverty programs; development now means a reversal of primitive accumulation' (Sanyal 2007, 174). Anti-poverty programmes are interpreted as instruments for securing the hegemony of capital accumulation through 'the management of poverty' (Sanyal 2007, 191).

Drawing on Sanyal as well as Polanyian notions of 'double-movements' (see Chapter 4), Partha Chatterjee argues, in an influential article, that neoliberalisation has brought 'the hegemonic hold of corporate capital over the domain of civil society' (Chatterjee 2008, 62). The hegemony of corporate capital implies, Chatterjee goes on to say, that processes of primitive accumulation divesting large sections of the population of their means of production will invariably continue; but in the context of Indian electoral democracy such processes will also necessarily entail a 'parallel process of the reversal of the effects of primitive accumulation' (Chatterjee 2008, 55). These latter reversals comprise exactly the various state-led schemes for public provision including the recent right to food (Chatterjee 2008, 55).

Ideas of the state intervening in order to reverse the effects of primitive accumulation bring us much closer to a properly contradictory approach to neoliberalisation. Yet there is reason to temper some of this bleakness. Without going any further into the rich debate on poverty in India (see e.g. Corbridge, Harriss, and Jeffrey 2012, 47–79), it is clear that significant numbers of Indians have indeed seen their lives improved during the period of neoliberalisation. It is also clear that, despite the country's steep economic growth rates, poverty reduction have not matched many other developing countries, and indeed fall short of many others (Drèze and Sen 2013). Moreover, as pointed out repeatedly throughout this book, class dynamics in the Indian countryside are complex, something that we risk hiding from view if we take primitive accumulation to be revolving exclusively around farmland rather than public assets more broadly, in line with David Harvey (2003). While farmland cannot be said to comprise a common point of contention for all of India's 'classes of labour' in the countryside, public assets arguably do.

These arguments imply that the state's social safety net is indeed expanding in proportion to primitive accumulation. However, this is not necessarily the case. For example, Eriksen (2017, 51) calculates social protection expenditure in India to show a clear downward trend since the 1980s –ambitious rights based schemes notwithstanding. Eriksen contends that the mobilisations involved should *not* be viewed as Polanyian counter-movements, as they neither lead to increased protections nor are they initiated 'from below' – but from elite activist circles (cf. Harriss 2011).[3] Rather than seeing the continuation or renewal of protectionist measures in line with Chatterjee and Sanyal, we can thus alternatively perceive state policies as related to 'capital's interest in state support' (Eriksen 2017, 41).

In sum, we need to foreground 'neoliberal contradictions' (Ahmed and Chatterjee 2016) in our view of the Indian state and economy: 'Thus electoral politics create political compulsions where capital-labour dialectics are contextually and temporarily resolved/synthesized in the form of policies that give a new lease of life to the accumulation process' (Ahmed and Chatterjee 2016, 345). A Gramscian perspective would moreover emphasise that we hold neoliberalisation as a hegemonic process involving 'unstable equilibria' – forms of class compromise – between dominant and subaltern groups (Gramsci 1971, 182). 'The negotiation of this equilibrium', write Nielsen and Nilsen, 'is ultimately intended to facilitate India's process of neoliberalisation in a context of advanced global capitalism' (Nielsen and Nilsen 2015, 206). *Ultimately* points

---

3   While Eriksen's calculations predate the recent welfare initiatives of Modi's government, we can expect patterns to continue, despite Modi's loud and perseverant rhetoric of welfare expansion. At the time of writing, for example, Indian reporters discovered underfunding in 71,9 percent of Modi's welfare schemes, in "one out of five schemes, the government spent less than half of what it promised in the budget" (Asopa and Jalihal 2024).

to the temporal dimension: the outcome in the longer term, in contradiction to the more short-term engagement with neoliberalisation's 'others' for gaining support and legitimacy through unstable equilibria. While Nielsen and Nilsen write in the context of land acquisition contestations, I will proceed to argue that similar processes underpin the ostensibly progressive 'right-to-food' legislation.

There is nothing particularly surprising to the finding that India neoliberalises in distinct ways: scholars of the political geography of neoliberalisation know it as a 'shape-shifting' process (Peck 2010) that generates 'hybrids' in 'actually existing neoliberalisms' (Peck and Tickell 2002). Neoliberalisation is 'always an incomplete process' where 'contradictory cohabitation represents the rule, rather than the exception' (Peck 2013, 140). Likewise, writes Peck with reference to Stuart Hall, hegemonies too are 'incomplete and contradictory'. This is a fruitful insight for food regime analysis: 'Hegemony is a tricky concept and provokes muddled thinking. No project achieves a position of permanent "hegemony". It is a process, not a state of being' (Hall 2011, 727–728).

4 The Right-to-Food in India

In the last two decades India has witnessed unprecedented legislative change strengthening civic rights. This 'new rights agenda' reflects the mounting pressure of civil society mobilisation, and popular expectations, for the Indian state to redress (some of the) grievances emergent from the proliferating inequities ensuing from neoliberalisation (Nilsen and Nielsen 2016; Ruparelia 2013). Among these inequities, India's blatant paradoxes of 'hunger amidst growth' have been widely observed. Food insecurity in the country remains endemic and a thorn in the eye for any official efforts at portraying India as a 'rising power' housing spectacular 'growth'. During the first period of Narendra Modi's regime, from 2014–2019, the "State of Food Security and Nutrition in the World" report documented a rise of 3,4 percent of food insecurity in the country (FAO et al. 2020). The "Global Hunger Index", moreover, places India at 111 out of 125 assessed countries.[4] As I will return to soon, the country's food insecurity clearly deteriorated during COVID-19, but it did so from an already alarmingly high level.

---

4 See Global Hunger Index Scores by 2023 GHI Rank – Global Hunger Index (GHI) – peer-reviewed annual publication designed to comprehensively measure and track hunger at the global, regional, and country levels.

It is in such a context that rights-based 'law-struggles' (Sundar 2011) around food must be understood. Concerted and sustained, though largely urban elite-based, activism and petitioning has been instrumental in effecting citizen rights coming to encompass not only food but, *inter alia*, the right to information, to rural work, to education. Legal activism in the realm of food, epitomised in the Right to Food Campaign emergent from civil society organisations across the country, took shape in the early 2000s in the effort to hold the state responsible in its obligations to provide protection in the face of famine and droughts in parts of the country. The campaign, spearheaded by social and legal activists as well as academics, worked through claim-making in courts as well as grassroots mobilisation and was influential in pressing the national government towards legislation, which eventually took the form of the National Food Security Act (NFSA) in September 2013. The campaign thus saw social activists working closely with parts of the judiciary – especially activist judges – as well as parts of the government by way of membership in the National Advisory Council headed, at the time of the introduction of the NFSA, by Sonia Gandhi of the Indian National Congress party (Banik 2016; Hertel 2015; Krishnan and Subramaniam 2014). Not only partaking in national law-struggles, the right to food has also, as Pritchard and colleagues (2016) show, become part of prominent multilateral agencies, as in the UN Special Rapporteur on the right to food.[5]

In essence, as the discussion above would indeed have us expect, the NFSA embodies contradictory dynamics. This is so both nationally, in terms of popular demands for redress of grievances through the state, and geopolitically, as India's protectionist measures in agriculture oppose WTO rules and India's confrontational stand in WTO negotiations thus have been instrumental in giving countries in the South a stronger platform for negotiating their national food security policies (Hopewell 2015; Pritchard et al. 2016). How, then, have the contradictions of neoliberalisation worked themselves out since the 2013 act was passed?

4.1   *Short-term Neoliberalisation*
Upon the inception of the NFSA, largely hidden from view by the accompanying global fanfare, forces in the Indian polity started work at pulling the act apart. This can in part be seen as related to the hurly-burly of electoral politics. While shunning from engaging at any length with ongoing debates on the politics behind the act, it is worth mentioning a few salient issues. First and foremost,

---

[5] See website: http://www.ohchr.org/EN/Issues/Food/Pages/FoodIndex.aspx.

the attacks have been focused on the food security architecture on which the act rests, namely, crucial parts of the Public Distribution System (PDS). During the heydays of the Indian developmental state in the 1960s a series of intricate measures were taken ostensibly to strengthen the provisioning of staple food to a burgeoning population. Central to such an agenda was the consolidation of the PDS aimed at procuring food grains – focused on wheat and rice from the heartland of the Green Revolution in Northwest India – for storage and distribution at subsidised rates (Landy 2009; Mooij 1998). I will return in the next section to the longer trajectory of the neoliberalisation of the PDS, adding for now that the 1990s saw the PDS shift from being a universal system to becoming 'targeted' in accordance with official poverty lines, providing subsidised grains only to particular sections of the population (Swaminathan 2000).

Passed just before national elections by the centrist Congress-led United Progressive Alliance (UPA) government, the NFSA was thereafter left to be implemented by Modi's Bharatiya Janata Party-led National Democratic Alliance (NDA) which came to power in 2014. The timing predictably enough led commentators of Indian politics to charge the UPA for 'populism' seeking electoral gains. Although the NDA did support the passing of the law in Parliament, the Congress in opposition has lambasted the government for failing to implement the law ever since (also predictably enough; see e.g. IANS 2016). Food activists, on their side, were disappointed by the final design of the NFSA – a far cry from the comprehensiveness and universality that the campaign had fronted (Hertel 2015). Yet they subsequently joined in criticising the government for failing to implement the law (e.g. Himanshu 2015; Mander 2015).

There is nothing novel about Indian governments not implementing ambitious schemes. In this case critics have perceived the government's neglect as a logical consequence of Modi and the NDA government's heavily pro-business political platform. While it is true that Modi's government rests on the promise of 'expedited neoliberalism' for the benefit of the corporate classes (Desai 2016, 26), and it is equally true that Congress does have more of an attachment to welfare and the rights agenda, it would be misleading to let the hurly-burly of electoral politics obstruct us from seeing underlying patterns. The NFSA rests on a steadily, yet messily neoliberalising food security apparatus. Here the Communist Party of India (Marxist), being the main dissenting voice in Indian parliamentary politics as far as the right to food is concerned, has been perceptive. Regardless of which party holds government, the Communist Party of India (Marxist) has insisted on viewing the NFSA as deeply flawed in its reliance on targeted PDS operations, promising to be a 'platform to push through neo-liberal reforms with legal sanction', as their Politburo put it back in 2011 (Politburo 2011).

The dissenters were onto something important. Consider the ways by which Modi's government has taken steps to steps to restructure the country's food security architecture. Shortly after assuming office in 2014, the NDA government assembled a High Level Committee to bring recommendations regarding possible restructurings of the Food Corporation of India (FCI). Established in 1964, at the initial stage of the Green Revolution, the FCI is in many ways the crucial agency to the country's food security system, being responsible for procurement, storage (as buffer stock) and distribution of food grains at subsidised prices (Minimum Support Price) (Dorin and Landy 2009). At least since the 1990s, the FCI has been repeatedly criticised – with good reason – for inefficiencies, waste, and corruption. The Modi government's turn to the FCI was thus not altogether unexpected. Among the recommendations of the High Committee was the partial outsourcing of food grain procurement and storage to *private* companies, a task hitherto consigned to the FCI but now being suggested restructured through competition in order to reduce state expenditure (Committee 2015). In March 2016 India's Food Minister Ram Vilas Paswan argued as follows for what is blatant privatisation:

> These players [private companies] have been engaged to expand the coverage of minimum support price (MSP) operations to such identified clusters of districts/parts of the district, where outreach of government agencies has been weak and state governments have consented for FCI to engage the private agencies to reach out to the paddy farmers for improvement.
> GOVERNMENT OF INDIA 2016

What ostensibly underlay the drive for dismantling the public nature of the FCI were two sets of arguments: First, the Committee held that the changed situation of excess food grain production in recent years has made obsolete a system intended for times of scarcity. Second, the Committee held that the dysfunctional nature of the FCI – and the PDS in general, only benefiting a small section of farmers, namely, to reiterate, those in the heartland of the Green Revolution – undermine their continued existence (Basu and Das 2015).[6] Rather than calling for expansion of public operations, which critics including

---

6 To what extent these arguments reflect reality is a question I leave aside for the moment. Important for our purposes are the *effects* of the arguments first and foremost. As to the argument of India becoming a perceived 'food surplus' producer, see Arindam Banerjee (2015) for

food activists pointed out as the pertinent response, the committee held cutbacks and narrowing of responsibilities in procurement as well as storage to be the way to 'efficiency'. The NFSA spawned loud debates in the Indian public as to the costs involved. Whereas many commentators seeking to criticise the initiative claimed it to be too expensive for an already cash-strapped bureaucracy, key persons in India's right to food movement such as Jean Drèze (2013) to the contrary held the NFSA to be a 'modest' initiative not actually involving any real expansion of public spending. Consonant with Eriksen's argument about the limited nature of counter-movements' abilities to bring about expansion in state welfare schemes, in real terms it is not the case that the NFSA involved a 'roll-out' of state provisioning.

The Committee further called for limiting the NFSA to cover only 40 percent of the population and, in the long term, replacing the PDS with a direct cash transfer system (Committee 2015). Critics on the electoral Left were swift in condemning the recommendations as a blueprint for 'destroying the food security edifice in India' (Gupta 2015) and it does seem pertinent to see the suggested restructuring as an end to a whole mode of state intervention in food, hollowing out the right-to-food agenda.

More recently, Modi's government has taken steps to incorporate the PDS in their flagship Aadhaar programme, a nationwide biometric ID system. In early 2017, the government started pushing towards making Aadhaar number a mandatory prerequisite for receiving grains through the PDS; a move that, in defiance of the Supreme Court, also can be seen as another step closer to ending subsidised grains distribution once and for all, to be replaced with cash transfers (Bera 2017). In April 2017, the central government moreover suggested that the states should reduce their subsidy expenditure through voluntary cash transfer schemes meant to 'persuade' the public to stop using the PDS (Das 2017). In 2018, the Indian Supreme Court permitted state governments to use Aadhaar to access public support programmes including the PDS, something that has been criticised by leading right-to-food activists for leading to starvation deaths for poor people lacking proper Aadhaar registration (see e.g. Bhatnagar 2018), and, less egregiously, found by scholars to involve routine delays for needy families (Chaudhuri 2022). The determined focus of Modi's regime on digitalisation here appears as a case of what Chantal Mouffe (2022) has called 'techno-authoritarianism', which articulates smoothly with Modi's

---

a thorough critique stressing that decreasing demand for food grains rather than increasing production is what has actually happened.

overall authoritarian neoliberalism (Sinha 2021), with potentially devastating consequences for India's poor and hungry majority.

While right to food activists have strongly opposed these moves – including by calling for withdrawal of links between Aadhaar and the PDS[7] – activists nevertheless appear to agree about the necessity of restructuring state intervention in food. Right to food activists have long called for the restructuring – in the form of decentralisation – of the FCI on the basis of real problems of wastage, inefficiency and dysfunctionality (Campaign 2010).[8] The activists' critique here seems to echo, in its implications while not in its triggering motivations, the view of dominant forces in the government and among policymakers that 'the time is appropriate for liberalising the foodgrains market' (Banerjee 2015, 42). Such shared views – approximating a sort of Gramscian 'common sense' – can arguably be seen as a prerequisite for neoliberalisation without strong dissent. Indeed, the crux of the dominant criticism of public distribution reminds us of criticisms of Fordism for its 'rigidities' paving the way for neoliberalisation in the West (Harvey 1989).

The disastrous effects of the COVID-19 pandemic in India sidelined these rather covert efforts at dismantling the food security edifice. COVID-19 led to the widely acknowledged fact that the Modi government vastly mismanaged its responsibilities for ensuring the right to food, not the least through its severe and authoritarian lockdown measures, among the strictest in the world (Drèze and Somanchi 2021), leading Alf Gunvald Nilsen to draw on Engels in discussing the Indian state's covid response in terms of concerted 'social murder' (Nilsen 2022). The COVID-19 response moreover starkly outlined the injustice of the 'targeted' distribution system, with reported dysfunctions and storage houses (*godowns*) holding rationed wheat that never reached starving populations (Harriss 2020), leading right to food activists to reassert their claims-making for universalised coverage (Nutrition 2020). This also affected a novel government scheme launched by prime minister Modi as part of the overall COVID-19 response, known as Pradhan Mantri Garib Kalyan Anna Yojana, comprising an additional food aid scheme worth USD 47 billion. Yet, in 2022, despite the continued hunger levels even after the end of the COVID-19

---

7 See for example press statement issued by the Right to Food Campaign in July 2017, at https://static1.squarespace.com/static/58b545dc59cc68c59cb75b8e/t/5979dbc9d482e9e56c8c816b/1501158349119/RFC+statement+against+Aadhaar+27th+July+2017.pdf.

8 This is not to say that criticisms of the FCI have been overall correct. As Chandrasekhar and Ghosh (2002, 160–162) point out, notwithstanding inefficiencies the FCI has managed to keep prices below market levels. Problems of food stocks in the midst of hunger, for example, have rather been effects of the limited ('targeted') design of the neoliberalised PDS itself.

crisis per se, the government announced it would scale back this additional food aid programme. Eventually, after considerable public criticism, the government reversed direction and, at the time of writing, promising that the free ration scheme would remain in place for the next five years, now to be merged with the NFSA. While this move, not unlike other schemes discussed above, may give the appearance of entailing an expansion of state provisioning, critical observers quickly noted how the implied merging of the free ration scheme with the NFSA would, in fact, amount to a significant *reduction* in overall provisioning, thus constituting a gross misrepresentation on the part of the government (Newsclick 2023).

The compulsions of electoral politics – facing upcoming elections in 2024 – were thus likely again triggering these moves, leaving wide open the possibility for the eventual termination of the free ration scheme, and thus, simultaneously, possibly jeopardizing or undermining the NFSA, albeit at a later stage. Of significance to broader food regime dynamics, Modi's move to cancel the food aid program was arguable linked to wheat price inflation following the country's much-publicised wheat export ban following the Ukraine war, in turn linked to the interests of export-oriented capitalist farmers, who were losing out on the wheat prices, while the country's classes of labour were starving (Montesclaros 2023).

The outcomes and broader significance of COVID-19 related turbulence in India's agro-food sector are still to be assessed in their overall reach, yet hunger and starvation will continue to challenge the hegemony of Modi's regime, and will continue to demand some sort of finely tuned management to ensure the persistence of compromise equilibria. There is, however, little reason to doubt that neoliberalisation will continue at pace, something that becomes even clearer once we look at the longer trajectory of opening new spaces for capital accumulation in agro-food over the last decades.

4.2 *Longer-term Neoliberalisation*

Since the end of state-directed developmentalism in the 1980s India has, as part of its overall programme of deregulating its economy, introduced numerous reforms in the agro-food sector. Yet unlike sectors such as IT, agriculture has been only gradually and highly selectively liberalised while maintaining forms of state protectionism such as subsidy regimes, trade regulations and minimum support prices (Frödin 2013), as witnessed in the recent farmer agitations against proposed accelerated deregulation. Protectionist state regulation in agriculture has indeed triggered criticism of India from the WTO (Hopewell 2018) – in our terms, noteworthy 'aberrations' from the hegemonic shape of the contemporary food regime. As we have seen, the Indian state's historical trajectory of engagement in agricultural production and distribution comprises a central reason for gradual and restrained neoliberalisation. Through this engagement, as Chapters 3–4 outlined, the broader trajectory of the postcolonial state came to rely, in the structure of its constitutive class allies, the demands for subsidies by dominant capitalist farmers (Mooij 1998). Looking more closely, however, it soon becomes apparent that the degree of 'aberration' is in fact limited. Although less visible than in the case of some of the country's more self-confident reforms, the opening up of domains of the agro-food system hitherto shielded from privatisation (Harvey 2005) has been a consistent process of transformation since the 1980s.

Apart from the PDS, agricultural markets in *dirigiste* India were subjected to state intervention in other ways as well. Foreign trade in food was strictly controlled and tariffed, and agricultural markets were comprehensively regulated – although in practice often erratically and dysfunctionally so, as the case of the FCI above also showed. The Agricultural Produce Market Committee (APMC) board is another key mechanism, ensuring (in principle if not always in practice) that agricultural produce was sold at state-regulated and licensed markets – known in Inda as the *mandi* system.[9] Some of these market protection measures have been maintained in unaltered form throughout the extended process of the opening of India's economy (Vijayshankar and Krishnamurthy 2012). The APMC, however, was amended by law in 2003 after mounting criticism both from within consecutive national and state governments as well as corporate actors, pushing towards removing the act altogether. The stated aim? To 'free' market access to farm produce, removing the 'inefficiency' of state regulation, thus facilitating more widely for contract farming and Foreign Direct Investments (FDI) through private capital (Singh 2013). In 2005, then Prime Minister Manmohan Singh of the Congress spoke of the APMC amendment as a step in the right direction, as it would, he was quoted by journalists to say, 'enable investments in market infrastructure and open up contract farming, he said, adding that both these areas would create avenues for private sector' (Bureau 2005). When the Modi government in 2020 turned precisely to the APMC and price regulations curtailing the practice of contract farming as key to its proposed legislative changes in the now-aborted farm laws, this move was in other words far from unprecedented.

In terms of financialised global markets, India's agro-food system has become increasingly integrated, thus partaking in a worldwide phenomenon

---

9   For a disaggregated analysis of the mandi system and its constitutive class relational dynamics of accumulation, see Sinha (2020b).

that many scholars perceive as a hallmark of the neoliberalisation of agriculture (Isakson 2014; Moore 2010) and of the contemporary food regime (McMichael 2013a, 100–103). In 2003, India allowed commodity futures trading in several agricultural items, despite government-appointed expert committees advising against the financialisation of staple foods. This triggered some critics to argue that 'it is clear from these developments that the government succumbed to the pressures of powerful lobbies and opened up important new avenues of profit making to speculators and traders' (Mahajan and Singh 2015, 40).[10]

Writing about the political economy of 'actually existing' food grains markets in West Bengal based on longitudinal fieldwork, Barbara Harriss-White holds liberalisation to be a 'much-misunderstood phenomenon. In reality, it consists not of abolishing regulation so much as making complex rearrangements of state regulation' (Harriss-White 2008b, 258). Within food grains markets, Harriss-White argues, forms of re-regulation were initiated already in the 1980s that 'occurred below the radar of most scholars' and 'shifted control from the public sector to private capital' (Harriss-White 2008b, 259). It is thus warranted to hold the opening for private capital in the rice-wheat complex as integrated in a broader trend of state 'roll-back', involving broad state withdrawals from the agro-food system, as discussed in Chapter 4.

The form of food security ensuing from such a policy regime falls into a global pattern of what Tony Weis calls 'market-based or commoditized food security' (Weis 2013, 76). It is unmistakable that state invervention in food security in India's rice-wheat complex for quite a long time has been 'meant to create a *favourable incentive environment* for the adoption of new technology based on high yielding varieties of wheat and rice' (Chand 2005, 1055 emphasis is mine). This is particularly evident upstream of the farm, as the country's agricultural policy since the Green Revolution of the 1960s has been 'input-centric' (Dasgupta 2013), leading to rapid commodification (see Table 2 below).

If we take 'the most fundamental agricultural input' (Kloppenburg 1988, 4), namely seeds, we find that, at the outset of liberalisation in 1991(at a time when the domestic market in seeds was under heavy state protectionism), the public sector had a 35% share of the market, Indian private companies 65%, while TNCs were insignificant. In 2009, public sector had declined to 20% and Indian firms to 54%, while TNCs had jumped up to 26% (Pray and Nagarajan 2014, 147). These numbers do not, however, differentiate between

---

10 The contested nature of the financialisation of agriculture in India is shown in the fact that the government banned futures trades in food commodities during the height of the global food crisis in 2007–8; the ban was lifted as soon as tensions lessened – to the great relief of traders and financiers (Reuters 2009).

TABLE 1   Input use in Indian agriculture, 1971–2011

Ag-inputs	1971	1981	1991	2001	2011
Quality seeds distribution ('000 tons)	52	450	575	918	2,773
Consumption of fertilisers (million tons)	2	5	12	18	28
Consumption of pesticides ('000 tons)	25.8	47.0	72.1	43.6	55.5
Sale of tractors (million units)	0.5	0.7	1.4	2.5	5.5

SOURCE: PRAY AND NAGARAJAN 2014

seeds. Official statements indicate that private sector investments have been most pronounced in high-value crops, leaving the rice-wheat complex to be dominated by public sector enterprise.[11] This is disputed by agrarian scholarship. Major crops, including wheat and rice, are predominantly of high-yielding varieties across India, entailing market dependency. Evidence shows that the private sector since liberalisation has risen to hold the majority share of the market in seeds (Mohanty and Lenka 2016, 172–173; Pal 2009, 97–100). The pattern is, as we can expect, uneven: the heartland of the Green Revolution (Punjab and Haryana, in particular) shows more developed private sectors in rice seeds (Pandey, Behura, and Velasco 2017). While the degree of market concentration surrounding seeds needs to be scrutinized further for making any clear assessment, an increased market competition is documented to have emerged (Spielman et al. 2014).[12]

International capital has clearly realised the potential of India's seed market for accumulation; a potential that has been out of reach until recently due to restrictions on FDI. Undergoing a process of gradual relaxing, in 2011 100 % FDI in development and production of seeds was introduced. Keeping in mind the caveat mentioned earlier in this book about the discrepancy between imaginaries of project growth and actual realities of dwindling and lacklustre

---

11   See government website: http://seednet.gov.in/Material/IndianSeedSector.htm.
12   Market competition around seeds, involving a complex multitude of commercial players, has also been described in ethnographic detail for the cotton sector by Andrew Flachs (Flachs 2019).

investments in India, A 2014 report by the Cereal Systems Initiative for South Asia[13] described the food grain seed sector as 'booming' and 'with future room for growth'. The report goes on to note: 'Only one-quarter of all seed transactions in India are conducted in the formal market, indicating that there are growth opportunities in the informal market where seed provisioning relies on farmer-to-farmer exchanges and farmer-saved seed in the informal market' (Spielman et al. 2014, 1–2).[14] While agricultural policy has thus clearly followed the neoliberal path of privatising assets and sectors, opening up hitherto shielded sectors to renewed capital accumulation (Harvey 2005), neoliberalisation has not led to the complete dismantling of the public sector in India's rice-wheat complex.

Returning briefly to the PDS in view of these longer-term processes, it is worth pointing out that, since the imposition of World Bank austerity demands and conditionalities for loans from the critical juncture of 1991, we find a discourse increasingly favouring private sector involvement in agriculture and the demand for 'efficiency' through market based solutions to food security. The 'roll-back' of the state from PDS commitments in the name of 'efficiency' involved its restructuring from being a universal food security apparatus to becoming a 'targeted' one, entitling only specified categories of people ('Below Poverty Level' according to the national poverty line) to subsidised food grains. 'Under the new "Targeted PDS" (the TPDS), the number of people the PDS reached was halved, food-prices doubled, grain consumption rates fell by 70% nationwide, and incidents of malnutrition, hunger, and starvation became increasingly widespread' (Moore 2014, 50). Intimately tied to this specific form of food security apparatus, recent right to food legislation must thus be seen as part of the contradictory logics of neoliberalisation. The right to food partakes in the formation of unstable equilibria between dominant and subaltern classes in the *ultimate* interest of capital accumulation. Yet, this perspective remains partial until we extend the spatial-temporal lens further to account for how capital accumulation in the rice-wheat complex fares in the broader trajectory of food regime patterning.

---

13   This is a partnership of CGIAR institutions with co-sponsorship from USAID and the Gates Foundation: http://csisa.org/.

14   With regard to the rice-wheat complex in particular, the report tells us that 'more than half of the rice seed planted in India in 2008–9 was purchased (rather than saved) by farmers', whereas 'farmers in India buy less than 20 percent of the wheat seed planted each year, preferring to save their own seed or exchange seed with neighbors' (Spielman et al. 2014, 3). What the report thus signals is: There is plenty of space for expanding accumulation!

5 The 'Long' Green Revolution, Crises and Commodity Frontiers

Independent India has based its agro-policies and food security architecture on the model of 'food = wheat + rice' (Dorin and Landy 2009, 231). As sketched out in Chapter 2, India's food grains – particularly wheat – have a long history of intertwinement with the workings of the food regime restructuring since the 19th century. The Punjab, in particular, was shaped as an agro-ecological region through its insertion in the first food regime of British hegemony, which was centrally revolving around the emergence of a world market in wheat, as an export zone (Jan 2019; Tirmizey 2023). As Mike Davis has documented in harrowing detail, the consequences of this form of incorporation in global commodity flows were dire as the 19th century ended with extreme droughts and widespread famine and starvation (Davis 2002). In the postcolonial period, India's rice-wheat complex was again constitutively reconfigured through its insertion in the workings of the so-called green revolution, again a crucial mechanism to the broader patterning of the global food regime – or, in Araghi's terms, the post-Second World War exception in which capital's food regime was kept at bay.

Returning to Raj Patel's (2013) notion of the 'long' green revolution of long-standing accumulation patterns involving both national and international capital flows, as introduced in Chapter 4, India's rich-wheat complex assumes its proper shape. And so, as this section will argue, another layer of explanation is added to the reasons why the Indian state is currently seeking an 'exit' of sorts from its long-held commitments even in the face of social movements' claims-making, as witnessed in the extensive yet often-clandestine efforts towards dismantling the food security apparatus explored above in this chapter. Part of the explanation has already been shown in the demands for unstable equilibria for securing the hegemony of neoliberalisation bringing expanded capital accumulation. But the story so far has left out something crucial: socio-ecological specificity. McMichael has recently called for more sustained emphasis on ecology as part of food regime analysis. 'Food regimes have ecological consequences', he writes (McMichael 2013a, 106). In pursuing this line of thinking further, this section continues where Chapter 4 ended in its emphasis on the dynamics of commodity frontiers and their cycles of boom and burst.

While the short-, medium- and long-term consequences of green revolution technologies on agrarian Punjab and surrounding areas have been subject of extensive scholarship that is beyond the scope of the present discussion, a short synoptic summary of some key insights is needed. Intervening in a specific part of agrarian India, namely the alluvial irrigated valleys in the heartland of the Green Revolution in the Northwest, the country's food security apparatus became inherently intertwined with the long-term socio-ecological trajectory of these agrarian environments. Capital-intensive, irrigated and mechanised farming based on the sustained use of agro-chemicals – termed, in Chapter 4, 'petrofarming' – was the recipe of the Green Revolution model. Initially generating increasing productivity and yields, evidence shows falling productivity in both rice and wheat over time, coupled with rising usage of agro-chemicals, leading to toxification with concomitant environmental degradation (soil depletion, salinity, groundwater depletion etc.) undermining continued accumulation. As a recent assessment puts it, 'the rice-wheat complex of northern India has become increasingly a technological treadmill, in which farmers have had to add ever larger quantities of inputs just to maintain production levels' (Pritchard et al. 2014, 56). The Green Revolution model in India is thus exemplary of the accelerating 'biophysical overrides' characterising industrialised agriculture across the globe – working through the 'web of life' (Moore 2015), it proves detrimental to the environment as well as accumulation (Weis 2013).

This brings us back to India's agrarian crisis, threatening social reproduction among the country's classes of labour. Viewed as a longer arc of accumulation that has become increasingly crisis-ridden, ongoing efforts at steering away from state engagements with a model that harks back to the initiation of the green revolution model throws new light on the dismantling of India's food security apparatus. Drawing on Harvey's (1982) notion of the 'spatial fix', Moore argues that capital invariably seeks to 'liberate' accumulation from the inflexibility and limitations that ensue from the production of historical natures – such as, in our case, rice-wheat monocultures of accelerating biophysical overrides (Moore 2015, 163). We have already seen the state seeking fixes through neoliberal technologies of outsourcing and 'roll-back'. Moreover, since the 1990s Indian governments have repeatedly been calling for a 'second green revolution' – a term that first appeared in the 1980s (e.g. Sharma 1988) – ostensibly to raise productivity, amounting to a spatial fix of shifting accumulation, primarily agribusiness-led, through industrial agricultural expansion to new areas that had hitherto been less mechanised and more reliant on mixed and traditional cropping patterns, particularly into rain-fed agricultural tracts in Eastern India. In line with Patel's view of the 'long' Green Revolution, the fix seeks a new trajectory for accumulation; rather than replicating the second food regime carryover of heavy state intervention, the new trajectory is based on inviting corporate agribusiness and public-private partnerships for a mode of agriculture more tightly integrated in global markets (Bajpai 2015).

These fixes – both aspirational and actually occurring – around a 'second green revolution' involve the search for 'commodity frontiers' both horizontal (land) and vertical (groundwater reserves) (Moore 2015, 249–255). The broader thrust towards new commodity frontiers in the context of a crisis-ridden agrarian landscape is the topic of the following chapter, taking these overarching dynamics much closer to the ground within lived realities of classes of labour in rural Karnataka.

6   Conclusion

In this chapter, I have offered a reinterpretation of the right-to-food agenda in India with a food regime lens. Whereas existing treatments thereof have perceived the right-to-food in the country, culminating in the landmark 2013 NFSA, as intrinsically 'progressive' and linked to a 'return' of sorts of the state in the realm of agro-food (as in the world economy more broadly), what this chapter has contributed with is a more challenging interpretation: the right to food may very well participate in, contribute to, and constitute a necessary coexistence with projects of neoliberalisation. To make space for such an analysis, predominant emphases in food regime literature of seeing the state as 'subordinated' to corporate interests, or 'withdrawn' in neoliberal onslaughts, needs to be questioned. As the political face of capital, the continued 'strong' state is indeed a defining feature of neoliberalism as a weapon against labour (Bonefeld 2010). Empirically, the chapter has scrutinised the recent right-to-food agenda in view of longer trajectories of capital accumulation in India's agro-food system, opening for an analysis that enables us to see continuities across time as capital's food regime struggles with the demolishment of remnants of the post-second world war exceptionalist phase.

This sort of synopsis may give the appearance of rather general and wide-ranging analytics, yet what this chapter has more properly sought to contribute, is a sustained embedding of broad food regime dynamics within historically-geographically specific empirical circumstances, in other words, a conjunctural analysis that seeks to make food regime analysis 'travel' without turning into a 'theoretical overstatement', as Said put it. In doing so, this chapter has sought to continue the project of downscaling food regime analysis that animates this entire book. Locating the struggles over the emergence of capital's food regime within the remnants of an older order in the specific conjuncture of the class relation as it has taken shape in postcolonial India over time, drawing on the longer narrative provided in earlier chapters of this book, this chapter has paid particular attention to scrutinizing the concepts of the state and neoliberalism in food regime analysis. While the role of the capitalist state has been subject of a still relatively small stream of critical writings in the last years, that have also contributed to downscaling food regime analysis beyond its hitherto 'global' fixation, the concept of neoliberalism has been relatively under-explored. What I have aimed to do, is to reveal some of the fruitfulness of mobilising historical-materialist geographical, thus dialectical, approaches to neoliberalisation to bring forwards food regime analysis in a distinctive and nuanced direction.

Centrally, this analysis has foregrounded *politics* amidst the messy and inextricably situated modes of existence of capital and of class struggle. The view of neoliberalisation put forward in the chapter does not favour 'easy' analyses, but rather invites scrutiny of complex negotiations over the direction of change in capital's food regime. This chapter has focused on the scale of Indian political negotiations over 'compromise equilibria' that work, in a longer perspective, towards ensuring capital accumulation for dominant class interests without fuelling unmanageable contestations from the majority of classes of labour. However, the analytics offered may have broader purchase. Most obviously, the empirical emphasis on right to food mobilisations invite scrutiny of similar 'law struggles' in other countries that address inequities in agro-food. Could such struggles also turn out to function in a broader sense within the making of 'unstable equilibria'? Furthermore, at the scale of 'global' civil society, how about mobilisations around legal charges against multinational corporations? And surrounding the very infrastructure of the global food regime's institutional apparatus, such as the WTO? I believe these questions can be fruitfully explored to 'ground' struggles in the contemporary food regime across different contexts and scales.

The downscaling that has been undertaken in this chapter has remained at the scale of national developments and their regional manifestations. In invoking, in the last section of the chapter, the recurrence of commodity frontiers amidst crisis-ridden patterns of accumulation in agrarian India, many questions remain open. Not the least, there is a pressing need to continue the movement towards the 'concrete' of 'many determinations' by descending to the ground of agrarian change. This is precisely what the next and penultimate chapter seeks to do, as it proceeds to examine how a specific commodity frontier plays out in rural Karnataka, South India.

CHAPTER 6

The Hybrid Maize Frontier

Having explored dynamics of agrarian crisis, neoliberalisation and the state in India at a national-scale oriented analytical level over the last chapters, the present chapter will take the downscaling of the global food regime further to the ground in rural South India.[1] Drawing on Araghi's under-acknowledged reconceptualisation of the food regime as the political face of global value relations, this chapter seeks to unravel further layers of complexity as '[g]lobal value relations include the politics of state relations, the world market, colonization and imperialism, and the (often geographically separated) labour regimes of absolute and relative value production' (Araghi 2003, 49). Tracing global value relations towards ground-level realities – centrally concerned with labour regimes, i.e. the combined material and ideational mechanisms that "bind capital and labor in a form of antagonistic relative stability in particular times and places" (Baglioni et al. 2022, 1) which were invoked in Chapter 2 but have so far remained implicit in the analyses in this book – does not, then, imply a reductive 'localism' but rather a dialectical approach to 'parts' and 'wholes' (Ollman 2003) that seeks to capture what Marx (1993b, 101) famously described as 'unity of the diverse'. In doing so, this chapter builds upon Bernstein's critique of food regime analysis where the macro-scale orientation reveals 'the need for it to connect with other currents of agrarian political economy' (Bernstein 2016a, 643). Specifically, Bernstein argues, this is needed to overcome the prevailing emphasis on certain 'determinations' over others. Contemporary agrarian change, he proceeds, demands analysis of:

> all three kinds of determinations, distinguished by their 'locus' – internal to the countryside, internal to 'national' economies and 'external' emanating from the world economy – are relevant to studying agrarian change today. The point is that the third kind of determination (world economy) does not make the others redundant but rather locates and elaborates them for the fruitful investigation of rural class formation, including 'peasant' differentiation, in changing historical conditions.
>
> BERNSTEIN 2016: 642

---

1 This chapter is a revised version of Jakobsen, Jostein (2020). The maize frontier in rural south India: exploring the everyday dynamics of the contemporary food regime. *Journal of Agrarian Change* 20(1): 137–162.

Taking a fieldwork-based approach, this chapter joins a still relatively small stream of recent scholarship that explores the ways the global food regime is articulated in specific, empirically grounded processes of agrarian change, efforts that have included geographical variation in studies from, amongst others, Cambodia (Green 2022), Lebanon (Martiniello and Kassem 2023) and India (Brown 2019; Tirmizey 2023). Specifically, the chapter traces booming maize cultivation in Karnataka, southern India. It thus seeks to operationalise Bernstein's invitation to rigorous analysis of multiple determinations through the lens of a single commodity. This, in turn, resonates with Friedmann's suggestion mentioned earlier in the book – from the prominent debate between McMichael, Bernstein and Friedmann in *Journal of Peasant Studies* that triggered much of the recent more empirically driven research into food regime analysis – to the effect that nuancing accounts of food regime transformations can fruitfully done along 'specific crops, regions and types of farmers' (Friedmann 2016, 675; see also Wang 2018).

This chapter thus engages the question of how new crops and regions are incorporated in capital's food regime understood in terms of global value relations. While the previous two chapters largely emphasised struggles over stagnating streams of accumulation amidst the remnants and debris after the post-WWII (anti-)food regime, we have also seen repeated indications that new accumulation patterns are being sought established through socioecological 'fixes' and commodity frontier dynamics. Hybrid maize in South India, this chapter argues, provides a novel lens into precisely how the commodity frontier is being articulated in contemporary rural India, paying sustained attention to historically-geographically specific dynamics of class and caste.

The following section starts by outlining the role of hybrid maize in the global food regime and in India's agrarian political economy writ large, providing necessary context for the analysis to come. Next, I provide an extended discussion of the key conceptual issue at play in this chapter: commodity frontiers. Here, I seek to outline how food regime analysis has hitherto approached the concept, which, unsurprisingly given the overall thrust of argument in this book, has been of the 'top-down' sort. I also pay notice to some underlying conceptual problems that I argue are in need of assessment in order to reshape commodity frontiers into a conceptual tool that can be applicable within the broader value-form theoretical approach suggested in this book. Following this conceptualisation, the chapter proceeds to lay out details about the methods and field site for the grounded research that has gone into this particular chapter. With all of this in place, the remainder of the chapter is devoted to the 'conjunctural' analysis of the hybrid maize commodity frontier, starting with a view of dynamics as they emanate 'from above' in the world of agribusiness, before turning sustained attention to dynamics 'from below' in the field in Karnataka. Following the self-consciously world-systemic focus in food regime analysis – as McMichael also recently reiterates as a key aspect of the approach as such, distinct from, and not reducible to, more localised research agendas (McMichael 2023) – less attention has been paid to the with processes 'from below' whereby new regions and crops are integrated in the contemporary food regime.

Shifting attention towards the mundane, everyday aspects of capitalist transformation has been suggested in recent critical agrarian studies. In her recent study of '[t]he emergence of capitalist relations in their routine but insidious form', Tania Li (2014, 8) similarly foregrounds the not-so-spectacular, arguing that such a focus has tended to be neglected in critical agrarian studies. Yet, the notion of the everyday invoked in this article does have parallels in recent rethinking of 'accumulation by dispossession' and 'land grabbing' (Hall 2013), including in the South Asian context where scholars have pointed to the everyday dimensions or 'routine processes' (De Neve 2015, 347) through local research (Adnan 2013; Vijayabaskar and Menon 2018). Whereas the food regime literature employs analytics 'from above', I argue that the expansion of maize in South India comes about at the conjuncture of processes 'from above' and very much localised 'everyday' processes 'from below' whereby maize is integrated in farmers' livelihoods. In the idiom of conjunctural analysis, this entails an examination of 'how multiple forces come together in practice to produce particular dynamics or trajectories' (Hart 2004, 97). Brought together, then, the chapter argues for a comprehensive analysis that is *only* attainable through a multiscalar approach to the 'concrete' in food regime analysis.

1   Hybrid Maize in the Global Food Regime

Hybrid maize is in many ways an emblematic crop for crucial contemporary food regime dynamics. With the reorganization of agricultural production across the Global South into global value chains over the last decades comes a strong centripetal force around an emergent porous agro-food-feed-fuel complex. Agrarian scholarship has pointed to the corporate-led, financialised expansion of 'flex crops and commodities' (Borras, McMichael, and Scoones 2010; Borras et al. 2016), where the worldwide increase in meat consumption constitutes a crucial nexus of expanded capital accumulation (Weis 2007, 2013). A increasingly important aspect of the contemporary food regime is thus what Tony Weis calls the corporate-dominated 'industrial grain-oilseed-livestock complex' (Weis 2007, 2013). Having established itself in its broad contours across much of the world after World War II (Friedmann 1993, 2009b), it is particularly in the neoliberal period that the complex has taken on properly *global* dimensions as countries in the South have experienced rapid 'meatification' of diets (Weis 2013). Coupled with the increasing corporate control that is exemplary of the contemporary 'corporate food regime' (McMichael 2013a), agricultural restructuring paradigmatically takes the commodity form of meat, fed on global supply chains of grains and oilseeds. As a key part of the industrial grain-oilseed-livestock complex, hybrid maize is thus instrumental in expanding the reach of global value relations that are at the heart of capital's food regime.

Although the common portrayal of India as a vegetarian country, including viciously so by Hindu nationalist forces under Modi's authoritarian populist regime, is misleading (Natrajan and Jacob 2018) and politically dangerous (Jakobsen and Nielsen 2023, 2024), India does distinguish itself as an diverging case in view of global tendencies towards rapid meatification. Per capita meat consumption remains among the world's lowest, revealing little increase over recent years in absolute numbers (FAOSTAT). Nevertheless, India is a significant meat producer and exporter in the Asian region, something that has arguably received less attention in studies of global agrarian transformation due to the overshadowing scale of processes in China (Jakobsen and Hansen 2020). This chapter locates the rapid rise of hybrid maize in view of these global patterns of meatification and agro-food transformation.

Unaccompanied by attention in agrarian scholarship, maize (*Zea mays*) has in recent years expanded at a rapid pace in India –especially its southern parts. Largely a monsoon (*kharif*) season crop, maize has emerged as the third most important crop categorised as 'food crop' by the Indian government, after rice and wheat, cultivated by an estimated 12 million households in the country in calculations made about ten years ago, a number which can thus be expected to have increased even further (Kumar, Srinivas, and Sivaramane 2013, 1; Modi 2014), estimated to comprise a production volume of 35.91 million tonnes in 2022–23.[2] Booming maize cultivation thus departs from a broad trend in India during the period of neoliberal reform of diversification away from what is classified as food crops (Mohanty and Lenka 2016). Whereas rice and wheat have shown low growth rates in the context of India's 'agrarian crisis' during the period of neoliberalisation since the early 1990s, which previous chapters have sought to explain as the decline of a longer 'petrofarming' cycle of accumulation initiated with the Green Revolution, maize stands clearly out with

---

2 See details at Maize (apeda.gov.in)

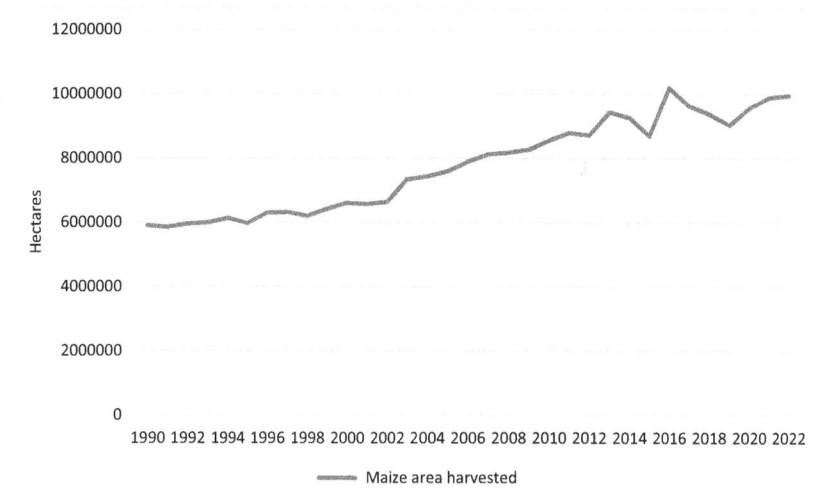

FIGURE 2   Maize area harvested, all-India (hectares)
SOURCE: DATA COMPILED FROM FAOSTAT BY THE AUTHOR

its 'impressive growth' (Kumar, Srinivas, and Sivaramane 2013, 6). From 1990 to 2016, the area harvested for maize in the country increased by 72,7 percent; wheat by 28,6 percent, and paddy a mere 0,6 percent. In the same period, total production of maize increased by 193 percent; production of wheat increased by 87,5 percent, whereas rice increased by 42,3 percent (FAOSTAT; see Figure 2 and Figure 3 below).

This staggering rise to prominence in cropping patterns has triggered Indian state officials, agribusinesses and media to speculate about the emergence of maize as India's 'new wonder crop' (Mukherjee 2013). Reflecting maize's central role as a profitable flex crop within a porous complex of commodities for multiple uses, moreover, Indian government officials at the time of writing recently launched a 'farm-to-fuel programme' through which support prices are to boost the production of maize for the country's agrofuel needs (Haq 2024a).

2   Commodity Frontiers

In McMichael's writings, the notion that the corporate food regime is expanding its reach across the global through 'frontier' dynamics appears as a closely linked part of an emphasis on dispossession. Broadly shared in much food regime literature (and beyond, in critical agrarian studies writ large), this

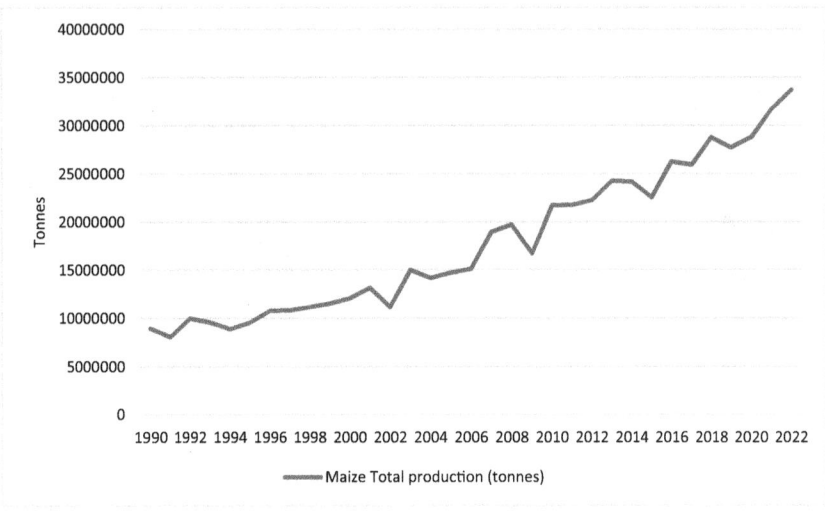

FIGURE 3   Maize production total, all-India (tonnes)
SOURCE: DATA COMPILED FROM FAOSTAT BY THE AUTHOR

entails an overall assessment of the contemporary conjuncture as one of escalating dispossession for rural populations worldwide (Friedmann 2005, 265; Pietilainen and Otero 2018; Bernstein 2016a; Dixon 2014; Araghi 2009). Focus has largely been on the spectacular and eye-catching: violent land grabs, corporate appropriation of crops and commons and other forms of 'accumulation by dispossession' (Harvey 2003) whereby populations and environments across the world are incorporated in the corporate food regime 'in letters of blood and fire' (Marx 1976, 875). And the frontier, as Rasmussen and Lund (2018) recapitulate, tends to be conceptualised in equally, if not even more so, exceptional imagery: violence, destruction, rupture are expected, indeed defining, features of the frontier. In McMichael's words, the 'corporate food regime' is characterised by 'the appropriation of agricultural resources for capitalist consumption relations' which, he says, 'is realised through an expanding foundation of human impoverishment and displacement, and the marginalisation of agrarian/food cultures' (McMichael 2005, 279). Seeking opportunities for 'spatial fixes' (Harvey 1982; McMichael 2013a, 109) for its inherent and accelerating contradictions through frontier processes, the expansion of the corporate food regime appears, first and foremost, as driven 'from above' (see e.g. McMichael 2012).

In dialogue with Jason Moore's world-ecology (as introduced briefly in Chapter 4), the expansion of the food regime thus appears to unfold through the incessant search for 'frontiers' for renewed capital accumulation in the face of crisis tendencies of socio-ecological exhaustion (McMichael 2013a, 109–130).³ 'Capitalism', writes Moore, 'is a frontier process' (Moore 2015, 107). By this he means to say that capitalism – as a world-ecological process of organising 'humanity-in-nature/nature-in-humanity' (Moore 2015, 49) – proceeds through incessantly expanding the scope of accumulation at the intersection of 'accumulation by exploitation' and 'accumulation by appropriation' (Moore 2015, 73). Where *exploitation* points to the extraction of surplus value from labour in the capitalist production process, by *appropriation* Moore points to 'nature's life-making capacities' where 'unpaid work/energy is appropriated in service to commodity production, and opens new opportunities for capital investment' (Moore 2015, 95). This happens through what Moore calls the 'Four Cheaps', i.e. 'those necessary elements of capitalist re/production – above all, labor, food, energy and raw materials' (Moore 2018, 241). Keeping these as cheap as possible through frontier processes of gaining access to relatively less capitalised natures (both human and extra-human) 'outside the centers of commodity production' (Moore 2018, 246) enables capital accumulation to thrive. Commodity frontiers are thus both geographically constituted and 'socio-ecological relations that unleash a new stream of nature's bounty to capital' (Moore 2010, 245).

Intrinsic to Moore's conception of commodity frontiers is the notion that the work of women has been, and is, central. The world-ecological perspective is thus a contribution to the feminist Marxist tradition of foregrounding the role of unpaid work to the expansion of global capitalism (Federici 2004; Mies 2014 [1986]; Bhattacharya 2017). Discussing the second food regime in the Philippines, Camba recently links this perspective to food regime analysis by thinking of the appropriation of paid and unpaid work in the capitalist world-ecology as the conjoined form whereby the global production of value channels into the food regime (Camba 2018). He discusses ways by which this 'nexus of paid and unpaid work' (Camba 2018, 4) functions as a form of subsidy to capital through examples such as draft animals' contribution to food production.

Further, in Moore's view, the neoliberal, contemporary phase of capitalism is marked by increasingly 'savage' accumulation strategies in the attempt at working against 'the relative contraction of opportunities for appropriation' (Moore 2015, 154). At times, Moore comes very close to saying that the current conjuncture is one where 'Cheap Nature' is exhausted and capital's incessant expansion through frontiers has reached its exhaustion on a global scale (Moore 2015, 89), something Chapter 4 criticised in dialogue with Saito's recent

---

3   For a succinct recent overview of commodity frontier literature, see Patel (2022).

eco-Marxist writings. Drawing on these ideas in Moore, McMichael argues that the current crisis of corporate food regime – including intersecting crises of accumulation, food, energy and climate – signals the 'under-reproduction of nature'; meaning exhaustion, either 'relative' or 'absolute'. A situation of relative exhaustion implies an increased press for frontiers as spatial fixes (McMichael 2013a, 115).

Where Harvey's notion of the spatial fix refers primarily to crisis of over-accumulation, the world-ecological notion incorporates under-reproduction akin to Ekers and Prudham's recent notion of 'socioecological fixes' (Ekers and Prudham 2017b, a). Frontier movements, then, are all about seeking relatively uncapitalised spaces where food, labour, energy, raw materials can be accessed at lower costs (Moore 2015). McMichael suggests that recent restructuring of the agro-food-feed-fuel complex into an interconnected, porous and speculative assemblage – taking such forms as biofuel booms and flex crops – represents one example of frontiers for capital (McMichael 2013a, 115–116). Building on these ideas, Marion Dixon has also argued for seeing corporate expansion in agro-food into desert regions in Egypt as an example of commodity frontier movements (Dixon 2017).

These contributions thus take us closer to Araghi's notion of labour regimes' role in global value relations, and thus a 'labour-centred approach to food regime analysis' (Rioux 2018, 716). Yet they remain relatively focused on dynamics 'from above' but also, and no less importantly, they lead directly into what I take to be rather problematic conceptual territory. Moore's idea of commodity frontiers can be fruitful for exploring dynamics of agro-industrial strategies vis-à-vis natural resources (Campling 2012; Barbesgaard and Whitmore 2023) and capital-labour dynamics amidst commodity booms (Martiniello 2021), but nevertheless, it comes with a controversial articulation of 'labour' and of 'value' – and, more deeply, of 'nature' and 'society' – subject of seemingly endless eco-Marxist debate and antagonism over the last years (for a couple of examples of contributions to this stream of debate, see e.g. Burkett 2018; Malm 2018; Heron 2021; Hornborg 2017; Moore 2022). While much of this debate is beyond the purview of this chapter, directly relevant is particularly the notion that frontiers work through 'appropriation' of the 'work' or 'unpaid labour' of non-human nature.

Undoubtedly this may appear an inviting way of conceiving dynamics of the global food regime, constituted as it is by the incorporation of landscapes of agrarian production, crops, whole ecologies, and so forth, in circuits of capital accumulation. However, this 'expansive' theory of value (Burkett 2018) sits uneasily with Marx's labour theory of value, despite Moore's (2015) well-formulated claims to the contrary. In short, a strong argument can be made that Marx's theory was one of the specifically *social* character of value, long recognised by eco-Marxist scholars such as Burkett in holding that capitalism indeed does not value nature (Burkett 1999). Or, as eloquently articulated by Moishe Postone, 'Value is peculiar in that, though a form of wealth, it does not express directly the relation of humans to nature but the relations among people as mediated by labor. Hence, according to Marx, nature does not enter directly into value's constitution at all' (Postone 1993, 195).

Moore is thus right in thinking of commodity frontiers in terms of the role of non-capitalist relations in capitalism, yet the value-theoretical scaffolding may need 'narrowing'. As Rebecca Carson recently argues, non-capitalist relations are crucial to capitalist reproduction, yet they remain non-capitalist insofar 'due to their irreducibility to capital's abstract form and not because they belong to a distinct social system' (Carson 2023a, 3). Valorisation, in this view, is restricted to the exploitation of the commodity labour power and the resultant creation of surplus value (ibid. p. 12). 'Expropriation', to the contrary, 'does not create surplus value', Carson writes, and 'occurs when capital takes from the social reproductive and natural resources of human life and nature without recourse to payment' (Carson 2023b, 55–56). Non-capitalist expropriation, then, is an 'immanent externality' to capital, not its 'outside', and indispensable to the functioning of capitalist reproduction. Yet it is *not – pace* Moore and others – an expanded form of valorisation unfolding in the realm of 'unpaid work' of non-human nature. Drawing upon this distinct conceptual pairing allows, I would suggest, a rigorous foundation in Marxist value-form theory, while maintaining the usefulness of commodity frontiers as analytical lens on to the uneven movement of capital across various domains. Relating this to Araghi's value-centered approach to food regimes, it is clear that commodity frontiers are implicated in seeking out 'cheap' labour and ecological 'surpluses', pointing to how 'the global food regime of capital is, through its impact on the value of labour-power and thus the production of surplus value, a historically specific constituent of global value relations' (Araghi 2012, 120).

With this reconceptualisation that puts much-needed 'constraints' on value-theoretical questions, it is possible to gain a more nuanced lens onto the mentioned interest in this chapter in everyday or mundane processes 'from below' whereby commodity frontiers unfold. While I take issue with Moore's framing of the 'appropriation' of the 'unpaid work' of nature, there is something important worth exploring more fully in how non-human nature's biophysical energies and qualities are expropriated. This brings attention to the specific use-values of maize. As I endeavour to show in empirical detail in this chapter, such use-values are indeed crucial to understanding the dynamics of the hybrid maize frontier in South India. In these terms, the maize boom parallels

Richa Kumar's findings from ethnographic fieldwork among soybean producers in Madhya Pradesh, where poorer farmers are found to grow soybean not for reasons of technical 'productivity' but due to it being 'a low-risk, high-return crop, making it an ideal choice for poor farmers' (Kumar 2016a, 90). In other words, profit is only part of the explanation for the spread of the crop. This means that we need to take the political ecology of maize seriously, something that can be fruitfully done by taking a 'crop-centred' approach (Fischer, Jakobsen, and Westengen 2022) that emphasises, as Sinha usefully articulates it in the context of paddy and cotton production in the Punjab, 'the dialectical relation between the physicality of the crop and the geographically and historically specific material relations within which they are embedded' (Sinha 2022, 146). Similarly to how the overall downscaling endeavour in this book refuses any 'localism', aiming instead for dialectical understanding of capital's valorization process, such attention to the materiality of the crop refuses what Marx called '[t]he crude materialism of the economists who regard as the *natural properties* of things what are social relations of production among people, and qualities which things obtain because they are subsumed under these relations' (Marx 1993b, 687, emphasis in original).

As I will proceed to show, the livelihood options of rural classes of labour are key to understanding how the crop's specific use-values contribute to the key dynamics of the commodity frontier. Nourished on regional patterns of uneven development (Neimark and Healy 2018), the maize frontier draws on how the crop fits into the drought-prone agrarian landscape, how it can feed livestock and be combined with wage labour. These socio-ecologically embedded material relations comprise reasons behind the maize boom that would remain invisible to more conventionally 'top down' food regime analysis, and are only, I would argue, demonstrable through fieldwork. In line with Bernstein's interventions, recounted above, I have sought to deploy a rigorous agrarian political economy approach to data collection. This warrants some more detailed description of methods and field site to provide necessary grounds for evaluating subsequent analysis.

3 Methods and Field Site

This chapter draws on fieldwork in a marginal part of Chamarajanagar district of southern Karnataka. Data was collected in September-October 2017 and February-March 2018. It draws, also, on contacts and networks established during a mapping visit in August-October 2016, during which I studied elementary Kannada in Bangalore. In this region, maize has risen to prominence in the last two decades. Along with neighbouring Andhra Pradesh, Karnataka is the leading maize producing state in the country. In Chamarajangar, the *kharif* acreage for maize expanded by a whopping 359 % between 1998 and 2014, propelling it from the seventh most to *the* most grown crop in the district.[4]

Mekkenur – meaning 'maize village' in Kannada from *mekkejola* (maize) and *uru* (village) – is the pseudonym I have given to the village where I located most of my field research. The village is located a few kilometers from the small town of Hanur, which is 150 km from Bengaluru by road, close to the Tamil Nadu border. In 2018, Hanur was granted the status of a separate *taluk* (administrative unit), while it hitherto has been part of Kollegal *taluk*. The marginal and inaccessible nature of the area comes across, for example, in the fact that in 2022 it was reported that administrative offices had still not been relocated from Kollegal (Ramesh 2022). Hanur is, in other words, a sleepy *mofussil* (provincial) town not wholly untypical for 'the India of the 88 percent' (Harriss-White 2002), accessible only by roads much less properly maintained than elsewhere in the district, where few outsiders would venture except on their way through to the popular pilgrim location Male Mahadeshwara Hills to the east. The 'backwater' quality of Hanur comes visibly to the fore in the absence of commercial accommodation; the only in existence at the time of my fieldwork was a small, miserly and congested 'guesthouse' located right next to the main road passing through town. Fortunately, during fieldwork in 2018, I was able to stay in a small local NGO office in Hanur through local contacts. I was unable to get a room in Mekkenur itself – villagers would not accommodate me, they said, due to the near total absence of toilet facilities. From this location, as I will get back to below, I could move around the rural vicinity (see Map 1 below).

A small town with a population of about 11,000 according to the latest census (2011), Hanur caters to the needs of the surrounding countryside by providing such facilities as banks (and moneylenders), schools, government offices, health and veterinary services, a plethora of small shops and eateries and – not the least – agro-shops where one can purchase necessary equipment for farming. The region surrounding Hanur is an understudied, economically 'backward' part of Karnataka, markedly different from the surrounding parts of southern Karnataka, which are relatively prosperous. This is partly due to different administrative histories; the Hanur/Kollegal region was part of the Coimbatore District of Madras Presidency during colonial times, whereas

---

4 These numbers are based on unpublished statistics gathered from Chamarajanagar district agriculture department.

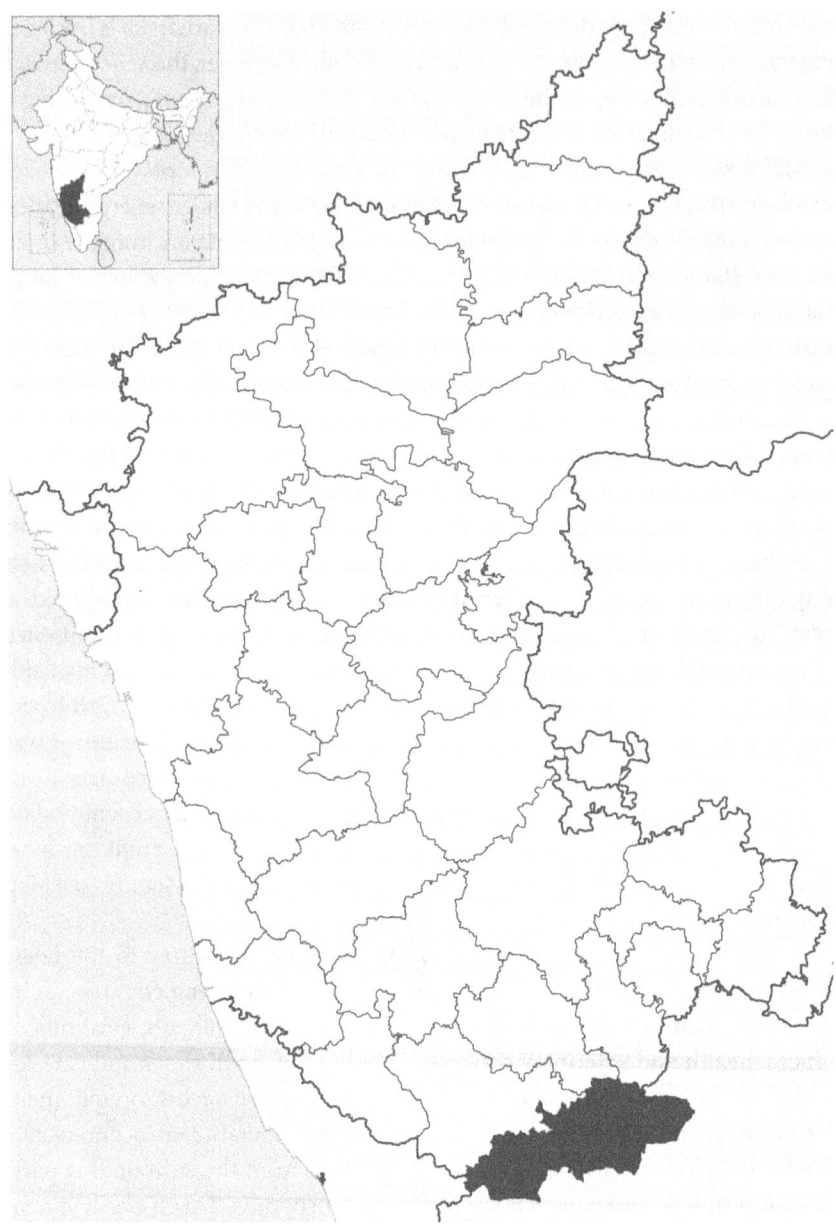

MAP 1   Map of Chamarajanagar district
SOURCE: WIKICOMMONS

surrounding areas were part of Mysore kingdom, known for its progressive administration (see e.g. Nair 2011). From my readings of scholarship from surrounding Mysore, I was in fact not aware of this before I met a man in his eighties in Mekkenur who told me his life story beginning in the Madras Presidency. The contemporary Hanur region has a significant Tamil population, and Tamil is widely spoken, increasingly so as one moves by road from Hanur towards the state border. According to the limited documentary sources I have been able to find about the (colonial) past of the field region, it appears to have been partly forested, with settlements known as dispersed, the population scarce, and the area considered remote (Nicholson 1887). Only nearer to Kollegal town did economic activities attract attention from outsiders, specifically in the form of Kollegal's famed silk industry (Charsley 1982). It thus follows that Mekkenur and the Hanur region surrounding it are peripheral and different from what we know about the nearby region from the established scholarship that is placed in former Mysore (Epstein 1973; Karanth 1995; Srinivas 1976; Hill 1982).

The 'backwardness' of the region is also tied to the agrarian context. Most of the region, including adjacent parts, is semi-arid. The Hanur region is, moreover, primarily rainfed, whereas many neighbouring areas have more developed irrigation. In Mandya district to the north, for example, there is canal irrigation, leading to the possibility to grow intensive sugar cane, which is a capital-intensive and (at least potentially) remunerative form of agriculture (see e.g. Taylor 2019). Things are different in predominantly rainfed areas. Importantly, there is a sense in which rainfed India has suffered a long-standing relative neglect in research compared to other agrarian zones of the country, bringing about what some scholars long ago called a 'delta bias' (Farmer 1980), further compounded by neglect on the part of the Indian state (Harriss 1984). This means that peripheral agrarian regions of India have been relatively understudied. 'Agrarian studies has concentrated primarily on regions where agricultural productivity was high, and where greater intensification of agriculture was evident', Agrawal and Sivaramakrishnan write (2000, 4), continuing to say that '[t]hus the fertile Indo-Gangetic plains have received the greatest analytical notice. Even in the Deccan and the south, irrigated agriculture in river valleys and coastal plains has attracted the most attention from historical and contemporary agrarian scholarship'. As a border zone with Tamil Nadu and, a bit further away, Kerala, moreover, the Hanur region is known as a peripheral area in another sense as well: the rainfed agricultural tracts are surrounded by hilly and partly forested tracts inhabited by the Soliga tribal group (*adivasis*). In these parts, which I also travelled by motorcycle and conducted interviews, swidden agriculture has been a traditional practice, only more recently shifting to settled farming, including of maize. Through relocation programmes associated with the establishment of national parks in the hilly and forested regions (see Map 2 below), Soliga settlements have been brough out of the forested tracts and onto the plains. In the forests, reports have for several years described covert activities by the Naxalite guerrilla movement, leading to occasional skirmishes with government forces.

Most of the data was collected in the village of Mekkenur supplemented by extensive travels, and visits to several villages, across the wider region. Having selected the region as a promising and understudied maize frontier, the village was chosen based on information and access provided by initial contacts in Hanur. Mekkenur is a village of 326 households and a population of 1368.[5] The dominant caste in the village is Lingayats, comprising some 100 households, residing in the central part of the village, leading in local politics and traditionally the main landholders.[6] Kurubas, which is an Other Backward Class (OBC) group, comprise some 20–30 households including descendants of a major landholder two generations back. The rest of the population consists of around 100 households of both Scheduled Castes (SCs) and Nayakas, which is a group categorised as Scheduled Tribe (ST). Due to the absence of village records showing landholdings and not having carried out a survey myself, I lack conclusive landholding evidence. Yet my findings clearly indicate that the STs and SCs in the village were in possession of plots of land that would be categorised as 'small and marginal' in government parlance (i.e. below 2 hectares) (India 2011). Indeed, small and marginal farmers predominate the agrarian scene in Kollegal taluk with as much as 87,4 percent of the landholdings (see Table 2 below). Group interviews revealed that, among the SCs, there was consensus that 4–5 families in the village were in the category of medium landholders, while STs did not have any substantial landholding families.

The majority of SC and ST landholdings were located at the outskirts of the village in places with less fertile (red) soil, whereas higher caste/class holdings were mainly located closer to the village in areas of more fertile (black) soil.[7] Following from land redistributions undertaken in the 1970s, higher castes had been able to retain their lands while lower castes were allocated former wasteland. Lower caste/class land was, moreover, close to hills and forests of surrounding uninhabited tracts where wild boars and other animals were frequently roaming as a nuisance for the farmers as they could eat and

---

5   These numbers are derived from the Village Accountant's office.
6   Lingayats are comprised of several sub-castes, where some are categorised as 'general category' and others 'other backward classes' in Karnataka.
7   This pattern is not untypical for class/caste stratification of landholdings in other parts of rainfed Karnataka (Pattenden 2016b).

THE HYBRID MAIZE FRONTIER

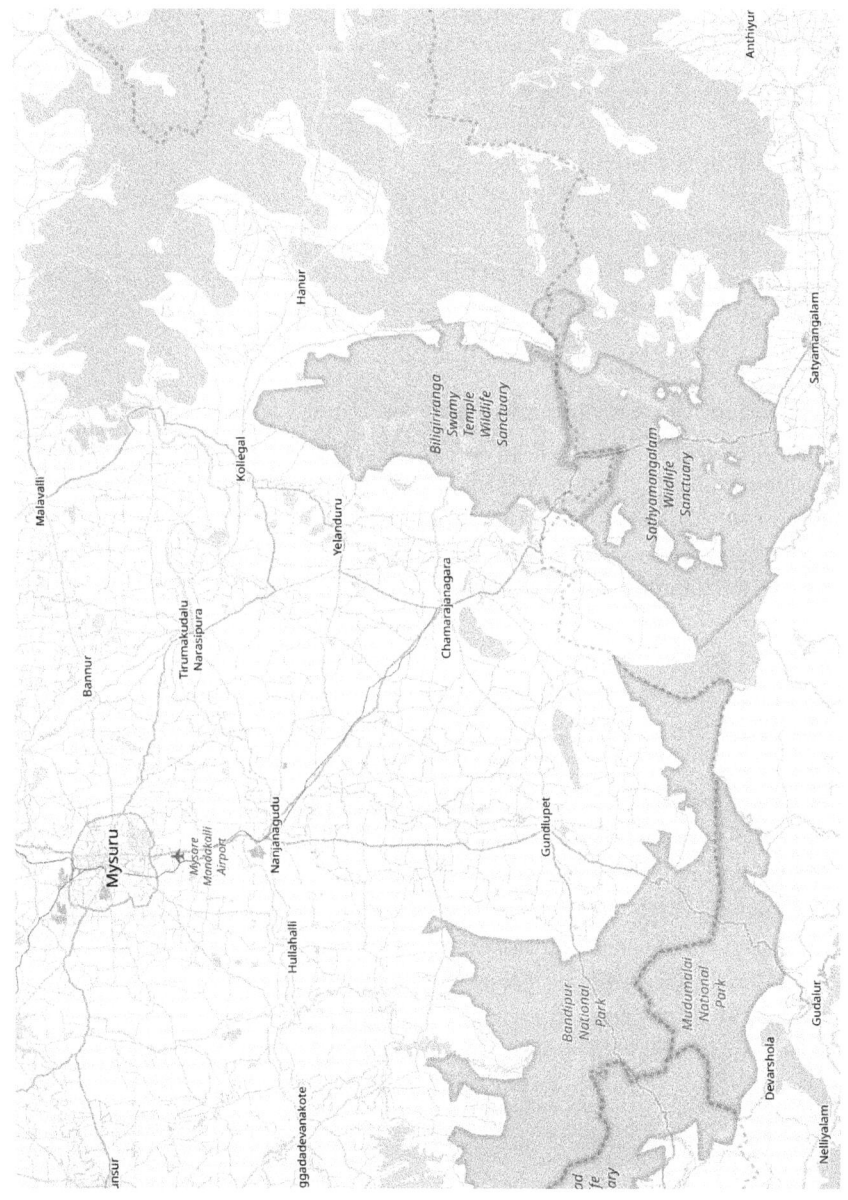

MAP 2 Map of broader field area

TABLE 2   Number and area of landholding by size group, Kollegal taluk

Type of holding (acres)	Total number of holdings	Percentage of total holdings	Percentage of land held
Marginal (0–2,5)	40592	61,5	27,5
Small (2,5–5)	17108	25,9	34,9
Semi-medium (5–10)	6826	10,3	25,2
Medium (10–20)	1317	1,9	9,9
Large (over 25)	88	0,1	2,2

SOURCE: KARNATAKA STATE AGRICULTURE CENSUS 2010–11

ravage crops. The threat from wild animals forced poor farmers in these parts to sleep in makeshift constructions during the season to protect their crops. Compounding my difficulties in determining landholdings was the fact that plots were 'dispersed', with single owners having smaller plots in more than one location around the village.[8] In group interviews across class/caste groups, the extent of landlessness in the village was calculated by villagers to be around 30–40 percent, with a slightly higher proportion of STs landless than other castes.

The region is prone to droughts. Agricultural officers stationed in Hanur calculated that the region is dependent on rainfed agriculture (*bejjalu*) on at least 70 percent of the acreage, pointing out that the extent of irrigation is unevenly distributed across villages in the region. Mekkenur has slightly more irrigation than some surrounding villages with rainfed land comprising 60 percent of the cropped acreage.[9] Irrigated agriculture (*neeravari*) is only available in the form of borewells, which have multiplied in recent years due to a particular government scheme (Ganga Kalyana) catering to SC and ST farmers as well as private investments by well-off farmers predominantly from dominant Lingayats and Kurubas. Through group interviews with farmers, I learned that borewell irrigation is now present in about 40 percent of Lingayat landholdings, 50 percent of Kuruba holdings, while 30 percent of SC and ST holdings.

---

8 According to Polly Hill's classic work from a dryland agricultural village south of Bangalore, 'dispersal of farm-plots' is a 'fundamental feature' of dryland agricultural systems (Hill 1982, 55).

9 Numbers are derived from the Village Accountant's office.

In Mekkenur I worked primarily through ethnographic methods, spending time with villagers to learn about their livelihoods and agricultural patterns. I quickly found that relying on 'interviews' strictly defined was deemed too time-consuming, or inconvenient, by villagers leading lives of hard and long working-hours. Instead of trying to arrange for lengthy sittings with villagers, I therefore spent most of the time chatting and engaging in semi-structured interviews with villagers at tea stalls, shops, streets and other public spaces, in people's houses as well as – crucially – traveling by motorcycle between agricultural fields, where I would be accompanying farmers and their livestock for some time, providing opportunities for informal interviewing in between chores. In so doing, I depended fully on my interpreter, without whom free-ranging conversations in Kannada would have been impossible.[10] Frequently, these interactions involved group discussions with villagers joining in the conversation while others departed, as the flow of life often looks like in a village setting. The body of data that I draw upon in this chapter thus has several strands to it. An important set involves semi-structured interviews with villagers across all caste groups in the village based on street-wise interactions, during which I collected key data about landholdings, cropping patterns and expenses, labour practices, livestock, as well as broader issues about the trajectory of socioeconomic change in the village. With a view for landholdings, these interviews are compiled in the table below (see Table 3 below). In addition, I had group discussions with women villagers through self-help groups. These meetings involved two meetings with 10 SC women each, and one meeting with 10 ST women. I also interacted with a large number of villagers of all castes in the course of my more ethnographically oriented fieldwork, but these interactions were looser and did not involve me collecting data about landholdings (and are thus not included in Table 3 below).

In addition to and complementing the material from Mekkenur, the chapter also draws on interactions with villagers in several other villages in the nearby region. These interactions would involve semi-systematic travels across the wider region around Hanur to map out differentiation in cropping patterns, irrigation, class/caste stratification, and so on. While the majority of these field visits to other villages were in the proximity to Mekkenur, travels included also further away to Soliga settlements to the south-west. Overall, this practice of moving about the landscape provided me with valuable overview of key patterns of agrarian change in the broader region to contextualise main findings.

---

10   I would like to express my gratitude to Dr. Y. D. Imran Khan for his invaluable contribution as my interpreter, guide and friend.

TABLE 3   Landholdings of respondents in Mekkenur

Caste	Marginal and small	Semi-medium and medium	Large	Landless	Number of villagers interviewed
Lingayat	7	10	1		18
Kuruba	8	1	2		11
Scheduled Caste	14	1		12	27
Scheduled Tribe	5	2		4	9

Moreover, I also interacted repeatedly with agro-shop keepers in Hanur, many of whom, as key intermediaries and 'merchants of knowledge' (Aga 2018) in the agrarian economy, were able to provide insightful details about agricultural patterns in the region. These conversations were also informal, often having myself sitting down at a chair in their shops, discussing with them over a cup of *chai* between customers. Similarly, I also met with agricultural department officers, veterinary hospital employees and others with expertise on things agrarian in Hanur. The last strand of data is a small set of semi-structured interviews conducted in Bengaluru with bureaucrats in the Agricultural Department, agricultural scientists and private seed company employees. This last group was mainly interviewed for data regarding the broader dimensions of India's – and Karnataka's – maize boom.

In what follows, I proceed to explore the maize frontier in two steps: first, I look at the way the frontier has taken shape 'from above' in the broader political economy, before I then shift lens to the localised dynamics 'from below' in the field region. These are the dialectically interrelated moments of the commodity frontier.

4   The Hybrid Maize Frontier Seen 'from Above'

The role of maize in the wider trajectory of agricultural transformation in India appears largely ignored, despite the long history of maize in the country. Some scholars have speculated (and later been refuted) about a pre-Columbian introduction of maize (Johannessen and Parker 1989), while others have argued for its introduction in the sixteenth century by the Portuguese (Singh 1977). Largely ignored is also the fact that maize was the (subsequently side-lined) starting point for the so-called green revolution in the country (Patel 2013). While we have come to know the story of the green revolution in India as one of wheat – and subsequently rice – it in fact started with maize. In the early 1950s, the Rockefeller Foundation in collaboration with the Indian government decided to initiate research in hybrid varieties of maize, building on the prior work of the Foundation in Mexico. This despite maize only comprising 3 percent of India's gross cropped area at the time (Lele and Goldsmith 1989, 314; Roy 2006, 128). One study of cropping patterns based on late 1950s government data shows that maize was a staple food in hilly and mountainous parts of northern India (Bhatia 1965). Prior to the recent expansion, maize was indeed mainly grown for human consumption (over 80 percent of the production, according to one study from the 1970s) in the form of unleavened bread in northern India (Singh 1977, 7). Seed development did, however, also happen, then under state-led R&D establishments and subject of the then-prevailing policies protecting domestic seed markets (Jakobsen and Westengen 2022). As we have seen in previous chapters, the slow and uneven disintegration of this mode of state involvement has been key to India's integration in capital's food regime in the post-1990 period.

The recent expansion of maize consequently follows a strikingly different trajectory from previous cultivation of the crop. Recounting parts of the argument made in previous chapters, the broad pattern of accumulation in agriculture following the so-called Green revolution has eventually run out of steam in the current conjuncture of agrarian crisis and neoliberal restructuring. Centred, as we have seen, on the country's longstanding rice-wheat complex, especially in irrigated landscapes, the trajectory has been one of deteriorating livelihoods and environments, sinking rates of profit, technological treadmills and accelerating 'biophysical contradictions' (Weis 2013). As some eco-Marxists would put it, the trajectory has jointly co-produced social and environmental changes, rather than seeing the environment as an 'external input' that has gradually been depleted (Moore 2015). Subsequently, efforts by the Indian state and various classes of agro-capital can be found devising attempts at socioecological fixes or searches for novel commodity frontiers to initiate new rounds of accumulation.[11] In arguing that hybrid maize constitutes one important emergent commodity frontier, I am also taking a cue from Indian environmentalists who already more than a decade ago critically noted that the rise of hybrid maize indicates that 'another revolution is in

---

11 To reiterate, as argued in Chapter 4, pointing to this broad tendency does not rule out differentiation or remaining ability to accumulate among certain classes of capital in agrarian India.

the making, but one formulated and directed by the private sector' (Narayan, Suchitra, and Sood 2011). Drawing on the reformulated approach to commodity frontiers sketched out above, the maize frontier emerges in semi-arid parts of southern India in particular that are less thoroughly capitalised than the homeland of the Green Revolution that gave rise to the trajectory of 'petro-farming', involving the relatively more accessible – for capital – expropriation of human reproductive work and of nature.

The explosive growth of maize in the context of an otherwise stagnant agricultural economy has triggered hopeful assessments that are expected parts of broader 'imaginaries' surrounding frontiers (Tsing 2003; Klinger 2018). More and faster growth of the crop appears the path of the future. Around ten years ago, several opinion pieces in Indian news outlets as well as academic publications put forward hybrid maize as a potential new 'miracle crop' (Mukherjee 2013) or 'wonder crop' (K et al. 2016) for the country. In the following years, maize has frequently been designated the 'crop of the future' among Indian policymakers and agribusinesses. The Indian Institute of Maize Research 'Vision 2050' report, for example, pictures a tripling of maize production by 2050, perceiving maize as *the* crop for a future of 'limited natural resources and a changing climate' (Research 2015, VII). Others, including India's Agriculture Minister, have talked of doubling maize production by 2025 (Sen 2016). At the time of writing, aims of doubling production have also been recently articulated by northern state government of Uttar Pradesh (Rawat 2023). While certainly celebrating the 'achievements' in production increase thus far, these narratives share features with what White and colleagues (2012) have identified as a widespread 'yield gap' narrative in corporate agricultural strategies. Seeing Indian maize as of today as suffering from a 'yield gap', the agribusiness sector in particular has been arguing for a cocktail of R&D in hybrids, public-private partnerships, export orientation and commodity chain integration as favoured strategies for achieving the desired expansion (KPMG 2014; Narayan, Suchitra, and Sood 2011).

The typically 'corporate food regime'-style concentration in the maize market, as with the industrial grain-oilseed-livestock complex more broadly, strongly differs from much of India's agrarian capitalism. As earlier chapters have outlined, the latter has hitherto been markedly decentralised with agribusiness 'dominated by small-scale, informal firms' (Frödin 2013, 230; see also Harriss-White 2002) that do not necessarily distinguish themselves radically from surrounding forms of predominant petty commodity production among classes of labour (Harriss-White 2012). While the Green Revolution-initiated accumulation cycle was based on heavy state involvement in the country's agro-food system, private and corporate capital drives the maize frontier – although, as we shall see shortly, under Narendra Modi's regime increasingly so in a closely knit state-capital nexus. As one high-ranking agricultural department official in Bangalore told me in an interview, the expansion of maize

> is more or less market-led, not government push. Diverse sectors – multinationals, who else – are the actual drivers. Not the government. In all other crops the government has tried to push but here it's market-led, although it's supported by government [...] it is a totally private, corporate sector which is pushing through the seed technology. In all of this, it has got a comparative advantage. So the push is from the corporate sector. Support of the mechanization: Again the corporate sector. It is some sort of global commodity.

Other agriculture department officials underlined the same point in several interviews: R&D units belonging to biotechnological seed companies drive technological development in the maize sector, as industry reports also corroborate (FICCI 2018). Furthermore, agriculture department and seed company informants in Bangalore variously estimated that the maize seed market houses somewhere between 30 and 50 companies. Among these we find that three of the top five companies are also members of the infamous 'Big Six' of world-leading agribusinesses controlling 60 percent of the global seed market (IPES-FOOD 2017, 21): DuPont Pioneer, DEKALB (a subsidiary of Monsanto/Bayer), and Syngenta. Apart from these we find the company Bisco, an Indian subsidiary of Limagrain which clocks in as the world's fourth largest seed company. The only domestic company on the top five is Kaveri Seeds, which is among the country's major agribusinesses with reported net sales of 669.89 *crore* rupees in 2016–17 (Limited 2017).

The private and corporate character of the hybrid maize frontier is also evident from the demand-side. The hybrid maize boom partakes in broader patterns of restructuring the global food regime that we have encountered earlier in this book, centred on the rise of the industrial grain-oilseed-livestock complex and the permeability of crops across food-fuel-feed complexes. The flexibility of maize comes across in reports acknowledging its manifold uses in the Indian context – in feed, particularly poultry feed, starch and other industrial products – as triggering its rise (FICCI 2015). Several sources agree that poultry feed comprises above 50 percent of the end-use for maize in the country

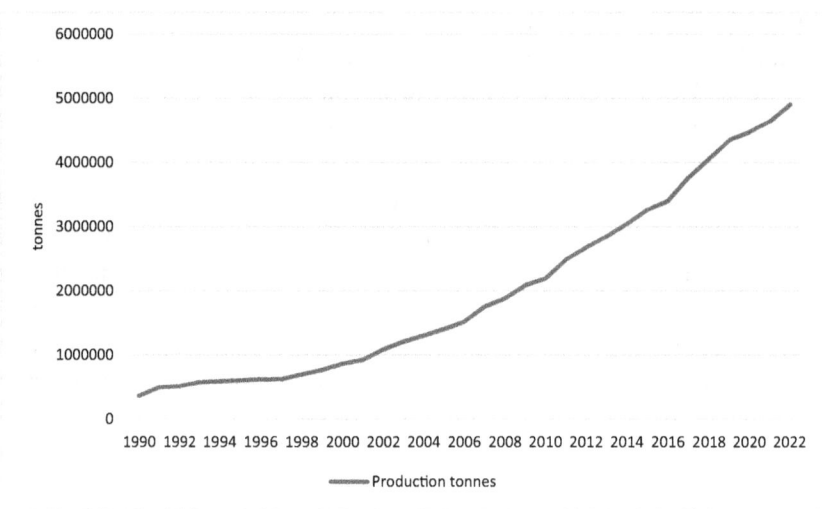

FIGURE 4   Chicken meat production in India (tonnes)
SOURCE: DATA COMPILED FROM FAOSTAT BY THE AUTHOR

(Modi 2014). It is thus clear that poultry is a major driver of the maize boom.[12] Although hitherto underexplored in agrarian studies scholarship, not unlike the maize frontier itself, data shows that poultry is booming (see Figure 4).

Production and consumption of poultry in the form of both chicken meat and egg increases rapidly in India; consumption has been calculated to increase by seven percent annually, totalling 4,5 million metric tons of chicken meat in 2016 (Intodia 2016; Gandhi 2018). Indeed, the poultry sector differs from other forms of agricultural production in India in being more industrialised with concentrated factory farms: 'About 90 percent of the more than two billion 'broiler' (meat) chickens produced in India each year are raised in industrial-style facilities' (MacDonald and Iyer 2012, 5). Although still low in comparative terms, middle-class lifestyle in urban India sees an increasing prominence of meat eating – which means primarily chicken as the favoured meat (Bruckert 2021). As any casual observer can readily acknowledge, Indian cities and towns of various sizes are now dotted with outlets selling fresh chicken meat. Since 2007–8, moreover, India has become a net exporter of maize, an export that reached 4,27 Mt in 2012–13, mainly to Southeast Asia (Kumar, Srinivas,

---

12   One important industry report holds the usage of maize for feed to be 'about 60 percent' including 47 percent for poultry and 13 percent for other livestock feed (FICCI 2018).

and Sivaramane 2013). The maize boom may in other words eventually have consequences far beyond India's borders, incorporating India in what can be conceptualised in an 'Asian meat complex' that is constitutive of broader food regime dynamics (Jakobsen and Hansen 2020).

In the last few years, Modi's government has been launching a renewed emphasis on ethanol production for biofuels. This is part of the Modi government's emphasis on 'self-sufficiency', a central trope to much of Modi's rhetoric throughout his period in power, yet markedly intensified as part of the regime's post-COVID-19 recovery efforts under the term 'Atmanirbhar Bharat' (Jakobsen and Nielsen 2024). Hybrid maize figures centrally in these governmental efforts towards augmenting biofuel production, with recent indications of state initiatives towards strengthening maize R&D and provide incentives towards increasing production (Haq 2024b, a). While it is still too early to tell how these governmental efforts affect agrarian production systems in the country, they do reveal an added layer of capital-state interests in the maize boom, resonating with the overall pro-corporate sector nature of Modi's regime and the documented close ties between large-scale capital and the state that, as indicated earlier in the book, have only intensified in the last few years (Chatterjee 2023; Sircar 2022).

The recent hybrid maize expansion has been dominated by a few Indian states, especially Karnataka and Andhra Pradesh, with around 38 percent of total production in 2011 (KPMG 2014, 12), which in turn are located in proximity to the leading poultry hub of Tamil Nadu. Karnataka's share of all-India maize production have been variously estimated at somewhere between 15 and 18 percent (Karnataka 2016) of total national production.[13] In these 'new' maize producing areas we find that 90–98 percent of the acreage currently is under hybrid varieties, whereas in 'older' maize areas (such as Rajasthan and Madhya Pradesh), hybrids account for only about 20 percent of the acreage (KPMG 2014, 13), and have seen stagnation and even negative growth rate in harvested areas (Jakobsen and Westengen 2022).

The new areas of maize expansion are predominantly semi-arid. It appears that a well-established agricultural sector conceptualisation of a spatial fix here is centred around the trope of 'diversification' in 'upland areas' as a form of 'exit' from environmental degradation following the Green revolution and its resultant pattern of 'petrofarming' (Joshi et al. 2005, 1). Hybrid maize is thus perceived as suitable for parts of the country where agriculture has hitherto

---

13   For details, see data provided by Indian Institute of Maize Research at India Maize Scenario – ICAR-Indian Institute of Maize Research.

been capitalised to only a relatively limited extent, thus offering the potential for a high 'ecological surplus', to put it in terms of Moore's commodity frontier analytics. Not only 'uplands' as referred to here, broad sections of semi-arid India are targeted: 'these hybrids have already made significant inroads into several parts of the country, especially in areas that face droughts, diminishing water resources and weather-related constraints' (Sud 2011). One agribusiness report holds that '[f]actors such as adaptability to diverse agro-climatic conditions, lower labour costs and lowering of water table in the rice belt of India have contributed to the increase in acreage' (KPMG 2014, 11). Note the mention of labour, which will assume central importance once we move to dynamics of the commodity frontier as seen 'from below'.

Two other points are also key: First, the notion of 'diversification' in the context of crisis – climate crisis, agrarian crisis – means that maize as a commodity frontier emerges from the socioecological particularities of agrarian change in contemporary India, where farmers in semi-arid parts in particular are in distress. In their way, informants in seed companies in Bangalore brought up the same point, one of whom emphasising that the strong growth of the maize sector has happened in a period also characterised by 'inconsistent rains' where, as he said, 'farmers were in need of new crops'. Second, the expansion of maize is framed as an incursion into areas relatively marginal to Indian agrarian capitalism. Semi-arid, lacking in irrigation facilities and generally marginalised in many ways, Barbara Harriss-White (2008a) has called these areas 'India's rainfed agricultural dystopia', characterised by

> an increasingly risk-beset, polarized and indebted agrarian capitalism dominated by micro-production and its credit and exchange relations. The mass of small-scale farms are not "un-incorporated", they are incorporated in a differentiated way such that much agriculture is a part-time component of a complex livelihood portfolio dominated by laboring.
> HARRISS-WHITE 2008a, 553

The production of the maize frontier thus happens through historically and discursively constituted regional patterns of uneven development (Neimark and Healy 2018).

4.1 *The Maize Frontier in Karnataka*

Most of Karnataka, barring parts along the coast and the Western Ghats, are largely semi-arid. This warrants common descriptions of agriculture in Karnataka as 'characterized by vast steppes of drought prone regions and sporadic patches of irrigated area' (Bhende 2013, 1), with only 36 percent of the net cultivated area under irrigation (Karnataka 2016). In Karnataka, we find that between 2005–6 and 2014–15, maize has been increasing rapidly in acreage, from 9,36 to 13,37 lakh hectares, making it the top crop in the state equal to paddy (Commission 2016). 90 percent of the production is in the kharif season, with most districts showing increased production except for the humid districts along the coast and in the Western Ghats (Karnataka 2016). Many of the other main agricultural crops – sorghum (*jowar*), rice, finger millet (*ragi*) and groundnut– have decreased over time, while there has been a strong growth in maize as well as sugarcane, cotton and some pulses (see Table 4 below). In addition, horticultural crops have increased, mirroring the mentioned all-India shift towards higher-value crops (Ramakumar 2017). Moreover, as argued by Sejuti Das Gupta (2024, 219), 'Karnataka was an early adopter of technology and private inputs', something we can surmise to have shaped these cropping changes.

Marginality is often a defining feature of frontiers. It is not uncommon to take frontiers as 'liminal' spaces closely associated with borders, hinterlands, unruly and remote spaces vis-à-vis state projects as well as capital (Rasmussen and Lund 2018; Tsing 2003; Cons and Eilenberg 2019). The same goes for the specific 'rainfed agricultural dystopia' that I will explore in what follows. Chamarajanagar is located in the southernmost part of Karnataka, bordering both Kerala and Tamil Nadu. The district was carved out of Mysore district in 1997 'to give a push to development' but continues, as widely perceived

TABLE 4   Major crops in Karnataka, decadal change (area in lakh hectares)

Crops	2005–6		2015–16	
	Area	Percent	Area	Percent
Maize	9,36	8	13,37	13
Jowar	14,85	13	13,27	13
Ragi	15,20	13	10,46	10
Cotton	4,13	4	8,76	9
Bengal gram	4,18	4	9,39	9
Tur	6,00	5	7,28	7
Ground nut	10,40	9	6,54	6
Sugar cane	2,21	2	4,80	5

SOURCE: COMMISSION 2016

in public, 'to languish as a backward region' (Krishna Kumar 2014). In 2005, Chamarajanagar was ranked 25th out of Karnataka's 27 districts in terms of human development, in stark contrast to neighbouring districts (Karnataka 2006). As described above in this chapter, only sections of Chamarajanagar was part of Mysore state prior to Independence, benefiting from the path-dependent effects of the development measures taken by the Mysore government. Much of Chamarajanagar was, however, very peripheral to Mysore, far from headquarters of administration. My field site was just beyond the border of Mysore kingdom and comprised a hilly and rainfed utmost periphery of Madras Presidency. The region is thus the product of long histories of being marginal to state projects. What this implies is that it differs markedly from what we know about the region more broadly. Landmark studies such as Srinivas' (1976) or Epstein's (1962, 1973) work from Mysore thus describe rather different patterns of change in much less marginal places. The closest existing scholarship comes is Charsley's study of sericulture in Kollegal town. Even here we do not, however, get any further glimpse of Kollegal's rural hinterlands. Charsley merely points out that 'Kollegal is the gateway to hilly country' to the east (Charsley 1982, 42). This hilly country is where I have studied the maize frontier.

5 The Hybrid Maize Frontier Seen 'from Below'

The wider region where the village of Mekkenur is located is popularly considered a backwater. It is, among other things, an infamous seat of 'black magic' and a concomitant discourse of fear. During my fieldwork, people kept telling me that state chief ministers have avoided the region due to fear of being cursed, and this part of Chamarajanagar came into the spotlight for allegations of black magic being used as part of the Karnataka state elections in 2018 and again in 2023. This historical and discursively produced marginality has only of late combined with any real interest shown in the region by outsiders, now in rather typical frontier-like ways. Over the last few years, several solar power plants have popped up across the region, as I discovered by traveling around the landscape. In a few kilometres' radius from Hanur, I mapped four solar plants, one of which was reported to spread over 450 acres of land, owned by a sub-company of the Adani Group, one of India's largest corporate conglomerates. Residents in the Hanur region explained that the entrance of solar companies in the last few years had raised price of land in the area significantly. Spending time in Hanur, I quickly started noticing migrant labourers from Jharkhand and other distant parts of India passing through on trucks heading for these solar plants. Casual visits to construction sites revealed that the migrant labourers were responsible for the demanding work of constructing masts, organized by 'supervisors' from Andhra Pradesh.

Other 'frontiersmen' were not hard to find either: land brokers, seen as 'urbanites' coming from Hanur town or farther afield, seemed to thrive in a recent situation of increasing land prices. The owner of my regular tea stall in Hanur, for example, revealed himself to be doubling as land broker. Outsiders – 'businessmen' from Bangalore with fancy cars – are buying land, unlike earlier. From what I have gathered, rates have increased rapidly in recent years, but the extent to which land is sold is still low (see also the relevant discussion in Vijayabaskar and Menon 2018). The plots that I discovered to be sold to outsiders were all classified locally as 'wastelands' (see for example Baka 2013, 2017). Although an unqualified number, one interviewee estimated that some 25–30 individuals from Mekkenur had sold plots of land over the last years. When traveling across agricultural fields, even in rather remote areas adjacent to forests and hills, I would several times encounter cars from Bengaluru by the wayside, and strikingly urban-looking men in white shirts vising plots of land fenced off with barbwire yet nothing being cultivated, or the land being used for intensive floriculture, otherwise uncommon in the area, with the deployment of local people as wage labourers. Inquiring casually into these developments, some of these urbanites narrated to me that they had grown interested in agriculture and wanted to establish themselves as 'part-time farmers' in the region, and had great hopes for their plots of land. Residents of Mekkenur had rather different interpretations: Rumours held that land was being bought speculatively by people in Bengaluru for the purpose of security for loans in banks for other investments, and other speculative ventures.

5.1 *Local Markets and Dealers in Hybrid Maize*

Hybrid maize has expanded rapidly over the last two decades in this region. Moving across Hanur town, I found every single agro-shop advertising for hybrid maize and keeping seed packets upfront in the stores, indicative of the crop's dominance in the agrarian economy and its prominence among agribusinesses operating in the region (see Figure 5 below).

In keeping with the overall picture of the industrial grain-oilseed-livestock complex in South India, shopkeepers explained that the market in hybrid maize seeds in Hanur is packed with as much as 15 supplying companies, of which the major ones are Kaveri, Pioneer and DEKALB (i.e. Monsanto/Bayer). Most farmers in Mekkenur reported that they would go to Hanur to purchase seeds from the town's agro-shops. And not any of the shops; customer relations appeared rather well-established, underwritten by informal credit relations,

FIGURE 5　Agro-shop in Hanur showcasing hybrid maize seeds
PHOTO BY THE AUTHOR

and thus relations of debt for farmers, something that resonates with findings about petty agro-dealers in other parts of India (Aga 2018). Class/caste relations were clearly underpinning these personalised ties between agro-shops and farmers. Among Hanur's agro-shopkeepers, the most prevalent caste was Naidus, one of the region's dominant castes, some of whom identified as being 'from Andhra'. In addition to owning shops, Naidus were well-known among the main landowners besides the Lingayats employing other castes as agricultural labour. Additionally, Naidus were reported to be key owners of machinery such as tractors and bulldozers that farmers would rent from them for seasonal tasks. In conversations, shopkeepers often displayed a rather caste-wise typical top-down – variously condescending or sympathetic – view of the region's farmers and their problems. As I probed their views as to why and how hybrid maize has been booming in the area, explanations emphasising farmers' lacking knowledge of seed varieties, fertilisers and machinery would repeatedly surface. In these narratives, farmers appeared to act herd-like in their choices: 'If one farmer goes for a new seed, all farmers will,' as one shopkeeper put it.[14] Furthermore, such narratives would stress farmers' tendency to over-use fertilisers and herbicides, as well as blaming farmers for neglecting to alternate between crops on single plots of land, leading to exhaustion of the soil. On irrigated land, shopkeepers explained, some farmers reduce the time in-between crops to maximize turnover, even though this leads to problems of insects. Shopkeepers linked these alleged farmers' practices to rising problems of a specific fungus disease – downy mildew – in maize cultivation, only surfacing in the last years.

In addition to supplying farmers directly, shopkeepers also reported of a system of sub-dealers for different seeds and agro-implements of other kinds with whom they had purchase agreements on discounted rates, and also smaller outlets in some villages supplied directly by agro-companies, i.e. circumventing the local agro-shops. These sub-dealers, many of whom were reported to live in the villages, were actively promoting company seeds, and hybrid maize varieties in particular although not exclusively, directly vis-à-vis farmers through outreach activities and farm visits. These localised sub-dealers operated (perhaps unsurprisingly enough given the workings of power in local systems of stratification in India) as dealers-cum-moneylenders, and I witnessed at least one instance in Mekkenur of severe local hostility to such an actor who was reported to take as much as ten percent interest.

---

14   For a different view of 'herd' dynamics in Indian farmers' seed choices, see Stone et al. (2014).

According to one sub-dealer, it is particularly the smaller maize companies that engage in active 'marketing', whereas the bigger companies presumably already have strong enough market shares to be able to direct their efforts elsewhere. Some of the main seed companies, on the other hand, organise 'demonstration plots' in agricultural fields, in which they invite farmers from nearby areas to come and observe seeds in action. Such demonstration plots, as I discovered by visiting several over the course of fieldwork, involved companies supplying inputs to farmers operating and working the plots, with occasional visits thereafter by company representatives. Demonstration plots were supplied with banners, signposts and other forms of notifications of the company and specific variety of hybrid maize seed grown. These plots, moreover, were without exceptions found on the land of big farmers, some of whom had leased this land in addition to their own land. Demonstration plots, moreover, were solely directed at irrigated farmers, the significance of which will be clearer in what follows.

The market for maize is likewise tightly integrated in the industrial grain-oilseed-livestock complex. Predominantly, the produce is sold to poultry companies across the border in Tamil Nadu, which was also referred to the as the key destination for the local cotton production. Other destinations for the regional maize crop that was mentioned in interviews included glycose production and other forms of industrial uses in factories in Tamil Nadu. One of the key companies sourcing maize in Mekkenur as well as surrounding villages was Suguna Food, India's leading poultry company, headquartered in Coimbatore. Villagers would emphasise the benefit of the 'good market' and 'demand' from poultry companies keeping prices relatively stable. While the possibility did exist for farmers to sell maize on state regulated markets, this was markedly disfavoured. Farmers found that the state administered market would entail additional expenses for transportation, but also that requirements and standards for the quality and quantity of the produce were unfeasible to manage, especially for rainfed farmers. Unlike state markets, private buyers of maize were reported to arrive with lorries at the farm to buy the maize produce directly. These buyers could be representatives of poultry companies or intermediaries generically referred to as 'middlemen from Tamil Nadu', both of which were described as offering acceptable prices. Alternatively, farmers reported selling to local middlemen from their own or nearby villages, based on relations of trust (and, one may add, undoubtedly local power relations with their hierarchies and structures of dominance). In either case, it was clear that the proximity to the booming poultry market just across the border in neighbouring Tamil Nadu was significant, indeed decisive, providing this remote region with an advantage: 'The market is good here', as one agricultural department officer explained to me with reference to transborder dynamics. Most of the farmers I talked to expressed lack of interest in *who* the buyer is or what the maize is used for: 'We don't know, we just sell it, we don't know where it will go', said a couple of farmers. Rather, the sense was that the market in maize was beneficial enough that they could easily sell to whomever 'came first', as farmers would say. All of this, in short, was seen by respondents as contrasting sharply with other agricultural commodities that were sold on state-run markets with fluctuating prices, greedy traders, unreliable price-setting and the added expenses of transporting the produce to the market.

5.2 The Making of the Boom

While the industrial grain-oilseed-livestock complex is centrally involved in the logics of maize cultivation in the region, in villagers' own view of the maize boom, it did not in fact start with the expanding reach of this complex into their surroundings. Instead, what villagers uniformly emphasised was a rather everyday initiation of the boom as hybrid maize first started being cultivated by neighbouring 'Tibetan refugees', as they were called. These Tibetans, residing in a cluster of resettlement groups some 30 km from Hanur, first started cultivating hybrid maize in their intensively irrigated fields 20–30 years ago. The common story was that villagers in Mekkenur and surroundings 'learned that the Tibetans were benefiting from growing maize', as many farmers said, and so they simply imitated them. This was the indeed the standard narrative that I was told innumerable time whenever the topic of maize surfaced. As I eventually discovered, the very first person to have picked up hybrid maize near Mekkenur was a Lingayat major landholder who told me that he learned of it around the year 2000 from relatives living close to the Tibetans. Others told similarly of having heard stories or personally observed the Tibetans as the explanation for the spread of maize.

Today, maize (*mekkejola*) is by far the most widespread crop in Mekkenur and nearby villages. Prior to the initiation of my fieldwork, in the agricultural year of 2016–17 – which, as I will return to below, was a year of drought – 66 percent of the cultivated irrigated land and 82 percent of the cultivated rainfed land in Mekkenur was growing maize.[15] Maize, then, has displaced traditional crops, in particular *ragi* (finger millet), which used to be the main rainfed crop in the village and surrounding region. In the agricultural year of 2016–17, ragi was only grown on 30 acres of rainfed land, a mere 7,5 percent of the size of rainfed land growing maize that year.[16] Elderly informants narrated social change

---

15   Data compiled from the Village Accountant's office.
16   Data compiled from the Village Accountant's office.

in the village as a transition from growing ragi for own consumption in their youth to agricultural commercialisation where food is bought on the market. Ragi was also the staple food and *ragi mudde* (balls of ragi) remains the daily dinner. An SC man in his eighties, for example, summarized his childhood succinctly as follows: 'In my childhood we had ragi. Growing, harvesting, eating. No saving of money'. Other farmers explained that ragi used to be commonly grown and the main food eaten up till around 10–12 years ago, with rice being infrequently consumed, mostly for rituals. I found many farmers growing ragi on a small section of their land (no more than one quarter of the land) for own consumption but that was about it. As a subsistence crop, ragi seeds are not purchased but saved from year to year, and ragi produce only very rarely being sold on any market.

Yet the making of the maize boom in the Hanur region is not a story of straightforward monocultural appropriation. Villagers could easily list up to 18 different rainfed and 5 irrigated crops (including 'vegetables' as a covering term for many varieties) being cultivated. Villagers as well as agro-shop keepers were very careful in explaining how maize is put to use as part of a wider portfolio of crops. The integration of maize in a broader combination of multiple crops is particularly widespread, I learned, for farmers having at least part of their land under irrigation. Throughout my fieldwork, I did not find a single irrigated farmer who had shifted fully into maize. In contrast, rainfed farmers were in many cases found to be exclusively, or primarily, relying on maize. This gives rise to a puzzle: when prompted, *not a single* farmer – neither irrigated nor rainfed – held maize to be outright profitable. A seemingly indifferent shrug often accompanied statements to the effect of maize's profitability. This, to be clear, was in sharp distinction to how farmers would point to profitability in crops such as bananas (see more below). So, even though the market, as we have seen, being intertwined with the industrial grain-oilseed-livestock complex, is facilitating farmers to convert into maize, its significance should not be exaggerated. In what follows, I will seek an explanation to this puzzle in the conjuncture of forces and processes on the ground that has rendered maize 'somewhat' useful to the livelihoods particularly for rainfed farmers in Mekkenur.

5.3 *The Rainfed Dystopia and Classes of Labour*

The Hanur region fits the 'agricultural dystopia' scenario mentioned earlier well: rainfed conditions have made farming increasingly risky and unprofitable in a context of unpredictable rainfalls, that is, in a version of the variegated 'climates of uncertainty' (Matthan 2023) increasingly characteristic of agrarian India's predicament. Informants in their fifties and above told me of life-long experience of failing monsoons, but sharply deteriorating rainfall starting only in recent years. When I started fieldwork in 2017, the region was experiencing its first proper monsoon in 4–5 years. The years before had, in other words, been unusually dry. During this extended drought, whole villages had abandoned agriculture; lands were left fallow and many villagers migrated temporarily to casual worksites from Bangalore to coffee estates in Kodagu.[17] Moreover, the vagaries and uncertainties of the climate extend even further: when it *does rain,* villagers held it to be all-too-common that it rains *too much,* for example in heavy downpours reappearing after sowing, thus spoiling a good part of the crops. In nearby villages where there is even less irrigation than in Mekkenur, recent years' droughts saw whole villages being temporarily deserted. Traveling the region, I came across villages where people had not yet returned fully.

In this context of climatic unpredictability, livelihoods are far from dependent on agriculture. As in Harriss-White's characterisation of the rainfed dystopia recounted earlier, wage labour dominates livelihoods in Mekkenur. Indeed, one of the common narratives of socioeconomic change emphasised how the increasingly unpredictable weather conditions and more frequent droughts have led people away from agriculture as a main occupation. Middle-aged residents would describe their childhoods as situated within the 'olden days' model of an agricultural way of life that has since then passed. This narrative was shared across class and caste lines – even though the ramifications of livelihood diversifications have, as we shall see, played out in distinct ways. While India's classes of labour have recently been framed as 'farmer-labourers' (Lerche 2021), Mekkenur's fraction thereof is perhaps even better termed 'labourers-farmers'.

The only people I met whom considered themselves to be economically benefitting wholly from agriculture were a few major landowners having around or above 10 acres of land. In Kannada these are known as *dodda raitharu* – big farmers. They were cultivating a wide range of crops on irrigated lands, including bananas, turmeric, cotton and sugarcane, which they considered more profitable. Such varied cropping patterns were perceived by respondents as a necessary corollary of the vagaries of climate in reducing risks: 'If you have only one variety you can lose everything', one big farmer said. While some of these larger farms were found within Mekkenur itself – largely in the hands of Lingayats, as the demographics and landownership patterns would suggest (see

---

17   Many villagers told me that the rise, although still limited, in local land sales is linked to these recent droughts.

also Table 3 above) – more striking were the farms located outside of villages proper in the area, where larger tracts of land were being intensively taken up by irrigated agriculture, in many cases also distinct from other farmlands by being fenced off with barbwire. Dominant castes in the region like Naidus, Vokkaligas and many Tamils owned these farms, where owners would live on the farm itself rather than following the prevailing pattern of living in a separate house in the nearby village. People from Mekkenur would be employed as wage labourers.[18] 'Maize is not profitable!' dominant farmers would exclaim when I asked them for the reasons behind their cropping choices. To the extent that they did grow hybrid maize, it was only on selectively apportioned parts of their lands – based, as the following will show, on 'feeding' livelihoods more indirectly. While *dodda raitharu* had profit as their orientation in evaluating maize, other farmers emphasised that 'at least we get something' from maize, unlike other crops with their fluctuating price rates. Agro-traders in Hanur calculated input and output costs for maize, matter-of-factly ascertaining that this 'something' farmers do get is a paltry sum. These significant findings, I argue, entail that we need to look beyond 'profit' in explaining the everyday dynamics of the maize boom (see also Kumar 2016a). Labour patterns, as indicated, are key.

Dominant farmers were able to produce commodities profitably by employing agricultural labour (*kuli*), primarily among the classes of labour residing in Mekkenur, hired on daily wages. Rainfed farmers only cultivate their lands for half the year or less, leaving them in a position where they can take up agricultural labour in the remaining months, i.e. for much of the year in total. In the regional market for labour, residents from other villages were also an option for hire, but several dominant farmers told me that they prefer local agricultural labourers from Mekkenur as they can be paid less and can return to their own houses for lunch, whereas hired labourers from other villages would need to have meals served.[19] Statements such as these, I suggest, point towards very localised patterns of dominance and hierarchy influencing the leverage held by dominant class/caste actors in controlling the labour force – that is, important yet insidious mechanisms of the labour regime (Pattenden 2016c, 2018b; Çelik 2023). Hired workers from other villages were, also, regularly trucked across the landscape by employees, entailing additional expenses and efforts. Local women appeared sought-after as agricultural labourers as they were paid

---

18   Several older agricultural labourers would describe patterns of bonded labour being prevalent on such farms 20 years ago or more.

19   Landowners told me that agricultural labourers from other villagers were paid Rs 50 more per day – but I have not had this corroborated by *labourers* themselves.

markedly less than men were (while men from the village were, at the time of fieldwork, paid Rs. 200 per day, women were paid Rs. 120).[20]

In conversations, dominant farmers would constantly bring up 'the labour problem'. They regularly talked about how, as one elderly Kuruba man put it, 'as compared to farmers, agricultural labourers will get good income now'. Never actually backing up such remarks with any proof, dominant farmers conveyed a sense of frustration in such terms, as commercial agriculture demands investments in seeds, equipment as well as *labour* – all overshadowed by the prospect of failing rains. Overlooking their lands where small groups of 5–8 agricultural labourers would be toiling in the heat, I met several dominant farmers who complained about how labourers have turned 'difficult to monitor'. If you try to press them to work harder, faster, or longer, they simply leave, landowners complained. This narrative was held up against a conveyed sense of a past in which landowners could pay workers in advance and be certain that the work would be done without complications. Many respondents, including agricultural labourers themselves, described wages as having risen lately (during my fieldwork in 2018, women would confirm that their wages had increased from 120 to 150 rupees per day only in the last six months). While this predictably enough reinforced complaints among dominant farmers, it ramified very differently among workers: lower caste/class respondents held the view that wages presently were at such a level that rainfed farmers refrained from hiring agricultural labourers altogether, relying now on their household labour power entirely in working their agricultural lands.

Across the class/class spectrum, these changes to agricultural wage labour were perceived as related to broader transformations to the agrarian system over the course of the last two generations. Where there was previously a sense in which dominant landowners had a certain personalised command over lower caste/class villagers which included the ability to recruit them as agricultural labourers throughout the year, the present scenario was described as one in which this command has weakened markedly. Dominant farmers, as we have seen, complained about increasing difficulties securing sufficient agricultural labour for their crops, and, moreover, a labour-force that now protested or refused if they would try to press the number of hours or the workload involved.[21] Lower caste/class respondents, however, described a situation

---

20   How this discussion fits into a broader pattern of feminisation of agriculture is beyond the scope of this chapter. For an overview of relevant literature, see Pattnaik et al. (2018). More broadly, the gender dimension here may point to the need for more substantial conceptualisation in a food regime approach (Mincyte 2024).

21   Research from surrounding parts of South India, including Taylor and Bhasme's (2018) recent work from Telangana, shows similar patterns of perceived 'labour shortage'.

where localised structures of domination have crumbled, allowing them to depart in search for other work if the conditions for agricultural labour locally do not fulfil their requirements. This is of course linked to changing labour markets and the 'incorporation' of a peripheral region, in Harriss-White's phrasing above, in a broader economy. In commodity frontier terms, these are significant dynamics. The incorporation of classes of labour in the region in a wider economy has important implications not only for the exploitation of paid work, but also, as I will return to below, the expropriation of reproductive work and of non-human nature.

Throughout fieldwork, I did not encounter a single extended household that did not include an element of paid work in its livelihood portfolio. Types of paid work, however, differed greatly across lines of class and caste. Dominant households in the village reported white-collar jobs including, for example, regular employment in banks and as engineers, as well as small-scale business in Hanur town (e.g. running restaurants or other shops) and income from legal and illegal practices running as 'contractors' with close links to the local state.[22] There are also a handful of small manufacturing units (coir, silk, jaggery, pani puri) in the village, all owned by Lingayats. Meanwhile, the majority of Mekkenur's population were involved in insecure, precarious and shifting paid work. As is typical of the country's classes of labour, the majority had agriculture as a component of a labour-oriented household economy. STs in the village reported on small-scale business both in Mekkenur (tea shops) and nearby Hanur as well as forms of labour migration – in many cases to Kodagu to work in coffee estates and, even more frequently, or to Bangalore to work in construction, garment factories and other casual and informal work. SCs in the village reported on similar employment patterns, only more starkly precarious, as local structures of caste domination work towards excluding SCs from regular employment in Hanur.

Excluded from avenues that are open to STs, then, SCs have seemingly found labour migration even more pressingly necessary, resulting in widespread reports of household members working in Bangalore and elsewhere far away. In line with what we know about India's labour migrants at the bottom of the labour hierarchy (Breman 2010; Gidwani and Sivaramakrishnan 2003; Sarkar and Mishra 2021), Mekkenur's low caste migrants also circulate. While there were some cases of people having sent their children for higher education and thereafter resettling, in group interviews with SCs and STs I found

---

22 These forms of employment among the dominant classes appear similar to what Pattenden has found in villages across Karnataka (Pattenden 2016b).

that very few from their castes had been able to resettle because of labour migration. With widespread circulation, I often found households consisting of a middle-aged couple, in many cases at least one of them doing agricultural labour on the lands of higher castes and also looking after their own plots of land, as well as a daughter-in-law and children. The middle-aged couple's own children were working elsewhere. In other cases, middle-aged couples had their children working more nearby in the various forms of causal employment reported above, contributing somewhat more to agriculture although circumscribed by the extent to which wage labour kept them away from the village during the day.

One should be careful in making assessments to the effect that the highly mobile working patterns observed were of recent nature. In her classic study which includes fieldwork in the late 1970s in a village south of Bangalore, Polly Hill writes:

> Under our dry grain mode [i.e. rainfed agriculture of the sort described above] a great proportion of households are obliged to follow non-farming occupations, their grain production being altogether insufficient for household needs and farm-labouring being a highly seasonal occupation.
> HILL 1982, 141–142

This historical precedence might have had an impact on the proclivity for mobile adaptations at present. Yet village narratives insisted that the current situation in Mekkenur differs sharply from what went before: Informants in their fifties and above invariably told me of spending their lives up to adulthood in a village where people mostly worked on the local land, engaging in growing crops for their own consumption, and where insufficient infrastructure and transport, rudimentary education and few social ties limited interaction with a broader economy. To me it seems evident that this links to the Hanur region's marginality, generative of patterns of agrarian change different from less marginal nearby parts.

5.4   *Maize Materiality*

These working patterns among the majority – and among the lower castes with their primarily rainfed small plots in particular – puts clear constraints on the extent to which agriculture *can* be the central component of livelihoods. In the terms of this chapter, I suggest, this can be seen as constraints to the commodity frontier. As the above has revealed, working people's patterns of labour are mixed and shifting, only engaging in agriculture as part of a broader portfolio of income sources. Consequently, household members are often scattered across multiple locations. The land is unhospitable with its unpredictable and deteriorating rainfall. This is where the crop-specific properties of hybrid maize – its relational-material qualities, drawing on Marx's warning against 'crude materialism' invoked earlier – come to matter significantly to the trajectory of the commodity frontier.

Significantly, hybrid maize demands less labour and less water than competing crops in the region. For locals in Mekkenur these properties of maize enabled even classes of labour owning small plots of rainfed land to continue cultivating while maintaining their labour-oriented livelihoods. Compared to the traditional crop of ragi, for example, maize-sowing is done with less density making it easier to weed – a material relation that is significant to understanding the broader agrarian political economy of crops, as Sinha also shows in related ways from cotton and rice in the Punjab (Sinha 2022). Maize harvesting with manual cutting is done either based on household or hired labour, depending on the size of one's holding. As mentioned above, rainfed classes of labour reported that they never hired labourers on their maize plots. Villagers explained that a farming couple can harvest one acre of maize in one day on their own. For threshing, people use what is locally known as the *mekkejola machine*.[23] In comparison, no labour-saving machinery is available for the staple crop of ragi, something respondents pointed to as a clear detriment in the context of the so-called 'labour shortage' or 'labour problem' discussed above.

Planting of maize happens in July/August (provided the monsoon does come) with harvesting on rainfed land after 90–100 days and on irrigated land after 110–120 days. This means that maize is a *quick* crop. For classes of labour this is obviously useful in a way that I believe cannot be underestimated: After harvesting, rainfed farmers can then proceed to do *other work* for the rest of the year, i.e. up to nine months yearly. This gives hybrid maize a strong advantage as it is inserted into their wage labour-oriented livelihood portfolios. Adding to this, recent patterns of labour mobility as well as overall monetisation of reproduction in the Indian countryside have created a situation where all sections of villagers in Mekkenur are increasingly in need of cash. Middle aged and older respondents emphasised a generational change in household dependencies on cash for handling an expanding list of expenditures: Agriculture has become commercialised, demanding a steady stream of purchased inputs. School fees need to be paid, as children universally go to school, usually finishing at 7th

---

23 Farmers would rent the machine, most commonly from big farmers who own these, for 75 rupees per quintal at the time of my fieldwork. The machine is then connected to a tractor engine for running. There were four tractors in Mekkenur and more could be rented in nearby Hanur.

standard, while some also go to college. Villagers reported that expenses on weddings have increased. Houses are constructed, maintained and upgraded to modernized (*pucca*) standards. In short, the need for cash involves a plethora of daily, seasonal and periodic needs.[24] Hybrid maize fits very well into these compulsions facing rural households as a quick crop.

It is thus evident that the maize boom is grounded in the conjunctural articulation of changing agro-ecological conditions, localised patterns of wage labour, differentiation across class/caste lines and the pressures, constraints and compulsions emanating from the broader political economy. To reveal just how contingent yet structured the local conjuncture is, indicative evidence from visiting Soliga (Adivasi) hamlets in the even more peripheral parts of the region closer to Tamil Nadu can be considered. As mentioned earlier in the chapter, Soligas in the area traditionally used to live in the forested and hilly tracts, practicing shifting (swidden) agriculture, but were later relocated to the plains and provided plots of land. Here too hybrid maize has been expanding rapidly.

Not dissimilar to what we saw in Mekkenur, Soliga respondents also stressed livelihoods dominated by wage labour of the utmost precarious, shifting sort – even more starkly so than the SCs in Mekkenur – immersed in localised patterns of exploitation and dominance, where wage levels were reportedly lower as well than for other class/caste groups. Agricultural lands were predominantly rainfed, lacking the irrigation schemes reported from villages closer to Hanur, and markedly exposed to drought. Since relocation to the plains, Soligas reported of having found themselves caught in a web of loans and debts to local moneylenders – upper castes from nearby villages – to purchase required inputs for agriculture. Over the last decade, these purchases have come to include hybrid maize, as farmers purchase seeds from these moneylenders. Under these conditions, respondents told me, maize has taken on a rather different position than in Mekkenur: its 'quickness' came to use primarily to pay back loans, something that might work under conditions of stable climate but would collapse under drought, leading to rising levels of debts, undermining households' social reproduction.

5.5 The Multiple Use-Values of Maize

The crop-specific properties of maize have repeatedly been singled out by scholars as important in understanding the global expansion of the crop.

---

24 For discussions about rural India's relationship to cash and the increasing pressures the monetisation of social reproduction exerts on rural households, see Vasavi (2012).

'Planting corn', historian Fernand Braudel memorably wrote, 'is surely the simplest and most convenient way to obtain one's "daily bread". It grows very rapidly and requires minimal care' (Braudel 1977, 12).[25] Villagers in Mekkenur were very vocal about this. 'Maize is a good crop', said one ST man as he was grazing his sheep in the wastelands outside of Mekkenur. 'It is easy to cultivate. No need to take care like other crops'. In his classic *Corn & Capitalism: How a Botanical Bastard Grew to Global Dominance* Arturo Warman elaborates:

> Corn's high performance is attributable to its adaptability, its high yields relative to other cereals, its low labor inputs, and its short growth cycle. All these factors go far in explaining why peasant producers prefer corn over other crops. The combination of these factors acquires special significance when producers are severely restricted in their access to resources, restricted in the amount of time that they can wait to have food or obtain income, and restricted by conditions of poverty.
> WARMAN 2003, 94

In Mekkenur, maize came into competition with ragi, which, as already indicated, demands more labour, has less secure market and has lower yields as well. Respondents would emphasise that ragi only brings 5 quintals of yields per acre, which they calculated to be insufficient for making any profit whatsoever, hence useful merely for food. Maize, by contrast, would yield up to 20 quintals per acre on rainfed land. An elderly SC man in his eighties, who grows maize with his two sons on their 2 acres of land narrated the impact of these factors to his household's needs as follows:

> Now if my grandfather had given more land, we would have had more agriculture. But only we have 2 acres land […] I am using maize in that. If I cultivate maize in my land I am getting 40 quintals. Instead of that if I cultivate ragi only 10–15 quintals ragi will be there. But maize I can grow more compared to ragi. Maize can be grown in maximum. With this I am taking care of my family and I am looking after my children and my health. In this way I am leading my life and spending my time […] Whatever that may be in the agricultural land I am taking that. And apart from that I am working as agricultural labour and I am making 300 rupees. Daily 300 rupees I can get. I have cows and sheep, with that I will

---

25 See also related discussion of the properties of maize in India and Malawi in Jakobsen and Westengen (2022).

sell that milk and will get some money. My wife is also helping me to grazing and working in farm also. In my family everybody has to work. Otherwise it would not be possible to maintain life [...] See, I have two sons, they are also helping me. Apart from that I am going for grazing sheep. And we'll take milk from cows. And sell it for dairy. Like that my family is managing.

Returning to Warman's classic work on maize, in addition to the factors described above, he also notes maize's special ability to grow alongside other plants as well as its multiple uses as food, feed and fuel (Warman 2003). Under the contemporary food regime, this makes it a crucial flex crop (Borras et al. 2016) not only at the scale of the global political economy but also in everyday livelihoods. As the following will reveal, this involves, significantly, dynamics of expropriation of unpaid domestic work as well as non-human nature including, especially, bovines.

Dominant farmers were not the only ones to doubt the profitability of maize. For rainfed farmers, the 'gamble', as many put it, of erratic rainfalls weighed heavy.[26] As one ST man said, 'farmers can't know whether they will get benefits from maize in advance. It's like education – you won't know whether you'll pass'. Yet compared to other crops, people emphasised that price levels fluctuate less in a context where demand from the poultry industry is high.[27] The price paid for selling maize for the 'industrial grain-oilseed-livestock complex' is only part of the story, as respondents' constant references to livestock made clear. 'Their main motivation is livestock', Hanur's most experienced agro-shop dealer told me repeatedly. It took me a while to understand statements such as these, but gradually I came to see their importance. For example, a Kuruba farmer with 4.5 acres of land who grows bananas said that 'there are no benefits in maize. We are only cultivating maize for livestock. For that only purpose we are growing maize here'. Big farmers with irrigated lands tended to keep maize straws in heaps on their properties. Next to these, they would keep their cows by a shed or in the shade under a tree (see Figure 6 below). Within the village, too, heaps of maize straw were found next to the houses of the more prosperous villagers (I mainly found these heaps around the Lingayat section of the village, where there is more space next to houses) in order for them to feed

---

26   For discussions of agriculture as 'gambling' in India, with focus on Tamil Nadu farmers who cultivate ginger in parts of Karnataka under 'frontier' like conditions, see Münster (2015).
27   Farmers pinpointed the minimum price needed to avoid losses in maize at 1500 rupees per quintal.

FIGURE 6 Cows grazing on maize straw in Mekkenur
PHOTO BY THE AUTHOR

their cows nearby as well. Other villagers, with less space for keeping straw mounds by their houses, would keep maize fodder in sheds by their houses to feed their cows.

In commodity frontier terms, these findings point to what Camba (2018, p.4) describes as the 'nexus of paid and unpaid work' in the food regime. The expansion of maize draws – conjuncturally – on its crop-specific ability to 'feed' into a broad spectrum of livelihood needs in Mekkenur. Middle-aged women as well as their daughters-in-law would do a lot of the work of feeding, washing and milking cows near to their houses. Milking could also be done after finishing the day's paid work. As agriculture has become increasingly risky, precarious and unprofitable, villagers perceived the livestock economy as a safer option.[28] I discussed the livestock economy with informants across caste/class lines throughout my fieldwork and found clear trends: The largest

---

28 It is worth pointing out that the turn towards increased importance of livestock and dairy production is part of a broader Karnataka-wide pattern and that this has been fostered, in part, by policies implemented by Siddaramaiah's Congress government in the years 2013–18.

farmers who were reporting to be actually accumulation from agriculture did not keep much livestock, as they deemed it prohibitively expensive to maintain as it would require the hiring of additional labour. Medium-sized farmers, mostly among Lingayats and Kurubas, were found to own 2–6 cows, with those having more than two cows professing the ability to accumulate at least some money from selling milk. Rainfed and other small farmers, on the other hand, were reporting ownership of merely 1–2 cows per household, not enough to profit from selling milk beyond contributing to covering household needs.[29] Local experts on the livestock economy – including a veterinary and the manager of the village dairy – explained that labouring class households could not possibly afford more cows than that. With the cost of purchasing a cow at Rps. 15 000 during the time of fieldwork, such households would have to take loans, most commonly from local self-help groups. Repaying loans – not only for the purchase of livestock but for household loans more broadly – was commonly a main use of milk money, as women respondents in labouring class households explained. Without the source of feed from maize it would have been difficult for them to maintain this, albeit small, stream of income. In other words, barring the *dodda raithuru* whose cropping patterns, as we have seen, steer towards higher-value crops apart from maize, the livestock economy appeared important across the castes in Mekkenur, although in ways differentiated along caste/class lines.

Adding to this conjuncture is the fact that the region has for the last 10–15 seen the appearance of new breeds of what is commonly called 'hybrid cows', that is, non-native breeds of bovines (see also Narayanan 2023). These produce more milk than the local varieties of cows. Importantly, they do not eat ragi – but they 'love' eating maize, as villagers would put it. Unlike the local varieties of cows, hybrid cows do not need grazing, allowing households to keep their cows under the watch of daughters-in-laws, not affecting their ability to engage in other work. By way of contrast, local cows were reported to demand one person to graze ten cows full-time. Specialised shepherds were no longer to be found in the village, as labouring patterns had diversified and expanded geographically. To handle their bovines, agricultural labourers would often keep their livestock tied in the shade of some trees while working in the field. While both men and women were involved in the everyday activities of tending for livestock, numerous respondents emphasised that women have a particularly important role in such regard.

---

29 Villagers sold milk in a dairy co-operative that has a station in the village itself. Here villagers would sell milk for 27 rupees per litre.

For example, one middle-aged SC woman explained her role one evening as we were sitting outside her house chatting while she was milking her single cow. A rainfed household with 3 acres of land where they grow hybrid maize as well as ragi and horsegram, she explained that the economy of the cow is crucial to their livelihoods. Women take care of the cows, she said, often with the help of their children when they are not in school. Key here is the fact that milk sales, as indicated, are a quick source of cash. As Hanur's livestock veterinary told me, the cow is a 'quick source of income, income per week, as compared to crops, where you have to wait'. An experienced agro-trader in Hanur said that 'profit from maize is only for family maintenance. They can't purchase land, can't put their children to good schools or colleges. They can't save money from that. Only from milk they can save some'. Adding to this, in times of monsoon failure the livestock economy would provide at least some backing for households. All of this makes maize highly congenial under the present agrarian conjuncture in Mekkenur.

The crop-specific properties of maize go even further in allowing for its integration in villagers' livelihoods in ways that can be understood in terms of commodity frontier expropriations. As Warman noted above, maize grows very well with other crops. In Mekkenur this has been taken advantage of by intercropping maize with lablab beans (*avare*) and castor. These were formerly intercropped with ragi. Whereas the irrigated crops do not intercrop well,[30] rainfed farmers would be intercropping with maize, allowing them to add potential additional income from the intercropped crops without having to spend additional time working their land.

Take for example a young SC man who has 2,5 acres of rainfed land. When I came across him in his field one day in September 2017, maize covered his land fully. Meeting him again in March 2018, he was harvesting castor and *avare* from morning to evening from what was by then a veritable forest (see Figure 7 above). While harvesting, he would tie his cows to some of the trees. Harvesting together with his elderly father, he would not hire any agricultural labourers. He sold the castor harvest in Hanur, while the *avare* was for household consumption. He held that the intercropping of castor and maize gives a particular synergy in that castor yields better when intercropped with maize, not with other crops. Referring to the oil made from castor that one puts on one's head to cool the body, he explained that, similarly, castor would 'cool' the land and give good yield in maize. While these intercrops do demand some

---

30 In irrigated agriculture, farmers explained, the intercrops would grow too fast, causing problems for the maize. Moreover, irrigated farmers would plant a new crop after harvesting, which is ill-compatible with intercrops.

FIGURE 7   Working in the castor 'forest'/maize field
PHOTO BY THE AUTHOR

additional labour after the end of the maize harvesting season, I found that Mekkenur's castor and avare 'forests' would be mainly visited by women. Such multiple uses of maize thus tie intimately to the configuration of work patterns among labouring households in ways conducive to the making of maize as a food regime frontier at the intersection of processes 'from above' and 'from below' as well as the intersection of exploitation of wage labour and expropriation of unpaid work and non-human nature.

6   Conclusion

In this chapter, I have continued the trajectory of downscaling food regime analysis by focusing on a single crop and its role as part of a commodity frontier in southern India. Picking up the mantle where earlier chapters ended at more of a national scale analysis, pointing towards unfolding dynamics of commodity frontiers and their exhaustion as broadly constitutive to India's trajectory from the 'long' Green revolution to its contemporary contested incorporation in capital's food regime, this chapter has thus provided a crucially situated empirical analysis that further 'grounds' the book's earlier analyses. Whereas Chapter 4 scrutinized conceptualisations of 'crisis' and 'counter-movements' in food regime writings, and Chapter 5 continued to examine conceptualisations of the 'state' and 'neoliberalism', this chapter has continued examining key food regime analytics by looking at the concept of 'commodity frontiers', offering a novel interpretation of this concept that may, I have argued, allow it to be congruently articulated within the value-form attuned approach suggested in this book.

Specifically, the chapter has shown how the hybrid maize frontier operates across scales, from its role in the increasingly multipolar order of commodity complexes centered on the 'meatification' of diets, to its role in India as a 'flex crop' including multiple uses such as supplying the booming poultry industry and for biofuel. Proceeding towards the 'concrete', the hybrid maize frontier in Karnataka involves agribusiness and state collaborations facilitating expansion of the crop. However, and this is especially the area where this chapter seeks to distinguish itself among food regime writings, to gain a more comprehensive view of the 'concrete', the chapter has unfolded fieldwork-based insights about how the maize frontier comes into being in actually existing terms in a specific agrarian conjuncture, and its constitutive labour regime dynamics, in the village I have called Mekkenur and its surroundings in a remote part of southern Karnataka. This empirical analysis contributes to the hitherto relatively limited number of studies that seek to embed food regime analysis in empirical specificities at the very local scale. In so doing, the chapter has also contributed with novel insights into the agrarian political economy of hybrid maize in the country, so far largely overlooked in agrarian scholarship, as well as that of the Hanur region where I conducted fieldwork, which forms part of an understudied region of South India.

From the fieldwork material, it has become evident that hybrid maize has been booming with distinct commodity frontier dynamics in ways that would be inexplicable from a conventional food regime analysis that takes a view 'from above'. I have shown how the crop has been integrated in local market structures; how it can be combined with labour-oriented livelihoods in different ways across distinctions of class and caste, and particularly so among classes of labour including those involved in rainfed agriculture on small plots facing unpredictable weather conditions; how the relational-material qualities of maize makes it especially suited for integration in these livelihoods; and how the multiple use-values of hybrid maize enables classes of labour to 'feed' their livelihoods more broadly, including through application in their livestock economies, that is, in commodity frontier terms, pointing towards the broader relevance of the maize crop for the expropriation of domestic labour and non-human labour in expanding global value relations.

While bringing these dynamics 'from below' into the picture, the aim has not been that of a 'localist' analysis. To the contrary, what the chapter has been seeking to do, is reveal some of the intricate mechanisms and processes that comprise what Araghi thinks of as capital's food regime as global value relations. Pointing towards further research, I believe the analytical steps taken in this chapter – stressing the conjuncture of dynamics of commodity frontier expansions 'from above' and those 'from below' – can be fruitfully applied and experimented further with in other contexts, bringing other 'booming' crops and their specific relational-material qualities into food regime analysis.

CHAPTER 7

Concluding Reflections

In early 2024, Indian farmers returned to protests in the streets of the capital New Delhi. Among the demands in this round of agitations, farmers sought guaranteed minimum support prises, but also charging the government for failing to live up to earlier promises of loan waivers, signalling the pressing crisis-conditions ramifying across contemporary rural India. Claims were also made that the Modi government was in fact still seeking to implement the now-aborted farm laws, only this time clandestinely. The protests that erupted three years earlier, and with which this book opened, had in other words not led to anything like a conclusive nor sufficiently substantial 'victory' for the country's farmers – or classes of labour, as this book has argued is a more appropriate term – in their struggle with Modi's authoritarian populist regime. Like the previous round of protests and mobilisation, the 2024 cycle was also met with severe repression. Barriers of barbed wire and other barricades had converted the capital into what one journalist described as a 'fortress'. Internet services were blocked in certain areas. Tear gas, rubber bullets, batons and circling drones met the marching farmers, as they again gathered in the tens of thousands at the initiation of a coalition of farmers' unions and movements – a significant gathering of forces once again, albeit not of the massive scale witnessed in the 2020–21 agitations. Several protesters died during the course of the protests, some of whom in the course of direct confrontations with the police and security forces, as had also happened in the previous round of mobilisation, during which several hundred people died.

As I sat down to write this concluding chapter, India's 2024 national election had just passed, with Modi set to assuming the prime ministerial post for the third time, albeit losing a significant share of his support across the country in what opposition forces considered to be a major step forward for Indian democracy in the face of aggressively chauvinist Hindu nationalist forces. Before the elections, the latest wave of farmers' protests had largely subsided without the triggering drivers being solved, but instead rather temporarily *dis*solved in negotiations that as of yet remain indeterminate. The violence that the regime unleashed – in response to both waves of protest – was very much determinate, however. Although I am hesitant of projecting future political trajectories, expectations of further violent crackdowns on protests against Modi's regime, as well as broader intensification of repression and coercion wielded against popular opposition are, sadly and disturbingly, not far-fetched.

Conceiving, as this book has done, these waves of protests as signalling the uneven and contested integration of agrarian India into capital's food regime – something Modi's 2024 election promises of expediting further corporate presence in the country's agro-food sector attests to – the furtherance of violent repression may be interpreted as capital's forceful subordination of oppositional forces to its expansionary sway. As the expansion of capital's food regime involves both repression and concession (Clarke 1988, 141), this book has, as noted in Chapter 1, primarily addressed the 'concession' part of the couplet in its scrutiny of political struggles. At the current conjuncture, however, it is not unimaginable that the actions by Modi's authoritarian populist regime will provide impetus for more sustained analytical emphasis on the part 'repression' plays therein.

While this book has emphasised the politics of consent – and the role of the integral state, hegemonic projects, compromise equilibria and so forth – in the trajectory of capital's food regime, scholars have already over a number of years highlighted that the politics of coercion is on the rise under Modi (Sinha 2017, 2021; Chacko 2018; Mehta 2022). 'The neoliberal state', writes Brown (2018, 50) in a rare contribution to bringing India into food regime debates, 'has demonstrated a greater tendency to resort to force when hegemonic interests are compromised'. Conflict and the willingness to exert force is registered, for example, in the extensive brutalities enacted against the population – predominantly *adivasis* in Central-Eastern India but also broader sections of civil society – in the context of the protracted Maoist insurgency in the heartlands of India (Sundar 2016). And yet I would suggest, although more robust substantiation thereof remains to be done, that such increased prominence of repression, already markedly rising under Modi's by-now decade-long reign, may be not merely because of mounting pressure on Modi's regime – as witnessed by the dwindling popularity evidenced by the 2024 election results. In a more fundamental manner, rising repression may simultaneously index the 'long downturn' (Brenner 2006) of falling profitability for capital, leading to forceful attempts at rejuvenating accumulation, something we can see across the world in numerous authoritarian populisms.

Rather than expecting such developments to revolve primarily or only around the 'accumulation by dispossession' carried out by agribusiness in conjunction with the capitalist state, which, as we have seen in this book, is part of the routine analytical approach in food regime writings, what I would suggest is rather that we need to train a keen eye for how capital seeks 'the opportunistic exploitation of the new forms of freedom created by acts of violence and theft', as William Clare Roberts puts it in his recent reinterpretation of Marx's notion of primitive accumulation (Roberts 2016, 207). Amongst others, this interpretation invites scrutiny of specific strategies of accumulation pursued by specific classes of capital, rather than typically all-encompassing claims in much food regime writings about the dispossession that unfold in the present 'corporate food regime'. As such, food regime writings in their present shape are, moreover, leaning not only towards 'agrarian populism', as argued by Bernstein (2016a), but towards some of Marx's political opponents in his articulations of primitive accumulation. These 'moralistic socialists' critique of conquest and usurpation', as Arboleda (2020a, 173) puts it, do not grasp the essence of the capitalist mode of production in its *systemic* character, by which it comes to exert an external, 'mute' or 'dull' compulsion and domination over people (Bonefeld 2023; Mau 2023; Postone 1993). Unfolding repression and violence in contemporary – and possibly, ominously, near-future – India may precisely enable the further deepening of capital's systemic reach, and not only its more overt grabbing of resources.

Alternatively, shifting gear towards something of an optimism of the will, repression, and mounting protests from parts of the classes of labour in the country, may be interpreted as indexing growing cracks in Modi's authoritarian populism. These developments may thus at the least signal the structural possibility for the emergence of novel forms of counter-hegemonic mobilisation.[1] Indeed, as analyses in the book have indicated, the farmers' agitations over the last few years point in this direction. As I have sought to show, for food regime scholars to take steps towards not only comprehending but also aligning themselves politically with counter-hegemonic forces, these agitations – and other progressive mobilisations in contemporary rural India – should not be seen as 'peasants' seeking to protect a lost way of life of the land. Rather than united around 'farming' or the 'peasant way of life', what unites them – as a form of 'unity in separation' (Endnotes 2015) is their proletarianization and thus subsumption under capital. It is within such compulsions, constraints but also, more hopefully, spaces of opportunity that progressive counter-mobilisations may emerge. The search for a peasantry that somehow escapes the grasp of capital is futile – conceptually and politically obsolete. Understanding the underlying interests, mobilising tropes and 'politico-organisational' (Borras 2023b) challenges that classes of labour face in seeking progressive mobilisation in contemporary India is by no means an easy task. But there is no way around it.

---

1   See also reflections along similar lines in Jakobsen and Nielsen (2024, Chapter 5).

1   The Contributions of this Book

This book has sought to contribute to developing food regime analysis in a new direction that may enable an empirically and conceptually nuanced understanding of dynamics such as those sketched out above, arising from the conundrums of understanding and acting in response to unfolding agitations and mobilisations among classes of labour in India. Towards such a broad aim, I have argued for taking steps towards rethinking food regime analysis in distinct ways. This book has offered two main interlinked contributions, both of which in the spirit of immanent critique, namely 'undertaken from a standpoint that is immanent to, rather than outside, its object of investigation' (Postone 1993, 21). As such, the book is one of the relatively few systematic critiques of food regime analysis, which has hitherto been criticised to surprisingly limited extent despite its influential position within broad fields of scholarship on agrarian change in the contemporary world, as recently pointed out by Bernstein (2016a). In the Indian context, moreover, such engagement has been even more limited, with assessments of the food regime approach largely done in the 'external' and largely dismissive mode of critique (Lerche 2013). The first of the book's contributions is thus that it has argued that food regime analysis needs to downscale its analytical apparatus to account, in a new and dynamic way, for actually existing processes of agrarian change at scales different from the 'global' scale that much food regime writing has fixated on to date. The second contribution is that the book has sought to offer a sustained rethinking of the underlying conceptualisation of food regimes that may enable such a downscaled analysis, by emphasising global value relations, the value-form and class struggle.

The downscaling of food regime analysis has been outlined as a key gap in need of attention in recent scholarship (see e.g. Otero 2016; Wang 2018). My contribution to this field of study has been explicitly rooted in Marx's critique of political economy and its dialectical methodology. 'The concrete', Marx (1993b, 101) writes, 'is concrete because it is the concentration of many determinations, hence unity of the diverse'. This has been a guiding thread for analysis in this book, as the downscaling has involved bringing in new determinations in stepwise movement through scales of analysis from India's historical-geographical trajectory of change over the postcolonial period through to the materiality of a single commodity. Such determinations have been left rather unattended in food regime analysis' prevailing global fixation and bringing them into view has been a key aim of the book. As such, the chapters have unfolded as a gradual processes of enrichment of determinations in search of concrete analysis. Underlying this endeavor, moreover, has been a commitment to 'interpret actual conditions in the rural world' (Borras 2009, 17), which, I would argue, is at times at odds with the thrust of food regime writings, especially surrounding the contemporary 'corporate food regime', that have tended towards synoptic generalisations and overarching claims. The book can in this sense be read as a plead for grappling with what Marx describes as 'infinite variations and gradations in appearance, which can be ascertained only by analysis of the empirically given circumstances' (Marx 1993a, 927).

The gradual movement towards 'the concrete' started in Chapter 2, where I provided an extended discussion of existing food regime literature, its current streams of unresolved debate, and tangent bodies of scholarship. From this overview, I then took the first steps of pointing to conceptual issues that can aid the broader project of the book, including a closer look at a small stream of recent writings that do suggest downscaling food regime analysis, discussions of hegemony and the capitalist state and not the least, noting that labour has been strikingly under-acknowledged in the food regime literature.

From this conceptual outline in Chapter 2, which thus added conceptual specificity to several areas of concern to be covered more empirically later in the book, I then proceeded in Chapter 3 to present a broad contextualisation of postcolonial India's trajectory of agrarian change. Necessarily a partial and synoptic view of massively complex processes of change across a huge country of enormous social, political, economic and cultural variation, the chapter sought to embed the discussion in the book in a firm understanding of key dynamics pertaining in particular to the workings of the 'integral state' in Gramscian terms. In other words, the chapter provided a basis in the insights from South Asia Studies of broad processes of change to be revisited in different ways throughout the book.

Remaining chapters in the book then proceeded towards more pointed and analytically specific analyses. Chapter 4 focused on the conceptual couplet of 'crisis' and 'counter-movements' in food regime analysis through a sustained analysis of the country's ongoing agrarian crisis and surrounding contestations. The chapter continued the analysis of the integral state initiated in the previous chapter, bringing the dynamics of class struggle sketched out in Chapter 3 to bear on more recent developments. It thus revealed how capital's food regime faces a set of gradually exhausted accumulation patterns that were initiated under the 'exceptional' conditions of the earlier postcolonial period – what Araghi (2003) has usefully termed the 'anti-food regime'.

Subsequently, Chapter 5 continued exploring such struggles over the remnants of the prior period and capital's food regime's efforts at demolishing these altogether through an emphasis on concepts of neoliberalisation and the state. The chapter had as its empirical focal point recent right-to-food legislation in India, which has been portrayed in food regime writings as a 'progressive' island in a neoliberal ocean; or, alternatively, a sign of a broader 'return' of the state in the agro-food sector worldwide. The chapter challenged these accounts, revealing how the right-to-food agenda has instead functioned as part of a contradictory process of neoliberalisation and its political negotiations over consent. The chapter ended by revealing that the neoliberal state's efforts at 'exiting' exhausted accumulation patterns involves novel attempts at rejuvenating accumulation through the search for commodity frontiers, which was explored further in the penultimate chapter of the book.

Proceeding the downscaling efforts towards offer a more fully grounded empirical analysis, Chapter 6 took the journey towards the 'concrete' all the way down to fieldwork in a remote part of Karnataka, South India. The chapter explored the making of a specific commodity frontier, surrounding hybrid maize. As such, what this chapter did, was taking a pointed and historically-geographically specific approach to food regimes as global value relations, as in Araghi's formulation. Taking the interest invoked in Chapter 2 in dynamics of labour as a central entry point, the chapter analysed how the crop in question – hybrid maize – comes to expand not only through drivers 'from above' in the global food regime and its manifestations in India's agrarian political economy writ large, but simultaneously as seen 'from below' in localised processes of agrarian change, patterns of waged and unpaid work, among classes of labour in the countryside, and inextricable from the relational-material qualities of the crop.

Viewed as a sequence, then, the book's chapters descended from global dynamics to the materiality of, and everyday practices surrounding, a single crop. Where does that take us? 'From there the journey would have to be retraced', Marx writes, 'but this time not as a chaotic conception of the whole, but as a rich totality of many determinations and relations (Marx 1993b, 100). While I would be hesitant to claim that existing writings on food regimes has succumbed to Marx's fallacy of dealing in 'chaotic conceptions', it has been the argument of this book – central to its immanent critique – that several of the prevailing conceptualisations, claims and overarching statements in the food regime approach can benefit from some systematic rethinking. In this regard, the second, and interrelated, main contribution of the book has been to offer conceptual tools that can help 'retracing' such a journey: a set of concepts and theoretical lenses that can, I suggest, be fruitfully developed further, and of course experimented with, in other empirical contexts. 'As a rule', Marx (1993b, 104) goes on to write a few pages further down in the *Grundrisse*, 'the most general abstractions arise only in the midst of the richest possible concrete development, where one thing appears as common to many, to all'.

In this spirit, the downscaling exercise offered in this book should *not* be seen as 'localism' of any sort. Indeed, as McMichael (2023) argues in a recent contribution that includes a certain reckoning with recent years' efforts towards downscaling, the food regime approach has as its constitutive and distinguishing lens that it seeks world-historical understanding. To strengthen the food regime approach as an entrance for studying capitalism's unfolding trajectory within the realm of food and agriculture, then, would entail sharpening the global reach and ambition, not jettisoning it. In view of Marx's dialectical methodological principles quoted above, I hold that it is precisely through the enrichment of determinations through 'concrete' analysis that such a global reach may be furthered. What, then, would be some of the requisite 'general abstractions' where, as Marx holds, 'one thing appears as common to many'?

This question brings us back to the conceptual lens offered in this book, first presented in Chapter 1 under the heading of going 'beyond reifications'. With this framing, I sought to question the view of 'the' food regime as a 'structure' that has led to incessant debate as to whether 'it' is 'neoliberal', 'corporate' or whether there is a 'new' food regime on the horizon, arising with China's emerging role in the global political economy. These approaches and directions of debate risk reifying the food regime and, furthermore, has been intertwined with an exaggerated tendency to periodize in strong terms, emphasizing rupture in overall capitalist development. The underlying approach I have suggested in this book, shaping the downscaling venture through and through, marks a departure from these tendencies. This approach has been rooted in Araghi's (2003, 51) conceptualisation of food regimes as 'the political face of world historical value relations', which I have sought to bring into dialogue with a specific Marxist approach to value theory stressing the value-form, that has hitherto been under-acknowledged in agrarian studies and beyond. The value-form informed approach bears directly upon the issue of reification, as neatly worded in the introduction to the first volume of the series on Open Marxism: 'Once the relation between structure and struggle is seen in terms of form of mode-of-existence one can never return to ideas of the development of capitalism on the basis of distinct stages' (Bonefeld, Gunn, and Psychopedis 1992, XVII).

Araghi's notion of food regimes viewed in terms of value relations speaks to this concern in that it has provided a strong critical lens on prevailing periodization of food regimes. In Araghi's take, 'the food regime of capital' took first a liberal shape, and then a neoliberal one, whereas what prevalent scholarship has termed the 'second food regime' rather appears a phase of exception, even an 'anti-food regime' in which capital's food regime was kept at bey, centrally by way of state intervention and protectionism. This book has drawn significantly on Araghi's dissident view on this point, which has enabled an analysis of India's current and uneven incorporation in capital's food regime as one involving political struggles over remnants of the prior, exceptional phase that capital currently seeks to demolish once and for all. In this way, I have sought to distance my analysis from that of seeing food regimes in terms of relative stability, with periods of crisis in between. Rather, capital's food regime operates in and through crisis, like the capitalist mode of production more broadly, of which India's recent trajectory of agrarian change has provided vivid exemplification.

Proceeding along this analytical path, the notion of 'modes-of-existence' can be 'filled' in different ways, thought concrete analysis, holding that capital is global in *form* – yet its *content* is, as Marx held, that of infinite variations. This is not, however, to say that it is unstructured. As noted in Chapter 1, Araghi (2003, 49) writes that global value relations as a dialectically 'deep' concept 'should not be hypostazised and conflated with reality', and that '[p]recisely because deep concepts are not concrete, however, they must be historically concretized'. The value-form approach that I have been inspired by insists on the structur*ing* role of *class struggle*. 'The logic of capital', writes John Holloway, 'is not separate from struggle; it *is* struggle' (Holloway 2019, XII, emphasis in original). Everything is not in flux, far from it, under the capitalist mode of production. Class struggle, then, is key to understanding global value relations. With its attention to the central, intrinsic role of the capitalist state, class struggle has been the shaping analytical force behind this book, where I have insisted that class struggle is not properly grasped unless located within historically grounded patterns of change. In doing so, the book has disaggregated aspects of struggle that have, in much previous food regime writings, been approach at an overarching level, in keeping with the 'global' fixation. So, for example, rather than speak of the role of 'Capital' in general, the book has taken steps towards disentangling the agencies of specific capitals, in the form of variegated classes of capital in the Indian agri-food sector.

Moreover, and here I have only been able to scratch the surface on what may in fact prove to be a broader area of inquiry, taking capital's food regime to centre on value relations may integrate it more fully in the overall mechanisms of the capitalist mode of production, rather than perceiving of the food regime sequence as a distinct – and quite idiosyncratic – aspect thereof. What I have sought to bring out in this regard, more specifically, has been the implications of seeing capital's food regime as emergent in a phase of the capitalist mode of production, i.e. the post-1973 period, marked by significant falling rates of profit across different sectors, progressively so not only in the advanced capitalist economies of the West but worldwide, amounting to what Brenner

(2006) has termed the 'long downturn'. Although countries of so-called emerging economies such as India may appear to break with this pattern, I have indicated that such is not necessarily the case. Instead, several aspects of agrarian change in India over the last several decades, involving the 'exhaustion' of patterns of accumulation that arose during the so-called Green revolution, have brought capital on to a downward trajectory. Under conditions of distress, decline and crisis, the book has probed some of the ways capital's food regime goes on search for renewed opportunities for accumulation, including through new commodity frontiers. Capital's food regime, then, seeks to deepen and strengthen its global reach in and through the capitalist stagnation witnessed in the long downturn – the general dynamics and specific manifestations of which are still relatively under-acknowledged in the field of agrarian studies and beyond. Much of these fields, including the approach taken in food regime analysis, has rather tended to emphasise capitalist 'expansion' for the period of neoliberalisation globally, often in dialogue with notions such as Harvey's 'accumulation by dispossession'. Shifting analytics to the rather different dynamics of capitalist stagnation under the long downturn may, I suggest, provide a novel angle on global agrarian transformations that has so far been relatively under-explored.

Consequently, I suggest that commodity frontiers constitute a significant area of concern for furthering food regime analysis along the line of global value relations, offering ample opportunities for 'concrete' analysis. Other approaches, such as recent critical economic geographers' rethinking of 'global value chains' along Marx's notions of circuits of capital (Baglioni and Campling 2017), have paid increased attention to commodity frontiers as central to the workings of contemporary capitalist restructuring, both in food and agriculture and beyond (Werner 2022). The immanent critique offered in this book has emphasised the need to sustained concrete analysis of dynamics of commodity frontiers that are invisible to analysts 'from above', demanding scrutiny of empirically grounded realities 'from below'. This book has sought to demonstrated that an approach to global value relations understood in such terms demands sustained attention to historical-geographical specificity and rigour no less than conceptual drive and ambition, refusing to dispense with the overall aim of bringing to view the systemic workings of the capitalist mode of production.

References

Adnan, Shapan. 2013. "Land grabs and primitive accumulation in deltaic Bangladesh: interactions between neoliberal globalization, state interventions, power relations and peasant resistance." *The Journal of Peasant Studies* 40 (1):87–128.

Adnan, Shapan. 2016. "Alienation in Neoliberal India and Bangladesh: Diversity of mechanisms and theoretical implications." *South Asia Multidisciplinary Academic Journal* (13).

Aga, Aniket. 2018. "Merchants of knowledge: Petty retail and differentiation without consolidation among farmers in Maharashtra, India." *Journal of Agrarian Change*, 18(3), 658–676. DOI: 10.1111/joac.12249.

Agrawal, Arun, and K. Sivaramakrishnan. 2000. "Introduction: Agrarian environments." In *Agrarian Environments: Resources, Representations, and Rule in India*, edited by Arun Agrawal and Sivaramakrishnan, 1–22. Durham: Duke University Press Books.

Aguilar-Støen, Mariel, and Jostein Jakobsen. 2023. "Will development kill us? Globalized livestock production in the" pandemic era"." In *Handbook on International Development and the Environment*, 185–198. Edward Elgar Publishing.

Ahmed, Waquar, and Ipsita Chatterjee. 2016. "Antinomies of the Indian State." In *The Palgrave Handbook of Critical International Political Economy*, edited by Alan Cafruny, Leila Simona Talani and Gonzalo Pozo Martin, 331–349. Palgrave Macmillan.

Akram-Lodhi, A. Haroon. 2021. "Contemporary pathogens and the capitalist world food system." *Canadian Journal of Development Studies/Revue canadienne d'études du développement* 42 (1–2):18–27.

Akram-Lodhi, A. Haroon, and Cristóbal Kay. 2010. "Surveying the agrarian question (part 2): current debates and beyond." *Journal of Peasant Studies* 37:255–284. DOI: 10.1080/03066151003594906.

Alami, Ilias, and Adam D Dixon. 2020. "State capitalism (s) redux? Theories, tensions, controversies." *Competition & change* 24 (1):70–94.

Altun, Sirma, Christian Caiconte, Madelaine Moore, Adam David Morton, Matthew Ryan, Riki Scanlan, and Austin Hayden Smidt. 2023. "The life-nerve of the dialectic: György Lukács and the metabolism of space and nature." *Review of International Political Economy* 30 (2):584–607.

Anderson, Kevin B. 2010. *Marx at the Margins: On Nationalism, Ethnicity, and Non-Western Societies*. Chicago: University of Chicago Press.

Anderson, Perry. 2017. *The H-Word: The Peripeteia of Hegemony*. London & New York: Verso.

Andreas, Joel, Sunila S Kale, Michael Levien, and Qian Forrest Zhang. 2020. "Rural land dispossession in China and India." *The Journal of Peasant Studies* 47 (6):1109–1142.

Anievas, Alex, and Kerem Nisancioglu. 2015. *How the West Came to Rule: The Geopolitical Origins of Capitalism*. London: Pluto Press.

Araghi, Farshad. 2000. "The great global enclosure of our times: Peasants and the agrarian question at the end of the twentieth century." *Hungry for profit: The agribusiness threat to farmers, food, and the environment*:145–160.

Araghi, Farshad. 2003. "Food regimes and the production of value: Some methodological issues." *The Journal of Peasant Studies* 30 (2):41–70. DOI: 10.1080/ 0306615041233131129.

Araghi, Farshad. 2009. "Accumulation by displacement: Global enclosures, food crisis, and the ecological contradictions of capitalism." *Review (Fernand Braudel Center)* 32 (1):113–146.

Araghi, Farshad. 2012. "The invisible hand and the visible foot: peasants, dispossession and globalization." In *Peasants and Globalization*, 111–147. Routledge.

Araghi, Farshad. 2016. "The rise and fall of the agrarian welfare state: peasants, globalisation, and the privatisation of development." In *Peasant Poverty and Persistence in the Twenty-first Century: Theories, Debates, Realities and Policies*, edited by Julio Boltvinik and Susan Archer Mann, 315–345. London: Zed Books.

Araghi, Farshad A. 1995. "Global depeasantization, 1945–1990." *The Sociological Quarterly* 36 (2):337–368.

Arboleda, Martín. 2020a. *Planetary Mine: Territories of Extraction under Late Capitalism*. London & New York: Verso.

Arboleda, Martín. 2020b. "Towards an agrarian question of circulation: Walmart's expansion in Chile and the agrarian political economy of supply chain capitalism." *Journal of Agrarian Change* 20 (3):345–363. DOI: https://doi.org/10.1111/joac.12356.

Arnold, David. 1984. "Gramsci and peasant subalternity in India." *The Journal of Peasant Studies* 11 (4):155–177. DOI: 10.1080/03066158408438246.

Arrighi, Giovanni. 2010. *The Long Twentieth Century: Money, Power and the Origins of Our Times*. Second ed. London & New York: Verso.

Asopa, Navya, and Shreegireesh Jalihal. 2024. Billboard governance: Under Modi, majority of 906 schemes faced funding squeeze. *The Reporters' Collective*.

Baglioni, Elena. 2015. "Straddling contract and estate farming: Accumulation strategies of Senegalese horticultural exporters." *Journal of Agrarian Change* 15 (1):17–42.

Baglioni, Elena, and Liam Campling. 2017. "Natural resource industries as global value chains: Frontiers, fetishism, labour and the state." *Environment and Planning a: Economy and Space* 49 (11):2437–2456.

Baglioni, Elena, Liam Campling, Neil Coe, and Adrian Smith. 2022. "Introduction: Labour regimes and global production." In *Labour Regimes and Global Production*, edited by Elena Baglioni, Liam Campling, Neil Coe and Adrian Smith, 1–26. Agenda Publishing.

Bailey, F. G. 1963. *Politics and Social Change: Orissa in 1959*. Berkeley: University of California Press.

Baines, Joseph. 2015. "Fuel, feed and the corporate restructuring of the food regime." *The Journal of Peasant Studies* 42 (2):295–321. DOI: 10.1080/03066150.2014.970534.

Bajpai, Vikas. 2015. "India's second green revolution: Portends for future and possible alternatives." *Agrarian South: Journal of Political Economy* 4 (3):289–326. doi: DOI: 10.1177/2277976016633343.

Baka, Jennifer. 2013. "The political construction of Wasteland: Governmentality, land acquisition and social inequality in South India." *Development and Change* 44:409–428. DOI: 10.1111/dech.12018.

Baka, Jennifer. 2017. "Making space for energy: Wasteland development, enclosures, and energy dispossessions." *Antipode* 49 (4):977–996. DOI: 10.1111/anti.12219.

Balagopal, K. 1987. "An ideology for the provincial propertied class." *Economic and Political Weekly*:1544–1546.

Banaji, Jairus. 1977. "Capitalist domination and the small peasantry: Deccan districts in the late Nineteenth Century." *Economic and Political Weekly* 12 (33/34):1375–1404.

Banaji, Jairus. 2022. "Indian big business: The evolution of India's corporate sector from 2000 to 2020." *Phenomenal World*.

Banerjee, Arindam. 2015. "Contestations over food subsidy policy: An examination of the high level committee recommendations." *Social Scientist* 43 (7/8):41–57.

Banik, Dan. 2016. "The Hungry Nation: Food policy and food politics in India." *Food Ethics* 1 (1):29–45. DOI: 10.1007/s41055-016-0001-1.

Barbesgaard, Mads, and Andy Whitmore. 2023. ""Blood on the floor": The nickel commodity frontier and inter-capitalist competition under green extractivism." *Journal of Political Ecology* 30 (1).

Bardhan, Pranab. 1998. *The Political Economy of Development in India*. Second ed. Delhi: Oxford University Press.

Bardhan, Pranab. 2010. *Awakening Giants, Feet of Clay: Assessing the Economic Rise of China and India*. Princeton: Princeton University Press.

Basile, Elisabetta, Barbara Harriss-White, and Christine Lutringer, eds. 2015. *Mapping India's Capitalism: Old and New Regions*. Basingstoke: Palgrave Macmillan.

Basole, Amit, and Deepankar Basu. 2011. "Relations of production and modes of surplus extraction in India: Part I – agriculture." *Economic and Political Weekly* XLVI (14):41–58.

Basu, Deepankar, and Debarshi Das. 2015. "A flawed approach to food security." *The Hindu*, February 17. http://www.thehindu.com/opinion/op-ed/comment-a-flawed-approach-to-food-security/article6902377.ece.

Baviskar, Amita, and Michael Levien. 2021. "Farmers' protests in India: Introduction to the JPS forum." *The Journal of Peasant Studies* 48 (7):1341–1355.

Baviskar, Amita, and Nandini Sundar. 2008. "Democracy versus economic transformation?" *Economic and Political Weekly* 43 (46):87–89.

Belesky, Paul, and Geoffrey Lawrence. 2018. "Chinese state capitalism and neomercantilism in the contemporary food regime: contradictions, continuity and change." *The Journal of Peasant Studies*:1–23. DOI: 10.1080/03066150.2018.1450242.

Benanav, Aaron. 2014. *A global history of unemployment: surplus populations in the World Economy, 1949–2010*: University of California, Los Angeles.

Benanav, Aaron. 2020. *Automation and the Future of Work*: Verso Books.

Benanav, Aaron, and John Clegg. 2010. "Misery and debt." *Endnotes* 2:20–51.

Bera, Sayantan. 2017. "Centre plans to make Aadhaar mandatory for food subsidy." *livemint*, January 20. http://www.livemint.com/Politics/Co6PIaqLpD2WLMD3Vyx vOO/Centre-plans-to-make-Aadhaar-mandatory-for-food-subsidy.html.

Bernards, Nick. 2021. "'Latent' surplus populations and colonial histories of drought, groundnuts, and finance in Senegal." *Geoforum* 126:441–450. DOI: https://doi.org/10.1016/j.geoforum.2019.10.007.

Bernstein, H. 1988. "Labour regimes and social change under colonialism". In *Survival and Change in the Third World*, B. Crow & M. Thorpe (eds), 30–50. New York: Oxford University Press.

Bernstein, Henry. 2006. "Is there an agrarian question in the 21st century?" *Canadian Journal of Development Studies / Revue canadienne d'études du développement* 27 (4):449–460. DOI: 10.1080/02255189.2006.9669166.

Bernstein, Henry. 2010. *Class Dynamics of Agrarian Change*. Halifax and Winnipeg & Sterling: Fernwood Publishing and Kumarian Press.

Bernstein, Henry. 2014. "Food sovereignty via the 'peasant way': a sceptical view." *The Journal of Peasant Studies* 41 (6):1031–1063. DOI: 10.1080/03066150.2013.852082.

Bernstein, Henry. 2015. "Some reflections on agrarian change in China." *Journal of Agrarian Change* 15 (3):454–477. doi: DOI: 10.1111/joac.12116.

Bernstein, Henry. 2016a. "Agrarian political economy and modern world capitalism: the contributions of food regime analysis." *The Journal of Peasant Studies* 43 (3):611–647. DOI: 10.1080/03066150.2015.1101456.

Bernstein, Henry. 2016b. "Revisiting agrarian transition: reflections on long histories and current realities." In *Critical Perspectives on Agrarian Transition: India in the Global Debate*, edited by B. B. Mohanty, 67–92. London & New York: Routledge.

Béteille, André. 1965. *Caste, Class and Power: Changing Patterns of Stratification in a Tanjore Village*. Berkeley & Los Angeles: University of California Press.

Bhatia, Shyam S. 1965. "Patterns of crop concentration and diversification in India." *Economic Geography* 41 (1):39–56. DOI: 10.2307/141855.

Bhatnagar, Guarev Vivek. 2018. "In Jharkhand, Suspected Starvation Deaths Indicate Failure of Governance: Right to Food Campaign," *The Wire*. June 21. https://thewire.in/government/jharkhand-starvation-deaths-right-to-food.

Bhattacharya, Tithi, ed. 2017. *Social Reproduction Theory: Remapping Class, Recentering Oppression*. London: Pluto Press.

Bhende, M. J. 2013. *Agricultural Profile of Karnataka State*. Bangalore: Institute for Social and Economic Changes.

Bieler, Andreas, and Adam David Morton. 2018. *Global Capitalism, Global War, Global Crisis*. Cambridge: Cambridge University Press.

Block, Fred. 2008. "Polanyi's double movement and the reconstruction of critical theory." *Revue Interventions économiques. Papers in Political Economy* (38).

Bonanno, Alessandro, and Douglas H. Constance. 2008. *Stories of Globalization: Transnational Corporations, Resistance, and the State*. Pennsylvania: The Pennsylvania State University Press.

Bond, Patrick. 2015. "BRICS and the sub-imperial location." *BRICS: An anti-capitalist critique*:15–26.

Bonefeld, Werner. 1992. "Social constitution and the form of the capitalist state." *Open Marxism* 1:93–132.

Bonefeld, Werner. 2004. "On postone's courageous but unsuccessful attempt to banish the class antagonism from the critique of political economy." *Historical Materialism* 12 (3):103–124.

Bonefeld, Werner. 2010. "Free economy and the strong state: Some notes on the state." *Capital & Class* 34 (1):15–24. DOI: 10.1177/0309816809353476.

Bonefeld, Werner. 2014. *Critical Theory and the Critique of Political Economy: On Subversion and Negative Reason*: Bloomsbury Publishing USA.

Bonefeld, Werner. 2023. *A Critical Theory of Economic Compulsion: Wealth, Suffering, Negation*: Routledge.

Bonefeld, Werner, Richard Gunn, and Kosmas Psychopedis. 1992. "Introduction." In *Open Marxism: Volume 1, Dialectics and History*, edited by Werner Bonefeld, Richard Gunn and Kosmas Psychopedis. London: Pluto Press.

Borras, Saturnino M. 2009. "Agrarian change and peasant studies: changes, continuities and challenges – an introduction." *The Journal of Peasant Studies* 36 (1):5–31. DOI: 10.1080/03066150902820297.

Borras, Saturnino M. 2023a. "Politically engaged, pluralist and internationalist: critical agrarian studies today." *The Journal of Peasant Studies*:1–41. DOI: 10.1080/03066150.2022.2163164.

Borras Jr, Saturnino M. 2023b. "Contemporary agrarian, rural and rural–urban movements and alliances." *Journal of Agrarian Change*, 23(3), 453–476.

Borras, Saturnino M., Jennifer C. Franco, Sergio Gómez, Cristóbal Kay, and Max Spoor. 2012. "Land grabbing in Latin America and the Caribbean." *The Journal of Peasant Studies* 39 (3–4):845–872. DOI: 10.1080/03066150.2012.679931.

Borras, Saturnino M., Jennifer C. Franco, S. Ryan Isakson, Les Levidow, and Pietje Vervest. 2016. "The rise of flex crops and commodities: Implications for research." *The Journal of Peasant Studies* 43 (1):93–115. DOI: 10.1080/03066150.2015.1036417.

Borras, Saturnino M., Philip McMichael, and Ian Scoones. 2010. "The politics of biofuels, land and agrarian change: editors' introduction." *The Journal of Peasant Studies* 37 (4):575–592. DOI: 10.1080/03066150.2010.512448.

Boyer, Robert. 2007. "Capitalism strikes back: Why and what consequences for social sciences?" *Revue de la régulation. Capitalisme, institutions, pouvoirs* (1).

Brass, Tom. 1995a. "Introduction: The new farmers' movements in India." In *New Farmers' Movements in India*, edited by Tom Brass, 3–27. London: Frank Cass.

Brass, Tom, ed. 1995b. *New Farmers' Movements in India*. London: Frank Cass.

Braudel, Fernand. 1977. *Afterthoughts on Material Civilization and Capitalism*. Baltimore and London: The John Hopkins University Press.

Breman, Jan. 2010. *Outcast Labour in Asia: Circulation and Informalization of the Workforce at the Bottom of the Economy*. New Delhi: Oxford University Press.

Brenner, Neil, Jamie Peck, and N. I. K. Theodore. 2010. "Variegated neoliberalization: geographies, modalities, pathways." *Global Networks* 10 (2):182–222. DOI: 10.1111/j.1471-0374.2009.00277.x.

Brenner, Robert. 2006. *The Economics of Global Turbulence: The Advanced Capitalist Economies from Long Boom to Long Downturn, 1945–2005*. London and New York: Verso.

Brown, Trent. 2013. "Agrarian crisis in Punjab and 'natural farming' as a response." *South Asia: Journal of South Asian Studies* 36 (2):229–242. DOI: 10.1080/00856401.2013.776002.

Brown, Trent. 2018. *Farmers, Subalterns, and Activists: Social Politics of Sustainable Agriculture in India*. Cambridge: Cambridge University Press.

Brown, Trent. 2019. "When food regimes become hegemonic: Agrarian India through a Gramscian lens." *Journal of Agrarian Change* 0 (0). DOI: 10.1111/joac.12344.

Brown, Trent. 2020. "When food regimes become hegemonic: Agrarian India through a Gramscian lens." *Journal of Agrarian Change* 20 (1):188–206. DOI: https://doi.org/10.1111/joac.12344.

Bruckert, Michaël. 2015. "Changing food habits in contemporary India. Discourses and practices from the middle classes in Chennai (Tamil Nadu)." In *Routledge Handbook of Contemporary India*, edited by Knut A. Jacobsen. Routledge.

Bruckert, Michaël. 2021. "Chicken politics: Agrifood capitalism, anxious bodies, and the new meanings of chicken meat in India." *Gastronomica: The Journal for Food Studies* 21 (2):33–46.

Buci-Glucksmann, Chrisine. 1980. *Gramsci and the State*. London: Lawrence and Wishart.

Burawoy, Michael. 2003. "For a sociological Marxism: The complementary convergence of Antonio Gramsci and Karl Polanyi." *Politics & Society* 31 (2):193–261. DOI: 10.1177/0032329203252270.

Burch, David, and Geoffrey Lawrence. 2009. "Towards a third food regime: behind the transformation." *Agriculture and Human Values* 26 (4):267. DOI: 10.1007/s10460-009-9219-4.

Bureau. 2005. "Free movement of agricultural products 16 States to amend APMC Act." *Business Line*, April 9. http://www.thehindubusinessline.com/todays-paper/free-movement-of-agricultural-products-16-states-to-amend-apmc-act/article2174194.ece.

Burkett, JB Foster P. 2018. "Value isn't everything." *Monthly Review* 70 (6):1–17.

Burkett, Paul. 1999. *Marx and Nature: A Red and Green Perspective*. New York: St. Martin's Press.

Bush, Ray, and Giuliano Martiniello. 2017. "Food riots and protest: Agrarian modernizations and structural crises." *World Development* 91:193–207. DOI: https://doi.org/10.1016/j.worlddev.2016.10.017.

Byres, T. J. 1985. "Modes of production and non-european pre-colonial societies: The nature and significance of the debate." *The Journal of Peasant Studies* 12 (2–3):1–18. DOI: 10.1080/03066158508438262.

Byres, Terence J. 1986. "The agrarian question, forms of capitalist agrarian transition and the state: An essay with reference to Asia." *Social Scientist*:3–67.

Byres, Terence J. 1995. "Preface." In *New Farmers' Movements in India*, edited by Tom Brass, 1–2.

Camba, Alvin A. 2018. "The food regime in late colonial Philippines: Pathways of appropriation and unpaid work." *Journal of Agrarian Change*:1–21. doi: DOI: 10.1111/joac.12269.

Campaign, Right to Food. 2010. An open letter to nac members from the right to food campaign.

Campling, Liam. 2012. "The tuna 'commodity frontier': business strategies and environment in the industrial tuna fisheries of the Western Indian Ocean." *Journal of Agrarian Change* 12 (2-3):252–278.

Campling, Liam. 2021. "The corporation and resource geography." In *The Routledge Handbook of Critical Resource Geography*, 188–200. Routledge.

Carroll, William K. 2010. "Crisis, movements, counter-hegemony: in search of the new." *Interface: A Journal for and about Social Movements* 2 (2):168–198.

Carson, Rebecca. 2023a. *Immanent Externalities: The Reproduction of Life in Capital*. Leiden: Brill.

Carson, Rebecca. 2023b. "Non-capitalist domination, rentierism, and the politics of class." *Crisis and Critique* 10 (1).

Çelik, Coşku. 2023. "Extractivism and labour control: Reflections of Turkey's 'Coal Rush' in local labour regimes." *Critical Sociology* 49 (1):59–76. DOI: 10.1177/08969205211046287.

Chacko, Priya. 2018. "The right turn in India: Authoritarianism, populism and neoliberalisation." *Journal of Contemporary Asia* 48 (4):541–565. DOI: 10.1080/00472336.2018.1446546.

Chand, Ramesh. 2005. "Whither India's food policy? From food security to food deprivation." *Economic and Political Weekly* 40 (11):1055–1062.

Chandra, Kanchan. 2015. "The new Indian State: The relocation of patronage in the post-liberalisation economy." *Economic and Political Weekly* L (41):46–58.

Chandrasekhar, C. P., and Jayati Ghosh. 2002. *The Market that Failed: A Decade of Neoliberal Economic Reforms in India*. New Delhi: LeftWord Books.

Chari, Sharad. 2004. *Fraternal Capital: Peasant-Workers, Self-Made Men, and Globalization in Provincial India*. Stanford: Stanford University Press.

Charsley, Simon R. 1982. *Culture and Sericulture: Social Anthropology and Development in a South Indian Livestock Industry*. London: Academic Press Inc.

Chatterjee, Elizabeth. 2023. "India's Oligarchic State Capitalism." *Current History* 122 (843):123–130.

Chatterjee, Partha. 1986. *Nationalist Thought and the Colonial World: A Derivative Discourse?*, London: Zed Books.

Chatterjee, Partha. 1997. "Development planning and the Indian State." In *State and Politics in India*, edited by Partha Chatterjee, 271–299. New Delhi: Oxford University Press.

Chatterjee, Partha. 2004. *The Politics of the Governed: Reflections on Popular Politics in Most of the World*. New York: Columbia University Press.

Chatterjee, Partha. 2008. "Democracy and economic transformation in India." *Economic and Political Weekly* 43:53–62.

Chaudhuri, Bidisha. 2022. "Programmed welfare: An ethnographic account of algorithmic practices in the public distribution system in India." *New Media & Society* 24 (4):887–902. DOI: 10.1177/14614448221079034.

Chawla, Prabhu. 1979. "Numbers' game." *India Today*, January 15. http://indiatoday.intoday.in/story/kisan-rally-fifty-lakh-farmers-participate-in-charan-singhs-political-circus/1/427069.html.

Chibber, Vivek. 2003. *Locked in Place: State-Building and Late Industrialization in India*. Princeton & Oxford: Princeton University Press.

Chibber, Vivek. 2013. *Postcolonial Theory and the Specter of Capital*. London and New York: Verso.

Claeys, Priscilla, and Marc Edelman. 2020. "The United Nations declaration on the rights of peasants and other people working in rural areas." *The Journal of Peasant Studies* 47 (1):1–68.

Clapp, Jennifer, Peter Newell, and Zoe W. Brent. 2018. "The global political economy of climate change, agriculture and food systems." *The Journal of Peasant Studies* 45 (1):80–88. DOI: 10.1080/03066150.2017.1381602.

Clarke, Simon. 1988. *Keynesianism, Monetarism and the Crisis of the State*: Elgar Aldershot.

Clarke, Simon. 1991. "The State debate." In *The State Debate*, edited by Simon Clarke, 1–69. London: Palgrave Macmillan UK.

Clarke, Simon. 1993. *Marx's Theory of Crisis*. London: Palgrave Macmillan.

Commission, Karnataka Agriculture Price. 2016. Decadal shift in cropping pattern in Karnataka: Research report July 2016. Government of Karnataka.

Committee, High Level. 2015. *Report of the High Level Committee on Reorienting the Role and Restructuring of Food Corporation of India*. New Delhi: Government of India.

Cons, Jason, and Michael Eilenberg. 2019. "Introduction: On the new politics of margins in Asia: mapping frontier assemblages." *Frontier Assemblages: The Emergent Politics of Resource Frontiers in Asia*:1–18.

Corbridge, Stuart, and John Harriss. 2000. *Reinventing India: Liberalization, Hindu Nationalism and Popular Democracy*. Cambridge, UK: Malden, MA: Polity Press.

Corbridge, Stuart, John Harriss, and Craig Jeffrey. 2012. *India Today: Economy, Politics and Society*. Cambridge, UK; Malden, MA: Polity.

Cousins, Ben, Saturnino M. Borras, Sérgio Sauer, and Jingzhong Ye. 2018. "BRICS, middle-income countries (MICs), and global agrarian transformations: internal dynamics, regional trends, and international implications." *Globalizations* 15 (1):1–11. DOI: 10.1080/14747731.2018.1429104.

Cowan, Thomas. 2018. "The Urban village, agrarian transformation, and Rentier Capitalism in Gurgaon, India." *Antipode* 50 (5):1244–1266. DOI: 10.1111/anti.12404.

Cullather, Nick. 2010. *The Hungry World: America's Cold War Battle against Poverty in Asia*. Cambridge, US & London, England: Harvard University Press.

D'Costa, Anthony, and Achin Chakraborty, eds. 2017a. *The Land Question in India: State, Dispossession, and Capitalist Transition*. New Delhi: Oxford University Press.

D'Costa, Anthony, and Achin Chakraborty. 2017b. "The land question in India: State, dispossession, and capitalist transition." In *The Land Question in India: State, Dispossession, and Capitalist Transition*, edited by Anthony D'Costa and Achin Chakraborty, 16–49. New Delhi: Oxford University Press.

D'Costa, Anthony P. 2014. "Compressed capitalism and development: Primitive accumulation, petty commodity production, and capitalist maturity in India and China." *Critical Asian Studies* 46 (2):317–344. DOI: 10.1080/14672715.2014.898458.

D'Costa, Anthony P. 2016. "Compressed capitalism, globalisation and the fate of Indian development." In *Globalisation and the Challenges of Development in Contemporary India*, edited by Sita Venkateswar and Sekhar Bandyopadhyay, 19–39. Singapore: Springer Singapore.

Dale, Gareth. 2010. *Karl Polanyi: The Limits of the Market*. Cambridge, UK & Malden, US: Polity Press.

Dale, Gareth. 2012. "Double movements and pendular forces: Polanyian perspectives on the neoliberal age." *Current Sociology* 60 (1):3–27. DOI: 10.1177/0011392111426645.

Damodaran, Harish. 2008. *India's New Capitalists: Caste, Business, and Industy in a Modern Nation*. New Delhi: Permanent Black.

Damodaran, Harish. 2020. "From "Entrepeneurial" to "Conglomerate" capitalism." *Seminar*.

Das, Arghyadeep, Shruti Mohapatra, and Neela Madhav Patnaik. 2021. "Feminization of Indian agriculture: a review." *Agricultural Reviews* 42 (4):434–439.

Das, Sandip. 2017. "After LPG success, Narendra Modi government wants public to give up food subsidies." *Financial Express*, April 25. http://www.financialexpress.com/economy/after-lpg-success-narendra-modi-government-wants-public-to-give-up-food-subsidies/640917/.

Das Gupta, Chirashree. 2016. *State and Capital in Independent India: Institutions and Accumulation*. Cambridge: Cambridge University Press.

Dasgupta, B. 1977. *Agrarian change and the new technology in India* , Geneva: United Nations Research Institute for Social Development

Dasgupta, Sejuti. 2013. "With flowers and capsicum in the driver's seat, food sovereignty is impossible: A comparison of the politics of agricultural policy in two Indian states, Gujarat and Chhattisgarh." *Food Sovereignty: A Critical Dialogue*, Yale University.

Davis, Mike. 2002. *Late Victorian Holocausts: El Nino Famines and the Making of the Third Wold*. London and New York: Verso.

Davis, Mike. 2006. *Planet of Slums*. London: Verso.

de LT Oliveira, Gustavo, and Ben M McKay. 2021. "BRICS and global agrarian transformations." In *Handbook of Critical Agrarian Studies*, 316–323. Edward Elgar Publishing.

De Neve, Geert. 2015. "Predatory property:Urban land acquisition, housing and class formation in Tiruppur, South India." *Journal of South Asian Development* 10 (3):345–368. DOI: 10.1177/0973174115606335.

Denning, Michael. 2010. "Wageless life." *New Left Review* 66 (6):79–97.

Desai, Radhika. 2016. "The slow-motion counterrevolution: Developmental contradictions and the emergence of neoliberalism." In *Social Movements and the State in India: Deepening Democracy?*, edited by Kenneth Bo Nielsen and Alf Gunvald Nilsen, 25–51. London: Palgrave Macmillan UK.

Desmarais, Annette Aurelie. 2007. *La Vía Campesina: Globalization and the Power of Peasants*. Halifax & London: Fernwood Publishing & Pluto Press.

Dixon, Marion. 2014. "The land grab, finance capital, and food regime restructuring: the case of Egypt." *Review of African Political Economy* 41 (140):232–248. DOI: 10.1080/03056244.2013.831342.

Dixon, Marion. 2017. "Plastics and agriculture in the desert frontier." *Comparative Studies of South Asia, Africa and the Middle East* 37 (1):86–102. DOI: 10.1215/1089201x-3821321.

Dixon, Marion W. 2018. "Chemical fertilizer in transformations in world agriculture and the state system, 1870 to interwar period." *Journal of Agrarian Change* 0 (0). doi: DOI: 10.1111/joac.12259.

Dorin, Bruno. 2017. "India and Africa in the global agricultural system (1961–2050): Towards a new sociotechnical regime?" *Economic and Political Weekly* LII (25 & 26):5–13.

Dorin, Bruno, and Claire Aubron. 2016. "Croissance et revenu du travail agricole en Inde. Une économie politique de la divergence (1950–2014)." *Économie rurale* 352 (2): 41–65.

Dorin, Bruno, and Frédéric Landy. 2009. *Agriculture and Food in India: A Half-century Review from Independence to Globalization*. New Delhi: Manohar.

Drèze, Jean. 2013. "The food security debate in India." *The New York Times*, July 9. https://india.blogs.nytimes.com/2013/07/09/the-food-security-debate-in-india/?_r=0.

Drèze, Jean, and Amartya Sen. 2013. *An Uncertain Glory: India and its Contradictions*. Princeton: Princeton University Press.

Drèze, Jean, and Anmol Somanchi. 2021. "The COVID-19 crisis and people's right to food." *SocArXiv*.

Edelman, Marc. 2024. *Peasant Politics of the Twenty-First Century: Transnational Social Movements and Agrarian Change*. Cornell University Press.

Edelman, Marc, and Saturnino M. Borras Jr. 2016. *Political Dynamics of Transnational Agrarian Movements*. Rugby: Fernwood Publishing & Practical Action Publishing.

Editorial. 2018. "The land conundrum." *Economic and Political Weekly* 53 (42).

Ekers, Michael, and Scott Prudham. 2015. "Towards the socio-ecological fix." *Environment and Planning A* 47 (12):2438–2445. DOI: 10.1177/0308518X15617573.

Ekers, Michael, and Scott Prudham. 2017a. "The metabolism of socioecological fixes: Capital switching, spatial fixes, and the production of nature." *Annals of the American Association of Geographers*:1–19. DOI: 10.1080/24694452.2017.1309962.

Ekers, Michael, and Scott Prudham. 2017b. "The socioecological fix: Fixed capital, metabolism, and Hegemony." *Annals of the American Association of Geographers*:1–18. DOI: 10.1080/24694452.2017.1309963.

Endnotes. 2015. *Endnotes #4: Unity in Separation*: Endnotes.

Epstein, T. Scarlett. 1962. *Economic Development and Social Change in South India*. Manchester: Manchester University Press.

Epstein, T. Scarlett. 1973. *South India: Yesterday, Today and Tomorrow: Mysore villages revisited*. London & Basingstoke: Mcmillan.

Eriksen, Stein Sundstøl. 2017. "From state-led development to embedded neoliberalism: India's industrial and social policies in comparative perspective." In *Industrialising Rural India: Land, Policy and Resistance*, edited by Kenneth Bo Nielsen and Patrik Oskarsson, 40–63. London and New York: Routledge.

Escher, Fabiano. 2021. "BRICS varieties of capitalism and food regime reordering: A comparative institutional analysis." *Journal of Agrarian Change* 21 (1):46–70. DOI: https://doi.org/10.1111/joac.12385.

FAO, IFAD, UNICEF, WFP, and WHO. 2020. *The State of Food Security and Nutrition in the World 2020. Transforming Food Systems for Affordable Healthy Diets.* Rome: FAO.

Fares, Tomaz Mefano. 2023. "China's financialized soybeans: The fault lines of neomercantilism narratives in international food regime analyses." *Journal of Agrarian Change* 23 (3):477–499. DOI: https://doi.org/10.1111/joac.12536.

Farmer, B. H., ed. 1980. *Green Revolution? Technology and Change in Rice-Growing Areas of Tamil Nadu and Sri Lanka*. London: Palgrave Macmillan.

Federici, Silvia. 2004. *Caliban and the Witch: Women, the Body and Primitive Accumulation*. New York: Autonomedia.

FICCI. 2015. India Maize Summit '15.

FICCI. 2018. Maize Vision 2022. The Federation of Indian Chambers of Commerce and Industry.

Fischer, Klara, Jostein Jakobsen, and Ola T Westengen. 2022. "The political ecology of crops: From seed to state and capital." *Geoforum* 130:92–95.

Flachs, Andrew. 2016a. "The green revolution." In *Encyclopedia of Food and Agricultural Ethics*, edited by Paul B. Thompson and David M. Kaplan, 1–7. Dordrecht: Springer Netherlands.

Flachs, Andrew. 2016b. "Redefining success: the political ecology of genetically modified and organic cotton as solutions to agrarian crisis." *Journal of Political Ecology* 23:50. DOI: https://doi.org/10.2458/v23i1.20179.

Flachs, Andrew. 2019. *Cultivating Knowledge: Biotechnology, Sustainability, and the Human Cost of Cotton Capitalism in India*. University of arizona Press.

Foster-Carter, Aidan. 1978. "The modes of production controversy." *New left review* 107 (1):47–78.

Frankel, Francine R. 2005. *India's Political Economy, 1947–2004*. Second ed. New Delhi: Oxford University Press.

Friedmann, Harriet. 1987. "International reigmes of food and agriculture since 1870." In *Peasants and Peasant Societies*, edited by Teodor Shanin, 227–264. Oxford: Basil Blackwell.

Friedmann, Harriet. 1992. "Distance and durability: Shaky foundations of the world food economy." *Third World Quarterly* 13 (2):371–383.

Friedmann, Harriet. 1993. "The political economy of food: A global crisis." *New Left Review* 197 (1):29–57.

Friedmann, Harriet. 2005. "From colonialism to green capitalism: Social movements and emergence of food regimes." In *New Directions in the Sociology of Global Development*, edited by Frederick H. Buttel and Philip McMichael, 227–264. Oxford: Elsevier.

Friedmann, Harriet. 2009a. "Discussion: moving food regimes forward: reflections on symposium essays." *Agriculture and Human Values* 26 (4):335. DOI: 10.1007/s10460-009-9225-6.

Friedmann, Harriet. 2009b. "Feeding the empire: The pathologies of globalized agriculture." *Socialist Register* 41 (41).

Friedmann, Harriet. 2016. "Commentary: Food regime analysis and agrarian questions: widening the conversation." *The Journal of Peasant Studies* 43 (3):671–692. DOI: 10.1080/03066150.2016.1146254.

Friedmann, Harriet, Benoît Daviron, and Gilles Allaire. 2016. "'Political economists have been blinded by the apparent marginalization of land and food'. An interview with Harriet Friedmann." *Revue de la régulation. Capitalisme, institutions, pouvoirs* (20).

Friedmann, Harriet, and Philip McMichael. 1989. "Agriculture and the state system: The rise and decline of national agricultures, 1870 to the present." *Sociologia Ruralis* 29 (2):93–117. DOI: 10.1111/j.1467-9523.1989.tb00360.x.

Frödin, Olle. 2013. "Modernization, neo-liberal globalization, or variegated development: the Indian food system transformation in comparative perspective." *International Review of Sociology* 23 (1):221–242. DOI: 10.1080/03906701.2013.771047.

Fuller, C. J., and Veronique Benei, eds. 2001. *The Everday State and Society in Modern India*. London: Hurst & Co Ltd.

Gandhi, Maneka. 2018. "India's meat industry growing rapidly, but depleting a third of world's fresh water reserves." *Firstpost*, February 20.

Gidwani, Vinay, and Priti Ramamurthy. 2018. "Agrarian questions of labor in urban India: middle migrants, translocal householding and the intersectional politics of social reproduction." *The Journal of Peasant Studies* 45 (5–6):994–1017. DOI: 10.1080/03066150.2018.1503172.

Gidwani, Vinay, and K. Sivaramakrishnan. 2003. "Circular migration and rural cosmopolitanism in India." *Contributions to Indian Sociology* 37 (1–2):339–367. DOI: 10.1177/006996670303700114.

Gill, Bikrum. 2016. "Can the river speak? Epistemological confrontation in the rise and fall of the land grab in Gambella, Ethiopia." *Environment and Planning A: Economy and Space* 48 (4):699–717. DOI: 10.1177/0308518x15610243.

Goodman, David, and Michael Watts. 1994. "Reconfiguring the rural or fording the divide?: Capitalist restructuring and the global agro-food system." *The Journal of Peasant Studies* 22 (1):1–49. DOI: 10.1080/03066159408438565.

Goswami, Manu. 2004. *Producing India*. Chicago: University of Chicago Press.

Gramsci, Antonio. 1971. *Selections from the Prison Notebooks*. New York: International Publishers.

Green, W. Nathan. 2021. "Placing Cambodia's agrarian transition in an emerging Chinese food regime." *The Journal of Peasant Studies*:1–24. DOI: 10.1080/03066150.2021.1923007.

Green, W. Nathan. 2022. "Placing Cambodia's agrarian transition in an emerging Chinese food regime." *The Journal of Peasant Studies* 49 (6):1249–1272.

Guha, Ranajit. 1997. *Dominance without Hegemony: History and Power in Colonial India*. Cambridge, US & London, UK: Harvard University Press.

Gulati, Ashok, and Tim Kelley. 1999. *Trade Liberalization and Indian Agriculture: Cropping Patten Changes and Efficiency Gains in Semi-Arid Tropics*. New Delhi: Oxford University Press.

Gunn, Richard. 1987. "Notes on class." Common Sense.

Gupta, Akhil. 1998. *Postcolonial Developments: Agriculture in the Making of Modern India*. Durham, NC: Duke University Press Books.

Gupta, Akhil, and K. Sivaramakrishnan. 2011. "Introduction: The state in India after liberalization." In *The State in India after Liberalization: Interdisciplinary Perspectvies*, edited by Akhil Gupta and K. Sivaramakrishnan, 1–27. Oxford and New York: Routledge.

Gupta, Dipankar. 2005. "Whither the Indian village? Culture and agriculture in 'Rural' India." *Economic and Political Weekly* 40 (8):751–758.

Gupta, Priyanshu, and Manish Thakur. 2017. "The changing rural-agrarian dominance: A conceptual excursus." *Sociological Bulletin* 66 (1):42–57. DOI: 10.1177/0038022916687062.

Gupta, Sejuti Das. 2024. *Class, Politics, and Agrarian Policies in Post-Liberalisation India*. Cambridge: Cambridge University Press.

Gupta, Smita. 2015. Dismantling food security in India.

Hall, Derek. 2013. "Primitive accumulation, accumulation by dispossession and the global land Grab." *Third World Quarterly* 34 (9):1582–1604. DOI: 10.1080/01436597.2013.843854.

Hall, Stuart. 2003. "Marx's notes on method: A 'Reading' of the '1857 introduction'." *Cultural Studies* 17 (2):113–149. DOI: 10.1080/0950238032000114868.

Hall, Stuart. 2007. "Epilogue: Through the prism of an intellectual life." In *Culture, Race, Politics and Diaspora: The Thought of Stuart Hall*, edited by Brian Meeks, 269–291. London: Kingston.

Hall, Stuart. 2011. "The neo-liberal revolution." *Cultural Studies* 25 (6):705–728. DOI: 10.1080/09502386.2011.619886.

Hansen, Arve, Jostein Jakobsen and Ulrikke Wethal. 2021. New geographies of global meatification: The BRICS of the industrial meat complex. In *Changing Meat Cultures: Local Cuisines, Global Capitalism and the Consumption of Animals*. Editors: Arve Hansen and Karen Lykke Syse, 35–59. London: Rowman & Littlefield.

Haq, Zia. 2024a. "For energy security, Indian govt looks at maize." *Hindustan Times.* https://www.hindustantimes.com/india-news/for-energy-security-indian-govt-looks-at-maize-101705431383724.html.

Haq, Zia. 2024b. "Govt plans to procure more maize to ramp up production of ethanol." *Hindustan Times,* March 05. https://www.hindustantimes.com/india-news/govt-plans-to-procure-more-maize-to-ramp-up-production-of-ethanol-101709579087613.html.

Harriss, Barbara. 1984. *Exchange Relations and Poverty in Dryland Agriculture.* New Delhi: Concept Publishing Company.

Harriss, J. 2020. ""Responding to an epidemic requires a compassionate state": How has the Indian state been doing in the time of COVID-19?" *J Asian Stud* 79 (3):609–620. DOI: 10.1017/s0021911820002314.

Harriss, John. 1982. *Capitalism and Peasant Farming: Agrarian Structure and Ideology in Northern Tamil Nadu.* Bombay: Oxford University Press.

Harriss, John. 1999. "Comparing political regimes across Indian states: A preliminary essay." *Economic and Political Weekly* 34 (48):3367–2277.

Harriss, John. 2011. "How far have India's economic reforms been guided by compassion and justice? Social policy in the Neoliberal Era." In *Understanding India's New Political Economy: A Great Transformation?*, edited by Sanjay Ruparelia, Sanjay Reddy, John Harriss and Stuart Corbridge, 127–140. London: Routledge.

Harriss, John. 2013. "Does 'Landlordism' still matter? Reflections on agrarian change in India." *Journal of Agrarian Change* 13:351–364. DOI: 10.1111/joac.12024.

Harriss-White, Barbara. 2002. *India Working: Essays on Society and Economy.* Cambridge; New York: Cambridge University Press.

Harriss-White, Barbara. 2008a. "Introduction: India's rainfed agricultural dystopia." *The European Journal of Development Research* 20 (4):549–561. DOI: 10.1080/09578810802493291.

Harriss-White, Barbara. 2008b. *Rural Commercial Capital: Agricultural Markets in West Bengal.* New Delhi: Oxford University Press.

Harriss-White, Barbara. 2012. "Capitalism and the common man: Peasants and petty production in Africa and South Asia." *Agrarian South: Journal of Political Economy* 1:109–160. DOI: 10.1177/2277976012001000201.

Harriss-White, Barbara. 2017. "Constructing regions inside the nation: Economic and social structure of space in agrarian and cultural regions." *Economic and Political Weekly* LII (46):44–55.

Harriss-White, Barbara, and Judith Heyer, eds. 2015. *Indian Capitalism in Development.* London & New York: Routledge.

Hart, Gillian. 2004. "Geography and development: critical ethnographies." *Progress in Human Geography* 28 (1):91–100. DOI: 10.1191/0309132504ph472pr.

Harvey, David. 1982. *The Limits to Capital.* Oxford: Basil Blackwell.

Harvey, David. 1989. *The Condition of Postmodernity: An Enquiry into the Origins of Cultural Change*. Cambridge MA and Oxford UK: Blackwell.

Harvey, David. 2001. "Globalization and the spatial fix." *Geographische Revue* 2 (3):23–31.

Harvey, David. 2003. *The New Imperialism*. New York: Oxford University Press.

Harvey, David. 2005. *A Brief History of Neoliberalism*. Oxford: Oxford University Press.

Harvey, David. 2006. *Spaces of Global Capitalism: Towards a Theory of Uneven Geographical Development*. London & New York: Verso.

Hasan, Zoya. 2012. *Congress after Indira: Policy, Power, Political Change (1984–2009)*. New Delhi: Oxford University Press.

Henderson, Christian. 2021. "The rise of Arab Gulf agro-capital: continuity and change in the corporate food regime." *The Journal of Peasant Studies*:1–22. DOI: 10.1080/03066150.2021.1888723.

Henderson, Christian, and Rafeef Ziadah. 2023. "Logistics of the neoliberal food regime: circulation, corporate food security and the United Arab Emirates." *New Political Economy* 28 (4):592–607.

Heron, Kai. 2021. "Dialectical materialisms, metabolic rifts and the climate crisis: a Lacanian/Hegelian perspective." *Science & Society* 85 (4):501–526.

Herring, Ronald J. 1983. *Land to the Tiller: The Political Economy of Agrarian Reform in South Asia*. New Haven: Yale University Press.

Herring, Ronald J., and Rina Agarwala, eds. 2008. *Whatever Happened to Class? Reflections from South Asia*. Delhi: Daanish Books.

Hertel, Shareen. 2015. "Hungry for justice: Social mobilization on the right to food in India." *Development and Change* 46 (1):72–94. DOI: 10.1111/dech.12144.

Hill, Polly. 1982. *Dry Grain Farming Families: Hausand (Nigeria) and Karnataka (India) compared*. Cambridge: Cambridge University Press.

Himanshu. 2015. "Reforming food corporation of India." *livemint*, February 18. http://www.livemint.com/Opinion/P6WkypbSfm8edngoBdH16K/Reforming-Food-Corporation-of-India.html.

Hindu, The. 2016. "Jat quota protests: What is it all about?" *The Hindu*, February 20. http://www.thehindu.com/specials/jat-quota-protests-what-is-it-all-about/article14091994.ece1.

Hobsbawm, Eric. 2010. *Age of Capital: 1848–1875*: Hachette UK.

Holloway, John. 2019. *We Are the Crisis of Capital: A John Holloway Reader*: PM Press.

Holloway, John, and Sol Picciotto. 1977. "Capital, crisis and the state." *Capital & Class* 1 (2):76–101. DOI: 10.1177/030981687700200104.

Holt Giménez, Eric, and Annie Shattuck. 2011. "Food crises, food regimes and food movements: rumblings of reform or tides of transformation?" *The Journal of Peasant Studies* 38 (1):109–144. DOI: 10.1080/03066150.2010.538578.

Hopewell, Kristen. 2015. "Different paths to power: The rise of Brazil, India and China at the world trade organization." *Review of International Political Economy* 22 (2):311–338. DOI: 10.1080/09692290.2014.927387.

Hopewell, Kristen. 2016. *Breaking the WTO: How Emerging Powers Disrupted the Neoliberal Project*. Standard: Stanford University Press.

Hopewell, Kristen. 2018. "Recalcitrant spoiler? Contesting dominant accounts of India's role in global trade governance." *Third World Quarterly* 39 (3):577–593. DOI: 10.1080/01436597.2017.1369033.

Hopewell, Kristen. 2021. "Heroes of the developing world? Emerging powers in WTO agriculture negotiations and dispute settlement." *The Journal of Peasant Studies*:1–24. DOI: 10.1080/03066150.2021.1873292.

Hornborg, Alf. 2017. "Dithering while the planet burns: Anthropologists' approaches to the anthropocene." *Reviews in Anthropology* 46 (2–3):61–77. DOI: 10.1080/00938157.2017.1343023.

Hules, Magdalena, and Simron Jit Singh. 2017. "India's land grab deals in Ethiopia: Food security or global politics?" *Land Use Policy* 60:343–351. DOI: https://doi.org/10.1016/j.landusepol.2016.10.035.

Hung, Ho-fung. 2015. *The China Boom: Why China Will Not Rule the World*: Columbia University Press.

IANS. 2016. "BJP destroying pro-poor policies launched by Congress: Rahul" *Business Standard*, February 5. http://www.business-standard.com/article/news-ians/bjp-destroying-pro-poor-policies-launched-by-congress-rahul-116020600248_1.html.

Inden, Ronald B. 1990. *Imagining India*. Oxford, UK & Cambridge, US: Blackwell Publishers.

Government of India. 2011. Agriculture Census 2010–11.

Government of India. 2017. *Economic Survey 2016–17*. New Delhi: Ministry of Finance Department of Economic Affairs Economic Division.

Press Trust of India. 2016. "Govt ropes in 3 private players for rice procurement." *India Today*, March 4. http://indiatoday.intoday.in/story/govt-ropes-in-3-private-players-for-rice-procurement/1/612167.html.

Intodia, Vijay. 2016. *Poultry and Poultry Products Annual 2016*. Global Agricultural Information Network: USDA Foreign Agricultural Service.

IPES-FOOD. 2017. Too big to feed: Exploring the impacts of mega-mergers, consolidation and concentration of power in the agri-food sector.

Isakson, S. Ryan. 2014. "Food and finance: the financial transformation of agrofood supply chains." *The Journal of Peasant Studies* 41 (5):749–775. DOI: 10.1080/03066150.2013.874340.

Iyengar, Rishi 2015. "Riots Break out in India over a dominant caste's attempt to Gain 'Backward' status." *Time*, August 26. http://time.com/4011001/hardik-patel-protest-arrest-gujarat-obc/.

Jaffrelot, Christophe. 2015. "The class element in the 2014 Indian election and the BJP's success with special reference to the hindi belt." *Studies in Indian Politics* 3 (1):19–38. DOI: 10.1177/2321023015575211.

Jaffrelot, Christophe. 2017a. "The return of kisan politics." *The Indian Express*, June 24. http://indianexpress.com/article/opinion/columns/the-return-of-kisan-politics-4719127/.

Jaffrelot, Christophe. 2017b. "Toward a hindu state?" *Journal of Democracy* 28 (3):52–63.

Jaffrelot, Christophe. 2021. "Modi's India: Hindu nationalism and the rise of ethnic democracy."

Jakobsen, Jostein. 2018. Towards a Gramscian food regime analysis of India's agrarian crisis: Counter- movements, petrofarming and Cheap Nature. *Geoforum*, 90, 1–10.

Jakobsen, Jostein. 2019a. "Neoliberalising the food regime 'amongst its others': the right to food and the state in India." *The Journal of Peasant Studies* 46 (6):1219–1239. DOI: 10.1080/03066150.2018.1449745.

Jakobsen, Jostein. 2019b. "Review of farmers, subalterns, and activists: Social politics of sustainable agriculture in India, by Trent Brown." *Journal of Agrarian Change*. DOI: 10.1111/joac.12342.

Jakobsen, Jostein. 2020. "The maize frontier in rural South India: Exploring the everyday dynamics of the contemporary food regime." *Journal of Agrarian Change* 20 (1):137–162.

Jakobsen, Jostein. 2021. "New food regime geographies: Scale, state, labor." *World Development* 145:105523. DOI: https://doi.org/10.1016/j.worlddev.2021.105523.

Jakobsen, Jostein. 2023. "The international development of food and agriculture: global food regimes, environmental change and new configurations of power." In *Handbook on International Development and the Environment*, 170–184. Edward Elgar Publishing.

Jakobsen, Jostein, and Arve Hansen. 2020. "Geographies of meatification: an emerging Asian meat complex." *Globalizations* 17 (1):93–109. DOI:10.1080/14747731.2019.1614723.

Jakobsen, Jostein, and Kenneth Bo Nielsen. 2023. "Bovine meat, authoritarian populism, and state contradictions in Modi's India." *Journal of Agrarian Change* 23 (1):110–130.

Jakobsen, Jostein, and Kenneth Bo Nielsen. 2024. *Authoritarian Populism and Bovine Political Economy in Modi's India*. London: Routledge.

Jakobsen, Jostein, Kenneth Bo Nielsen, Alf Gunvald Nilsen, and Anand Vaidya. 2018. "Mapping the world's largest democracy (1947–2017)." *Forum for Development Studies*:1–26. DOI: 10.1080/08039410.2018.1465461.

Jakobsen, Jostein, and Ola T. Westengen. 2022. "The imperial maize assemblage: maize dialectics in Malawi and India." *The Journal of Peasant Studies* 49 (3):536–560. DOI: 10.1080/03066150.2021.1890042.

Jan, Muhammad Ali. 2019. "The complexity of exchange: Wheat markets, petty-commodity producers and the emergence of commercial capital in colonial Punjab." 19 (2):225–248. DOI: 10.1111/joac.12302.

Jeffrey, Craig. 2010. *Timepass: Youth, Class, and the Politics of Waiting*. Stanford, California: Stanford University Press.

Jenkins, Rob. 1999. *Democratic Politics and Economic Reform in India*. Cambridge: Cambridge University Press.

Jodhka, Surinder S. 1998. "From "book view" to "field view": Social anthropological constructions of the Indian village." *Oxford Development Studies* 26 (3):311–331. DOI: 10.1080/13600819808424159.

Jodhka, Surinder S. 2017. "Revisiting the rural in 21st century India." *Economic and Political Weekly* 51 (26–27):5–7.

Johannessen, Carl L., and Anne Z. Parker. 1989. "Maize ears sculptured in 12th and 13th century A.D. India as indicators of pre-columbian diffusion." *Economic Botany* 43 (2):164–180. DOI: 10.1007/bf02859857.

Jones, Lee. 2020. *Beyond China, Inc.: Understanding Chinese Companies*. Transnational Institute.

Jones, Lee, and Shahar Hameiri. 2021. *Fractured China: How State Transformation Is Shaping China's Rise*. Cambridge: Cambridge University Press.

Joshi, P. K., N. P. Singh, N. N. Singh, R. V. Gerpacio, and P. L. Pingali. 2005. *Maize in India: Production Systems, Constraints, and Research Priorities*. Mexico: International Maize and Wheat Improvement Center.

K, Murdia, Ranjeeta Wadhwani, N. Wadhawan, Preeti Dixit-Bajpai, and S. Shekhawat. 2016. "Maize utilization in India: An overview." *American Journal of Food and Nutrition* 4:169–176. DOI: 10.12691/ajfn-4-6-5.

Kalaiyarasan, A., and M. Vijayabaskar. 2021. "Why does the 'provincial propertied class' remain provincial? Reading the agrarian question of capital through caste." *Urbanisation* 6 (1):16–34. DOI: 10.1177/24557471211021506.

Kandikuppa, Sandeep. 2022. "Class and vulnerability to debt in rural India: A statistical overview*." *Rural Sociology* 87 (2):454–488. DOI: https://doi.org/10.1111/ruso.12425.

Karanth, G. K. 1995. *Change and Continuity in Agrarian Relations*. New Delhi: Concept Publishing Company.

Karnataka, Government of. 2006. *Karnataka Human Development Report 2005*. Bangalore: Government of Karnataka.

Karnataka, Government of. 2016. *Profile of Agriculture Statistics: Karnataka State*. Bengaluru: Karnataka State Department of Agriculture.

Kaviraj, Sudipta. 1988. "A critique of the passive revolution." *Economic and Political Weekly* 23 (45/47):2429–2444.

Kaviraj, Sudipta 2017. "Three planes of space: Examining regions theoretically in India." *Economic and Political Weekly* LII (46):56–63.

Kennedy, Jonathan, and Lawrence King. 2014. "The political economy of farmers' suicides in India: Indebted cash-crop farmers with marginal landholdings explain state-level variation in suicide rates." *Globalization and Health* 10:16. DOI: 10.1186/1744-8603-10-16.

Kennedy, Loraine. 2014. *The Politics of Economic Restructuring in India: Economic Governance and State Spatial Rescaling*. London & New York: Routledge.

Khadse, Ashlesha, Peter Michael Rosset, Helda Morales, and Bruce G. Ferguson. 2017. "Taking agroecology to scale: The zero budget natural farming peasant movement in Karnataka, India." *The Journal of Peasant Studies*:1–28. DOI: 10.1080/03066150.2016.1276450.

Klinger, Julie Michelle. 2018. *Rare Earth Frontiers: From Terrestrial Subsoils to Lunar Landscapes*: Cornell University Press.

Kloppenburg, Jack. 1988. *First the Seed: The Political Economy of Plant Biotechnology, 1492–2000*. Cambridge: Cambridge University Press.

Kohli, Atul. 1987. *The State and Poverty in India: The Politics of Reform*. Cambridge: Cambridge University Press.

Kohli, Atul. 2012. *Poverty Amid Plenty in the New India*. Cambridge; New York: Cambridge University Press.

Kothakapa, Gouthami, and Rahul A. Sirohi. 2023. "'Capital as power': an alternative reading of India's post-2011 economic slowdown." *Area Development and Policy* 8 (1):37–59.

Kothari, Rajni. 1964. "The congress 'system' in India." *Asian Survey* 4 (12):1161–1173. DOI: 10.2307/2642550.

KPMG. 2014. India maize summit '14. KPMG, FICCI, NCDEX.

Krishna Kumar, R. 2014. "Chamarjanagar's saga of backwardness continues." *The Hindu*, November 2. http://www.thehindu.com/news/cities/bangalore/chamaraj anagars-saga-of-backwardness-continues/article6555738.ece.

Krishnan, Preethi, and Mangala Subramaniam. 2014. "Understanding the state: Right to food campaign in India." *The Global South* 8 (2):101–118.

Krishnan, Varun. 2018. "What the agriculture census shows about land holdings in India " *The Hindu*, October 3. https://www.thehindu.com/sci-tech/agriculture/ind ian-farms-getting-smaller/article25113177.ece.

Kumar, Ranjit, K. Srinivas, and N. Sivaramane. 2013. Assessment of the maize situation, outlook and investment opportunities in India. In *Country Report – Regional Assessment Asia (MAIZE-CRP)*. Hyderabad: National Academy of Agricultural Research Management.

Kumar, Richa. 2016a. "The perils of productivity: Making 'good farmers' in Malwa, India." *Journal of Agrarian Change* 16 (1):70–93. DOI: 10.1111/joac.12084.

Kumar, Richa. 2016b. *Rethinking Revolutions: Soyabean, Choupals, and the Changing Countryside in Central India*. New Delhi: Oxford University Press.

Kumar, Satendra. 2022. *New Farm Bills and Farmers' Resistance to Neoliberalism*. New Delhi, India: Sage Publications Sage India.

Landes, Maurice. 2008. *The Environment for Agricultural and Agribusiness Investment in India*. edited by Economic Research Service: United States Department of Agriculture.

Landy, Frédéric. 2009. *Feeding India: The Spatial Parameters of Food Grain Policy*. New Delhi: Manohar.

Lapegna, Pablo, and Tamara Perelmuter. 2020. "Genetically modified crops and seed/food sovereignty in Argentina: scales and states in the contemporary food regime." *The Journal of Peasant Studies* 47 (4):700–719. DOI: 10.1080/03066150.2020.1732933.

Lele, Uma, and Arthur A. Goldsmith. 1989. "The development of national agricultural research capacity: India's experience with the Rockefeller foundation and its significance for Africa." *Economic Development and Cultural Change* 37 (2):305–343.

Lerche, Jens. 2010. "From rural labour to classes of labour: class fragmentation, caste and class struggle at the bottom of the Indian labour hierarchy." In *The Comparative Political Economy of Development: Africa and South Asia*, edited by Barbara Harriss-White and Judith Heyer, 64–85. London & New York: Routledge.

Lerche, Jens. 2011. "Agrarian crisis and agrarian questions in India." *Journal of Agrarian Change* 11:104–118. DOI: 10.1111/j.1471-0366.2010.00295.x.

Lerche, Jens. 2013. "The agrarian question in Neoliberal India: Agrarian transition bypassed?" *Journal of Agrarian Change* 13 (3):382–404. DOI: 10.1111/joac.12026.

Lerche, Jens. 2014. "Regional patterns of agrarian accumulation in India." In *Indian Capitalism in Development*, edited by Judith Heyer and Barbara Harriss-White, 46–65. London & New York: Routledge.

Lerche, Jens. 2021. "The farm laws struggle 2020–2021: class-caste alliances and bypassed agrarian transition in neoliberal India." *The Journal of Peasant Studies* 48 (7):1380–1396.

Lerche, Jens, Alpa Shah, and Barbara Harriss-White. 2013. "Introduction: Agrarian questions and left politics in India." *Journal of Agrarian Change* 13:337–350. DOI: 10.1111/joac.12031.

Levien, Michael. 2018. *Dispossession without Development: Land Grabs in Neoliberal India*. New York: Oxford University Press.

Li, Tania Murray. 2014. *Land's End: Capitalist Relations on an Indigenous Frontier*. Durham and London: Duke University Press.

Limited, Kaveri Seed Company. 2017. Annual report 2016–17.

Lin, Scott Y. 2023. "Restoring the state back to food regime theory: China's agribusiness and the global soybean commodity Chain." *Journal of Contemporary Asia* 53 (2):288–310. DOI: 10.1080/00472336.2022.2032279.

Ludden, David. 1999. *An Agrarian History of South Asia*. Cambridge: Cambridge University Press.

Ludden, David. 2005. "Development regimes in South Asia: History and the governance conundrum." *Economic and Political Weekly* 40 (37):4042–4051.

MacDonald, Mia, and Sangamithra Iyer. 2012. *Veg or Non-Veg? India at the Crossroads*. Brighter Green.

Magnan, André. 2012. "Food regimes." In *The Oxford Handbook of Food History*, edited by J. M. Pilcher, 370–388. Oxford: Oxford University Press.

Magnan, André. 2016. *When Wheat Was King: The Rise and Fall of the Canada-UK Grain Trade*: Ubc Press.

Mahajan, Neeraj, and Kavaljit Singh. 2015. *A Beginner's Guide to Indian Commodity Futures Markets*. New Delhi: Madhyam.

Makki, Fouad. 2015. "Reframing development theory: the significance of the idea of uneven and combined development." *Theory and Society* 44 (5):471–497. DOI: 10.1007/s11186-015-9252-9.

Malm, Andreas. 2018. *The Progress of This Storm: Nature and Society in a Warming World*. London & New York: Verso.

Mander, Harsh. 2015. "Is the govt threatening to dismantle national food security act?" *Hindustan Times*, July 9.

Margulis, Matias E., Nora McKeon, and Saturnino M. Borras. 2013. "Land grabbing and global governance: Critical perspectives." *Globalizations* 10 (1):1–23. DOI: 10.1080/14747731.2013.764151.

Margulis, Matias E., and Tony Porter. 2013. "Governing the global land grab: Multipolarity, ideas, and complexity in transnational governance." *Globalizations* 10 (1):65–86. DOI: 10.1080/14747731.2013.760930.

Martiniello, Giuliano. 2021. "Bitter sugarification: sugar frontier and contract farming in Uganda." *Globalizations* 18 (3):355–371. DOI: 10.1080/14747731.2020.1794564.

Martiniello, Giuliano, and Julia Kassem. 2023. "The corporate food regime and Lebanon: Machgara and adverse incorporation." *The Journal of Peasant Studies*:1–21.

Marx, Karl. 1963. *Theories of Surplus Value, Part 1*. Moscow: Progress Publishers.

Marx, Karl. 1976. *Capital: A Critique of Political Economy (Volume 1)*. London: Penguin.

Marx, Karl. 1992. *Capital: A Critique of Political Economy (Volume 2)*. London: Penguin.

Marx, Karl. 1993a. *Capital: A Critique of Political Economy, Volume 3*. Penguin UK.

Marx, Karl. 1993b. *Grundrisse: Foundations of the Critique of Political Economy*. London: Penguin.

Marx, Karl, and Friedrich Engels. 1974. *The German Ideology*. 2d ed. London: Lawrence & Wishart London.

Matthan, Tanya. 2023. "Beyond bad weather: climates of uncertainty in rural India." *The Journal of Peasant Studies* 50 (1):114–135.

Mau, Søren. 2023. *Mute Compulsion: A Marxist Theory of the Economic Power of Capital*: Verso Books.

McCarthy, James. 2015. "A socioecological fix to capitalist crisis and climate change? The possibilities and limits of renewable energy." *Environment and Planning A: Economy and Space* 47 (12):2485–2502. DOI: 10.1177/0308518x15602491.

McKay, Ben M., Alberto Alonso-Fradejas, Zoe W. Brent, Sérgio Sauer, and Yunan Xu. 2016. "China and Latin America: towards a new consensus of resource control?" *Third World Thematics: A TWQ Journal* 1 (5):592–611. DOI: 10.1080/23802014.2016.1344564.

McKay, Ben M., Ruth Hall, and Juan Liu. 2016. "The rise of BRICS: implications for global agrarian transformation." *Third World Thematics: A TWQ Journal* 1 (5):581–591. DOI: 10.1080/23802014.2016.1362323.

McMichael, Philip. 2000. "Global food politics." In *Hungry for Profit: The Agribusiness Threat to Farmers, Food and the Environment*, edited by Fred Magdoff, John Bellamy Foster and Frederick H. Buttel. New York: Monthly Review Press.

McMichael, Philip. 2005. "Global development and the corporate food regime." In *New Directions in the Sociology of Global Development*, edited by Frederick H. Buttel and Philip McMichael, 269–303. Oxford: Elsevier Press.

McMichael, Philip. 2006. "Peasant prospects in the neoliberal age." *New Political Economy* 11 (3):407–418. DOI: 10.1080/13563460600841041.

McMichael, Philip. 2009a. "A food regime analysis of the 'world food crisis'." *Agriculture and Human Values* 26:281–295. DOI: 10.1007/s10460-009-9218-5.

McMichael, Philip. 2009b. "A food regime genealogy." *The Journal of Peasant Studies* 36 (1):139–169. DOI: 10.1080/03066150902820354.

McMichael, Philip. 2009c. "Interpreting the world food crisis of 2007–08." *Review (Fernand Braudel Center)* 32 (1):1–8.

McMichael, Philip. 2010. "Agrofuels in the food regime." *The Journal of Peasant Studies* 37 (4):609–629. DOI: 10.1080/03066150.2010.512450.

McMichael, Philip. 2012. "The land grab and corporate food regime restructuring." *The Journal of Peasant Studies* 39 (3–4):681–701. DOI: 10.1080/03066150.2012.661369.

McMichael, Philip. 2013a. *Food Regimes and Agrarian Questions*. Rugby, UK: PracticalAid Publishing.

McMichael, Philip. 2013b. "Land grabbing as security mercantilism in international relations." *Globalizations* 10 (1):47–64. DOI: 10.1080/14747731.2013.760925.

McMichael, Philip. 2016. "Commentary: Food regime for thought." *The Journal of Peasant Studies* 43 (3):648–670. DOI: 10.1080/03066150.2016.1143816.

McMichael, Philip. 2020. "Does China's 'going out' strategy prefigure a new food regime?" *The Journal of Peasant Studies* 47 (1):116–154. DOI: 10.1080/03066150.2019.1693368.

McMichael, Philip. 2021. "Food regimes." In *Handbook of critical agrarian studies*, 218–231. Edward Elgar Publishing.

McMichael, Philip. 2023. "Updating Karl Polanyi's 'double movement' for critical agrarian studies." *The Journal of Peasant Studies* 50 (6):2123–2144. DOI: 10.1080/03066150.2023.2219978.

McNally, David. 2017. "Intersections and dialectics: Critical reconstructions in social reproduction theory." In *Social Reproduction Theory: Remapping Class, Recentering Oppression*, edited by Tithi Bhattacharya, 94–112. London: Pluto Press.

Mehta, Pratap Bhanu. 2022. "Hindu nationalism: from ethnic identity to authoritarian repression." *Studies in Indian Politics* 10 (1):31–47.

Mezzadra, Sandro, and Brett Neilson. 2019. *The Politics of Operations: Excavating Contemporary Capitalism*. Durham & London: Duke University Press.

Mezzadri, Alessandra, and Lulu Fan. 2018. "'Classes of labour' at the margins of global commodity chains in India and China." *Development and Change* 49 (4):1034–1063. DOI: https://doi.org/10.1111/dech.12412.

Michael, Arndt, and Marcel M. Baumann. 2016. "India and the dialectics of domestic and international "land grabbing": Historical perspectives, current debates, and the case of Ethiopia." *India Review* 15 (1):112–135. DOI: 10.1080/14736489.2016.1129935.

Mies, Maria. 2014 [1986]. *Patriarchy and Accumulation on a World Scale: Women in the International Division of Labor*. London: Zed Books.

Mincyte, Diana. 2024. "Rethinking food regime as gender regime: agrarian change and the politics of social reproduction." *The Journal of Peasant Studies* 51 (1):18–36. DOI: 10.1080/03066150.2022.2157720.

Mines, Diane P., and Nicolas Yazgi, eds. 2010. *Village Matters: Relocating Villages in the Contemporary Anthropology of India*. New Delhi: Oxford University Press.

Modi, Ajay. 2014. "Amazing." *Business Today*, May 25.

Mody, Ashoka. 2023. "India's fake growth story." *Project Syndicate*.

Mohammad-Arif, Aminah. 2014. "Introduction. Imaginations and constructions of south asia: An enchanting abstraction?" *South Asia Multidisciplinary Academic Journal* (10).

Mohanty, B. B. 2016a. "Agrarian transition: from classic to current debates." In *Critical Perspectives on Agrarian Transition: India in the Global Debate*, edited by B. B. Mohanty, 1–41. London & New York: Routledge.

Mohanty, B. B., ed. 2016b. *Critical Perspectives on Agrarian Transition: India in the Global Debate*. London & New York: Routledge.

Mohanty, B. B., and Papesh K. Lenka. 2016. "Neoliberal reforms, agrarian capitalism and peasantry." In *Critical Perspectives on Agrarian Transition: India in the Global Debate*, edited by B. B. Mohanty, 164–195. New Delhi: Routledge.

Montesclaros, Jose. 2023. Why is India rolling back COVID-19 food aid? *East Asia Forum*.

Mooij, Jos. 1998. "Food policy and politics: The political economy of the public distribution system in India." *The Journal of Peasant Studies* 25 (2):77–101. DOI: 10.1080/03066159808438667.

Moore, Ilona Tamminen. 2014. "The Work of "Feeding the World:" from India's Green Revolution to the Paradox of Plenty." PhD, University of Minnesota.

Moore, Jason W. 2010. "Cheap food & bad money: Food, frontiers, and financialization in the rise and demise of neoliberalism." *Review (Fernand Braudel Center)* 33 (2/3):225–261.

Moore, Jason W. 2015. *Capitalism in the Web of Life: Ecology and the Accumulation of Capital*. London and New York: Verso.

Moore, Jason W. 2017. "The capitalocene part II: accumulation by appropriation and the centrality of unpaid work/energy." *The Journal of Peasant Studies*:1–43. DOI: 10.1080/03066150.2016.1272587.

Moore, Jason W. 2018. "The capitalocene part II: accumulation by appropriation and the centrality of unpaid work/energy." *The Journal of Peasant Studies* 45 (2):237–279. DOI: 10.1080/03066150.2016.1272587.

Moore, Jason W. 2022. "Anthropocene, capitalocene & the flight from world history: dialectical universalism & the geographies of class power in the capitalist world-ecology, 1492–2022." *Nordia Geographical Publications* 51 (2):123–146.

Morton, Adam David. 2007. *Unravelling Gramsci: Hegemony and Passive Revolution in the Global Economy*. London: Pluto Press.

Morton, Adam David. 2010. "The continuum of passive revolution." *Capital & Class* 34 (3):315–342. DOI: 10.1177/0309816810378266.

Morton, Adam David. 2013. "Traveling with Gramsci: The spatiality of passive revolution." In *Gramsci: Space, Nature, Politics*, edited by Michael Ekers, Gillian Hart and Alex Loftus, 65–83. Oxford: Wiley-Blackwell.

Mouffe, Chantal. 2022. *Towards a Green Democratic Revolution: Left Populism and the Power of Affects*: Verso Books.

Mukherjee, Sanjeeb. 2013. "Is maize India's new miracle crop?" *Business Standard*, August 12. Accessed 22.03.2018. http://www.business-standard.com/article/economy-policy/is-maize-india-s-new-wonder-crop-113081000571_1.html.

Mukherji, Rahul. 2014. *Political Economy of Reforms in India*. New Delhi: Oxford University Press.

Musto, Marcello. 2020. *The Last Years of Karl Marx: An Intellectual Biography*: Stanford University Press.

Münster, Daniel. 2012. "Farmers' suicides and the state in India: Conceptual and ethnographic notes from Wayanad, Kerala." *Contributions to Indian Sociology* 46:181–208. DOI: 10.1177/006996671104600208.

Münster, Daniel. 2015. ""Ginger is a gamble": Crop booms, rural uncertainty, and the neoliberalization of agriculture in South India." *Focaal: Journal of Global and Historical Anthropology* 2015 (71):100–113. DOI: 10.3167/fcl.2015.710109.

Münster, Daniel. 2016. "Agro-ecological double movements? Zero budget natural farming and alternative agricultures after the neoliberal crisis in Kerala." In *Critical Perspectives on Agrarian Transition: India in the Global Debate*, edited by B. B. Mohanty, 222–245. London and New York: Routledge.

Münster, Daniel, and Christian Strümpell. 2014. "The anthropology of neoliberal India: An introduction." *Contributions to Indian Sociology* 48 (1):1–16. DOI: 10.1177/0069966713502419.

Naidu, Sirisha C., and Lyn Ossome. 2016. "Social reproduction and the agrarian question of women's labour in India." *Agrarian South: Journal of Political Economy* 5 (1):50–76.

Nair, Janaki. 2011. *Mysore Modern: Rethinking the Region Under Princely Rule*. Minneapolis: University of Minnesota Press.

Narasimha Reddy, D., and Srijit Mishra, eds. 2009a. *Agrarian Crisis in India*. New Delhi; New York: Oxford University Press.

Narasimha Reddy, D., and Srijit Mishra. 2009b. "Agriculture in the reforms regime." In *Agrarian Crisis in India*, edited by D. Narasimha Reddy and Srijit Mishra, 3–44. New Delhi Oxford University Press.

Narayan, Sumana, M. Suchitra, and Jyotika Sood. 2011. "Maize mania." *Down to Earth*, 15 August. http://www.downtoearth.org.in/coverage/maize-mania-33801.

Narayanan, Yamini. 2023. *Mother Cow, Mother India: A Multispecies Politics of Dairy in India*: Stanford University Press.

Natrajan, Balmurli, and Suraj Jacob. 2018. "'provincialising'vegetarianism putting Indian food habits in their place." *Economic and Political Weekly* 53 (9):54–64.

Neimark, Benjamin D., and Timothy M. Healy. 2018. "Small-scale commodity frontiers: The bioeconomy value chain of castor oil in Madagascar." *Journal of Agrarian Change* 0 (0). DOI: 10.1111/joac.12231.

Neo, Harvey, and Jody Emel. 2017. *Geographies of Meat: Politics, Economy and Culture*. London & New York: Routledge.

Newsclick. 2023. "Right to food campaign raise concern over centre's 'misrepresentation' of PMGKAY." *Newslick*, 7 November. https://www.newsclick.in/right-food-campaign-raise-concern-over-centres-misrepresentation-pmgkay.

Nicholson, F. A. 1887. *Manual of the Coimbatore District in the Presidency of Madras*. Madras: Government Press.

Nielsen, Kenneth Bo. 2011. "Congress factionalism revisited: West bengal." In *Trysts with Democracy: Political Practice in South Asia*, edited by Stig Toft Madsen and Kenneth Bo Nielsen, 157–192. London: Anthem Press.

Nielsen, Kenneth Bo. 2018. *Land Dispossession and Everyday Politics in Rural Eastern India*. London & New York: Anthem Press.

Nielsen, Kenneth Bo, and Alf Gunvald Nilsen. 2015. "Law struggles and hegemonic processes in neoliberal India: Gramscian reflections on land acquisition legislation." *Globalizations* 12 (2):203–216. DOI: 10.1080/14747731.2014.937084.

Nilsen, Alf Gunvald. 2009. "'The authors and the actors of their own drama': Towards a Marxist theory of social movements." *Capital & Class* 33 (3):109–139. DOI: 10.1177/03098168090330030501.

Nilsen, Alf Gunvald. 2012. "Adivasis in and against the state: Subaltern politics and state power in contemporary India." *Critical Asian Studies* 44 (2):251–282. DOI: 10.1080/14672715.2012.672827.

Nilsen, Alf Gunvald. 2017. "Passages from Marxism to postcolonialism: A comment on Vivek Chibber's postcolonial theory and the specter of capital." *Critical Sociology* 43 (4–5):559–571. DOI: 10.1177/0896920515614982.

Nilsen, Alf Gunvald. 2021. "India's trajectories of change, 2004–2019." *Destroying Democracy: Neoliberal Capitalism and the Rise of Authoritarian Politics*:112.

Nilsen, Alf Gunvald. 2022. "India's pandemic: spectacle, social murder and authoritarian politics in a lockdown nation." *Globalizations* 19 (3):466–486.

Nilsen, Alf Gunvald, and Kenneth Bo Nielsen. 2016. "Social movements, state formation and democracy in India: An introduction." In *Social Movements and the State in India: Deepening Democracy?*, edited by Kenneth Bo Nielsen and Alf Gunvald Nilsen, 1–23. London: Palgrave Macmillan UK.

Noy, Itay. 2023. "Unpicking precarity: Informal work in eastern India's coal mining tracts." *Development and Change* 54 (1):168–191. DOI: https://doi.org/10.1111/dech.12739.

Nutrition, Global Network for the Right to Food and. 2020. "Right to food campaign kickstarts in India as gov't set to end COVID-19 rations despite widespread hunger." https://www.righttofoodandnutrition.org/right-food-campaign-kickstarts-india-govt-set-end-covid-19-rations-despite-widespread-hunger.

O'Connor, James. 1998. *Natural Causes: Essays in Ecological Marxism*. New York: Guilford Press.

Oliveira, Gustavo de L. T. 2018. "Chinese land grabs in Brazil? Sinophobia and foreign investments in Brazilian soybean agribusiness." *Globalizations* 15 (1):114–133. DOI: 10.1080/14747731.2017.1377374.

Oliveira, Gustavo de L. T., Ben M McKay, and Juan Liu. 2021. "Beyond land grabs: new insights on land struggles and global agrarian change." *Globalizations* 18 (3):321–338.

Ollman, Bertell. 2003. *Dance of the Dialectic: Steps in Marx's Method*. Urbana and Chicago: University of Illinois Press.

Omvedt, Gail. 1981. "Capitalist agriculture and rural classes in India." *Economic and Political Weekly* 16 (52):A140–A159.

Oskarsson, Patrik, Kuntala Lahiri-Dutt, and Patrick Wennström. 2019. "From incremental dispossession to a cumulative land grab: Understanding territorial transformation in India's north Karanpura coalfield." *Development and Change*, 2019, 50.6: 1485–1508. DOI: 10.1111/dech.12513.

Oskarsson, Patrik, and Kenneth Bo Nielsen. 2017. "Industrialising rural India." In *Industrialising Rural India: Land, Policy and Resistance*, edited by Kenneth Bo Nielsen and Patrik Oskarsson, 3–19. London & New York: Routledge.

Otero, Gerardo. 2012. "The neoliberal food regime in Latin America: state, agribusiness transnational corporations and biotechnology." *Canadian Journal of Development Studies / Revue canadienne d'études du développement* 33 (3):282–294. DOI: 10.1080/02255189.2012.711747.

Otero, Gerardo. 2016. "Review of Philip McMichael's food regimes and agrarian questions." *Journal of World-Systems Research* 22 (1):7. DOI: 10.5195/jwsr.2016.651.

Otero, Gerardo. 2018. *The Neoliberal Diet: Healthy Profits, Unhealthy People*: University of Texas Press.

Otero, Gerardo, and Pablo Lapegna. 2016. "Transgenic crops in Latin America: Expropriation, negative value and the state." *Journal of Agrarian Change* 16 (4):665–674. DOI: 10.1111/joac.12159.

Otero, Gerardo, Gabriela Pechlaner, and Efe Can Gürcan. 2013. "The political economy of 'food security' and trade: Uneven and combined dependency." *Rural Sociology* 78 (3):263–289. DOI: 10.1111/ruso.12011.

Pal, Suresh. 2009. "Managing vulnerability of Indian agriculture: implications for research and development." In *Agrarian Crisis in India*, edited by D. Narasimha Reddy and Srijit Mishra, 87–109. New Delhi: Oxford University Press.

Palmer, James. 2021. "Putting forests to work? Enrolling vegetal labor in the socioecological fix of bioenergy resource making." *Annals of the American Association of Geographers* 111 (1):141–156.

Pandey, Sushil, Debdutt Behura, and Maria Lourdes Velasco. 2017. "Transitions in rice seed provisioning in Odisha: Constraints and reform agenda." *Economic and Political Weekly* 52 (1):83–91.

Parenti, Christian. 2015. "The 2013 ANTIPODE AAG lecture the environment making state: Territory, nature, and value." *Antipode* 47 (4):829–848. DOI: 10.1111/anti.12134.

Patel, Raj. 2012. *Stuffed and Starved: From Farm to Fork: The Hidden Battle for the World Food System*. Second ed. London: Portobello Books.

Patel, Raj. 2013. "The long green revolution." *The Journal of Peasant Studies* 40 (1):1–63. DOI: 10.1080/03066150.2012.719224.

Patel, Raj. 2022. "Land in world-ecology perspectives." In *The Oxford Handbook of Land Politics*, edited by Saturnino M. Borras, Jr. and Jennifer C. Franco, 0. Oxford University Press.

Patel, Raj, and Jason W. Moore. 2017. *A History of the World in Seven Cheap Things: A Guide to Capitalism, Nature, and the Future of the Planet*: Univ of California Press.

Patnaik, Prabhat. 2014. "Imperialism and the agrarian question." *Agrarian South: Journal of Political Economy* 3 (1):1–15. DOI: 10.1177/2277976014530229.

Patnaik, Utsa. 1986. "The agrarian question and development of capitalism in India." *Economic and Political Weekly* XXI (18):781–793.

Patnaik, Utsa, ed. 1990. *Agrarian Relations and Accumulation: The "Mode of Production" Debate in India* Bombay: Published for Sameeksha Trust by Oxford University Press.

Pattenden, Jonathan. 2005. "Horizontality and the Political Economy of Social Movement: The Anti-Capitalist Globalisation Movement, the Karnataka State Farmers Association and Dynamics of Social Transformation in Rural South India." PhD, Department of Development Studies, School of Oriental and African Studies, University of London.

Pattenden, Jonathan. 2016a. "Blind alleys and red herrings? Social movements, the state, class alliances and pro-labouring class strategy." In *Social Movements and the State in India: Deepening Democracy?*, edited by Kenneth Bo Nielsen and Alf Gunvald Nilsen, 215–239. London: Palgrave Macmillan.

Pattenden, Jonathan. 2016b. *Labour, State and Society in Rural India: A Class-Relational Approach*. Manchester: Manchester University Press.

Pattenden, Jonathan. 2016c. "Working at the margins of global production networks: local labour control regimes and rural-based labourers in South India." *Third World Quarterly* 37 (10):1809–1833.

Pattenden, Jonathan. 2018a. "The politics of classes of labour: fragmentation, reproduction zones and collective action in Karnataka, India." *The Journal of Peasant Studies* 45 (5–6):1039–1059. DOI: 10.1080/03066150.2018.1495625.

Pattenden, Jonathan. 2018b. "The politics of classes of labour: fragmentation, reproduction zones and collective action in Karnataka, India." *Journal of Peasant Studies* 45 (5/6):1039–1059.

Pattenden, Jonathan, and Gaurav Bansal. 2021. "A new class alliance in the Indian countryside? From new farmers' movements to the 2020 protest wave." *Economic and Political Weekly* 56 (26–27).

Pattnaik, Itishree, Kuntala Lahiri-Dutt, Stewart Lockie, and Bill Pritchard. 2018. "The feminization of agriculture or the feminization of agrarian distress? Tracking the trajectory of women in agriculture in India." *Journal of the Asia Pacific Economy* 23 (1):138–155. DOI: 10.1080/13547860.2017.1394569.

Pechlaner, Gabriela. 2012. *Corporate Crops: Biotechnology, Agriculture, and the Struggle for Control*. Austin: University of Texas Press.

Pechlaner, Gabriela, and Gerardo Otero. 2008. "The third food regime: Neoliberal globalism and agricultural biotechnology in North America." *Sociologia Ruralis* 48 (4):351–371. DOI: 10.1111/j.1467-9523.2008.00469.x.

Pechlaner, Gabriela, and Gerardo Otero. 2010. "The Neoliberal food regime: Neoregulation and the new division of labor in North America." *Rural Sociology* 75 (2):179–208. DOI: 10.1111/j.1549-0831.2009.00006.x.

Peck, Jamie. 2010. *Constructions of Neoliberal Reason*. Oxford: Oxford University Press.

Peck, Jamie. 2013. "Explaining (with) neoliberalism." *Territory, Politics, Governance* 1 (2):132–157. DOI: 10.1080/21622671.2013.785365.

Peck, Jamie, and Nik Theodore. 2019. "Still neoliberalism?" *South Atlantic Quarterly* 118 (2):245–265. DOI: 10.1215/00382876-7381122.

Peck, Jamie, and Adam Tickell. 2002. "Neoliberalizing space." *Antipode* 34:380–404. DOI: 10.1111/1467-8330.00247.

Pedersen, Jørgen Dige. 2008. *Globalization, Development and the State: The Performance of India and Brazil since 1990*. London: Palgrave Macmillan.

Peet, Richard. 2007. *Geography of Power: The Making of Global Economic Policy*. London and New York: Zed Books.

Perkins, John H. 1997. *Geopolitics and the Green Revolution: Wheat, Genes, and the Cold War*. New York & Oxford: Oxford University Press.

Pietilainen, Emma Pauliina, and Gerardo Otero. 2018. "Power and dispossession in the neoliberal food regime: Oil palm expansion in Guatemala." *The Journal of Peasant Studies*:1–25. DOI: 10.1080/03066150.2018.1499093.

Pitts, Frederick Harry. 2019. "Value form theory, open Marxism & the new reading of Marx." In *Open Marxism IV: Against a Closing World*, 63–75. Pluto Press.

Polanyi, Karl. 2001 [1944]. *The Great Tranformation: The Political and Economic Origins of Our Time*. Boston: Beacon Press.

Politburo, Communist Party of India (Marxist). 2011. *Food Security Bill: Unacceptable*. Communist Party of India.

Postone, Moishe. 1993. *Title, Time, Labor, and Social Domination: A Reinterpretation of Marx's Critical Theory*. Cambridge: Cambridge University Press.

Poulantzas, Nicos. 1978. *State, Power, Socialism*. London: New Left Review Editions.

Pray, Carl E., and Latha Nagarajan. 2014. "The transformation of the Indian agricultural input industry: has it increased agricultural R&D?" *Agricultural Economics* 45 (S1):145–156. DOI: 10.1111/agec.12138.

Price, Pamela. 2011. "A political breakthrough for irrigation development: The Congress assembly campaign in Andhra Pradesh in 2003–2004." *Trysts with Democracy: Political Practice in South Asia*:135–56.

Price, Pamela, and Arild Engelsen Ruud, eds. 2010. *Power and Influence in India: Bosses, Lords and Captains*. New Delhi: Routledge.

Pritchard, Bill. 2009. "The long hangover from the second food regime: a world-historical interpretation of the collapse of the WTO Doha round." *Agriculture and Human Values* 26 (4):297. DOI: 10.1007/s10460-009-9216-7.

Pritchard, Bill, Jane Dixon, Elizabeth Hull, and Chetan Choithani. 2016. "'Stepping back and moving in': the role of the state in the contemporary food regime." *The Journal of Peasant Studies* 43 (3):693–710. DOI: 10.1080/03066150.2015.1136621.

Pritchard, Bill, Anu Rammohan, Madhushree Sekher, S. Parasumaran, and Chetan Choithani. 2014. *Feeding India: Livelihoods, Entitlements and Capabilities*. London and New York: Routledge.

Pye, Oliver. 2019. "Agrarian Marxism and the proletariat: A palm oil manifesto." *The Journal of Peasant Studies*:1–20. DOI: 10.1080/03066150.2019.1667772.

Ramachandran, V. K. 2011. "The state of agrarian relations in India today." *The Marxist* XXVII (1–2):51–89.

Ramakumar, R. 2017. "The agrarian economy of Karnataka." In *Socio-Economic Surveys of Three Villages in Karnataka: A Study of Agrarian Relations*, edited by Madhura Swaminathan and Arindam Das, 1–31. Delhi: Tulika Books.

Ramesh, S. 2022. "Despite granting taluk status, govt offices yet to be shifted to Hanur." *The Times of India*. https://timesofindia.indiatimes.com/city/mysuru/despite-granting-taluk-status-govt-offices-yet-to-be-shifted-to-hanur/articleshow/88864630.cms.

Ramprasad, Vijay. 2019. "Debt and vulnerability: indebtedness, institutions and smallholder agriculture in South India." *The Journal of Peasant Studies* 46 (6):1286–1307.

Rasmussen, Mattias Borg, and Christian Lund. 2018. "Reconfiguring frontier spaces: The territorialization of resource control." *World Development* 101 (Supplement C):388–399. DOI: https://doi.org/10.1016/j.worlddev.2017.01.018.

Rawat, Virendra Singh. 2023. "Uttar Pradesh govt aims to double maize output to 2.75 mt in 4–5 years." *Business Standard*, May 15. https://www.business-standard.com/economy/news/uttar-pradesh-govt-aims-to-double-maize-output-to-2-75-mt-in-4-5-years-123051500879_1.html.

Reboul, E., I. Guérin, and C. J. Nordman. 2021. "The gender of debt and credit: Insights from rural Tamil Nadu." *World Development* 142:105363. DOI: https://doi.org/10.1016/j.worlddev.2020.105363.

Research, Indian Institute of Maize. 2015. *Vision 20150*. New Delhi: Indian Council of Agricultural Research.

Reuters. 2009. "Wheat ban end, new govt to boost commodity futures trade." *livemint*, May 18. http://www.livemint.com/Money/AHzbDVincOwZEtKZImIcqN/Wheat-ban-end-new-govt-to-boost-commodity-futures-trade.html.

Ríos-Núñez, Sandra M., and Daniel Coq-Huelva. 2015. "The transformation of the spanish livestock system in the second and third food regimes." *Journal of Agrarian Change* 15 (4):519–540. DOI: 10.1111/joac.12088.

Rioux, Sébastien. 2018. "Rethinking food regime analysis: an essay on the temporal, spatial and scalar dimensions of the first food regime." *The Journal of Peasant Studies* 45 (4):715–738. DOI: 10.1080/03066150.2017.1351432.

Roberts, William Clare. 2016. *Marx's Inferno: The Political Theory of Capital*: Princeton University Press.

Roy, Tirthankar. 2006. *The Economic History of India, 1857–1947*. New Delhi: Oxford University Press.

Rudolph, Lloyd I., and Susanne Hoeber Rudolph. 1987. *In Pursuit of Lakshmi: The Political Economy of the Indian State*. Chicago & London: The University of Chicago Press.

Ruparelia, Sanjay. 2013. "India's new rights agenda: genesis, promises, risks." *Pacific Affairs* 86 (3):569–590.

Ruparelia, Sanjay. 2015. "'Minimum government, maximum governance': The restructuring of power in Modi's India." *South Asia: Journal of South Asian Studies* 38 (4):755–775.

Russi, Luigi. 2013. *Hungry Capital: The Financialization of Food*. Winchester, UK & Washinton, US: Zero Books.

Said, EW (1983) *The World, the Text and the Critic*. Cambridge, ma.: Harvard University.

Saito, Kohei. 2023. *Marx in the Anthropocene: Towards the Idea of Degrowth Communism*. Cambridge: Cambridge University Press.

Sanyal, Kalyan. 2007. *Rethinking Capitalist Development: Primitive Accumulation, Governmentality and Post-Colonial Capitalism*. London and New Delhi: Routledge.

Sarkar, Sudipta, and Deepak K. Mishra. 2021. "Circular labour migration from rural India: A study of out-migration of Male labour from West Bengal." *Journal of Asian and African Studies* 56 (6):1403–1418. DOI: 10.1177/0021909620967044.

Sayer, Derek. 1987. *The Violence of Abstraction: The Analytical Foundations of Historical Materialism*. New York: Basil Blackwell.

Searle, Llerena Guiu. 2019. *Landscapes of Accumulation: Real Estate and the Neoliberal Imagination in Contemporary India*: University of Chicago Press.

Sen, Amiti. 2016. "Maize cultivation needs to double by 2025: Agriculture minister." *The Hindu*, May 26.

Shah, Alpa. 2013. "The agrarian question in a maoist Guerrilla zone: Land, labour and capital in the forests and hills of Jharkhand, India." *Journal of Agrarian Change* 13:424–450. DOI: 10.1111/joac.12027.

Shah, Alpa. 2019. *Nightmarch: Among India's Revolutionary Guerrillas*. London: Hurst & Co.

Shah, Alpa, and Barbara Harriss-White. 2011. "Resurrecting scholarship on agrarian transformations." *Economic and Political Weekly* 46 (39):13–18.

Shah, Alpa, Jens Lerche, Richard Axelby, Dalel Benbabaali, Brendan Donegan, Jayaseelan Raj, and Vikramaditya Thakur. 2018. *Ground Down by Growth: Tribe, Class and Inequality in Twenty-First-Century India*. London: Pluto Press.

Shanin, Teodor. 1983. *Late Marx and the Russian Road: Marx and the 'Peripheries of Capitalism'*. Vol. null, *null*.

Sharma, K. K. 1988. "Survey of India (10): Wanted, a new green revolution – Agriculture / Farmers have been protesting over the lack of a fair deal." *Financial Times*, December 20.

Siegel, Benjamin Robert. 2018. *Hungry Nation: Food, Famine, and the Making of Modern India*. Cambridge: Cambridge University Press.

Simon, Roger. 2015. *Gramsci's Political Thought*. Third ed. London: Lawrence & Wishart.

Simpson, Edward. 2016. "Village restudies: Trials and tribulations." *Economic and Political Weekly* 51 (26–27).

REFERENCES

Singh, Bhag. 1977. *Races of Maize in India*. New Delhi: Indian Council of Agricultural Research.

Singh, David. 2022. "'This is all waste': emptying, cleaning and clearing land for renewable energy dispossession in borderland India." *Contemporary South Asia* 30 (3):402–419.

Singh, Sukhpal. 2013. "The practice of contract farming in India: making it inclusive and effective." *Food Chain* 3 (3):137–154. DOI: 10.3362/2046-1887.2013.014.

Singh, Tanya, Pritam Singh, and Meena Dhanda. 2021. "Resisting a "digital green revolution": Agri-logistics, India's new farm laws and the regional politics of protest." *Capitalism Nature Socialism* 32 (2):1–21.

Sinha, Aseema. 2005. *The Regional Roots of Developmental Politics in India: A Divided Leviathan*. Bloomington, IN: Indiana University Press.

Sinha, Aseema. 2015. "Scaling up: Beyond the subnational comparative method for India." *Studies in Indian Politics* 3 (1):128–133. DOI: 10.1177/2321023015575225.

Sinha, Shreya. 2020a. "Betting on potatoes: Accumulation in times of agrarian crisis in Punjab, India." *Development and Change* 51 (6):1533–1554.

Sinha, Shreya. 2020b. "The politics of markets: Farmer–trader relations under neoliberalism in Punjab, India." *Journal of Agrarian Change* 20 (2):255–269.

Sinha, Shreya. 2022. "From cotton to paddy: Political crops in the Indian Punjab." *Geoforum* 130:146–154. DOI: https://doi.org/10.1016/j.geoforum.2021.05.017.

Sinha, Subir. 2008. "Lineages of the developmentalist state: Transnationality and village India, 1900–1965." *Comparative Studies in Society and History* 50 (1):57–90. DOI: 10.1017/S0010417508000054.

Sinha, Subir. 2017. "'Histories of power', the 'universalization of capital', and India's Modi moment: Between and beyond Marxism and Postcolonial theory." *Critical Sociology* 43 (4–5):529–544. DOI: 10.1177/0896920516641732.

Sinha, Subir. 2021. "'Strong leaders', authoritarian populism and Indian developmentalism: The Modi moment in historical context." *Geoforum* 124:320–333.

Sircar, Neelanjan. 2022. "Corporate-controlled capitalism in India" *Seminar*.

Slobodian, Quinn. 2018. *Globalists: The End of Empire and the Birth of Neoliberalism*. Cambridge, Massachusetts: Harvard University Press.

Spielman, David J., Deepthi E. Kolady, Anthony J. Cavalieri, and N. Chandrasekhara Rao. 2014. Structure, competition and policy in India's seed and agricultural biotechnology industries. In CSISA *Research Note* The Cereals Systems Initiative for South Asia.

Srinivas, M. N. 1976. *The Remembered Village*. Berkeley, Los Angeles & London: University of California Press.

Srivastava, Ravi. 2012. "Changing employment conditions of the Indian workforce and implication for decent work." *Global Labour Journal* 3 (1):63–90.

Stock, Ryan. 2023. "Power for the plantationocene: solar parks as the colonial form of an energy plantation." In *Climate Change and Critical Agrarian Studies*, 225–247. Routledge.

Stock, Ryan, and Trevor Birkenholtz. 2021. "The sun and the scythe: Energy dispossessions and the agrarian question of labor in solar parks." *The journal of peasant studies* 48 (5):984–1007.

Stone, Glenn Davis, Andrew Flachs, and Christine Diepenbrock. 2014. "Rhythms of the herd: Long term dynamics in seed choice by Indian farmers." *Technology in Society* 36:26–38. DOI: 10.1016/j.techsoc.2013.10.003.

Sud, Nikita. 2009. "The Indian state in a liberalizing landscape." *Development and Change* 40 (4):645–665. DOI: 10.1111/j.1467-7660.2009.01566.x.

Sud, Nikita. 2017. "State, scale and networks in the liberalisation of India's land." *Environment and Planning c: Government and Policy* 35 (1):76–93. DOI: 10.1177/0263774X16655801.

Sud, Surinder. 2011. "'A-maizing' progress." *Business Standard*, 26 July.

Sudheesh, R. C. 2023. "Adivasi migrant labour and agrarian capitalism in southern India." *Journal of Agrarian Change* 23 (4):755–770. DOI: https://doi.org/10.1111/joac.12540.

Sundar, Nandini. 2011. "The rule of law and the rule of property: Law-struggles and the neo-liberal state in India." In *The State in India after Liberalization: Interdisciplinary Perspectives*, edited by Akhil Gupta and K. Sivaramakrishnan, 175–193. London: Routledge.

Sundar, Nandini. 2016. *The Burning Forest: India's War in Bastar*. New Delhi: Juggernaut.

Suri, K. C. 2006. "Political economy of agrarian distress." *Economic and Political Weekly* 41 (16):1523–1529.

Suwandi, Intan. 2019. *Value Chains: The New Economic Imperialism*: Monthly Review Press.

Swaminathan, Madhura. 2000. *Weakening Welfare: The Public Distribution of Food in India*. New Delhi: LeftWord Books.

Swaminathan, Madhura, and Sandipan Baksi, eds. 2017. *How Do Small Farmers Fare? Evidence from Rural India*. New Delhi: Tulika Books.

Taylor, Marcus. 2013. "Liquid Debts: credit, groundwater and the social ecology of agrarian distress in Andhra Pradesh, India." *Third World Quarterly* 34 (4):691–709. DOI: 10.1080/01436597.2013.786291.

Taylor, Marcus. 2014. *The Political Ecology of Climate Change Adaptation: Livelihoods, Agrarian Change and the Conflicts of Development*: Routledge.

Taylor, Marcus. 2019. "Hybrid realities: making a new green revolution for rice in South India." *The Journal of Peasant Studies*:1–20. DOI: 10.1080/03066150.2019.1568246.

Taylor, Marcus, and Suhas Bhasme. 2018. "The political ecology of rice intensification in South India: Putting SRI in its places." *Journal of Agrarian Change* 0 (0). DOI: 10.1111/joac.12268.

Taylor, Marcus, and Suhas Bhasme. 2021. "Between deficit rains and surplus populations: The political ecology of a climate-resilient village in South India." *Geoforum* 126:431–440.

Thomas, Peter D. 2009. *The Gramscian Moment: Philosophy, Hegemony and Marxism.* Chicago: Haymarket Books.

Thorner, Daniel. 1956. *The Agrarian Prospect in India.* New Delhi: Delhi School of Economics University Press.

Tilzey, Mark. 2018. *Political Ecology, Food Regimes, and Food Sovereignty: Crisis, Resistance, and Resilience.* UK: Palgrave Macmillan.

Tilzey, Mark. 2019. "Food regimes, capital, state, and class: Friedmann and McMichael revisited." *Sociologia Ruralis* 59 (2):230–254. DOI: 10.1111/soru.12237.

Tirmizey, Kasim Ali. 2023. "The geometry of (anti)imperialism in food regime analysis." *Environment and Planning A: Economy and Space* 0 (0):0308518X231214419. DOI: 10.1177/0308518x231214419.

Torrado, Marla. 2016. "Food regime analysis in a Post-Neoliberal Era: Argentina and the expansion of transgenic soybeans." *Journal of Agrarian Change*.

Touzard, Jean-Marc, and Pierre Labarthe. 2016. "Regulation theory and transformation of agriculture: A literature review." *Revue de la Régulation-Capitalisme, institutions, pouvoirs* 20.

Tsing, Anna Lowenhaupt. 2003. "Natural resources and capitalist frontiers." *Economic and Political Weekly* 38 (48):5100–5106.

Upadhya, Carol Boyack. 1988. "The farmer-capitalists of coastal Andhra Pradesh." *Economic and Political Weekly* 23 (27):1376–1382.

Vakulabharanam, Vamsi, and Sripad Motiram. 2011. "Political economy of agrarian distress in India since the 1990s." In *Understanding India's New Political Economy: A Great Transformation?*, edited by Sanjay Ruparelia, Sanjay Reddy, John Harriss and Stuart Corbridge, 101–127. London & New York: Routledge.

Varsney, Ashutosh. 1995. *Democracy, Development, and the Countryside: Urban-Rural Struggles in India.* Cambridge: Cambridge University Press.

Vasavi, A. R. 2012. *Shadow Space: Suicides and the Predicament of Rural India.* Gurgaon: Three Essays Collective.

Vergara-Camus, Leandro, and Cristóbal Kay. 2017. "Agribusiness, peasants, left-wing governments, and the state in Latin America: An overview and theoretical reflections." *Journal of Agrarian Change* 17 (2):239–257. DOI: 10.1111/joac.12215.

Vijayabaskar, M., and Ajit Menon. 2018. "Dispossession by neglect: Agricultural land sales in Southern India." *Journal of Agrarian Change*, 18(3), 571–587. DOI: 10.1111/joac.12256.

Vijayshankar, P. S., and Mekhala Krishnamurthy. 2012. "Understanding agricultural commodity markets." *Economic and Political Weekly* XLVII (52):34–37.

Walker, Kathy Le Mons. 2008. "Neoliberalism on the ground in rural India: Predatory growth, agrarian crisis, internal colonization, and the intensification of class struggle." *Journal of Peasant Studies* 35:557–620. DOI: 10.1080/03066150802681963.

Walker, Richard A. 2004. *The Conquest of Bread: 150 Years of Agribusiness in California* New York & London: The New Press.

Wallace, R. 2016. *Big farms make big flu: dispatches on influenza, agribusiness, and the nature of science*. NYU Press.

Wallerstein, Immanuel. 2004. *World-Systems Analysis: An Introduction*. Durham & London: Duke University Press.

Wang, Kuan-chi. 2017. "East Asian food regimes: agrarian warriors, edamame beans and spatial topologies of food regimes in East Asia." *The Journal of Peasant Studies*:1–18. DOI: 10.1080/03066150.2017.1324427.

Wang, Kuan-chi. 2018. "East Asian food regimes: Agrarian warriors, edamame beans and spatial topologies of food regimes in East Asia." *The Journal of Peasant Studies* 45 (4):739–756. DOI: 10.1080/03066150.2017.1324427.

Wang, Kuan-Chi, and Daniel Buck. 2024. "Relocating agrarian development in Asia: Food regimes, R&D programs, and the long twentieth century." *The Journal of Peasant Studies* 51 (1):212–236.

Warman, Arturo. 2003. *Corn & Capitalism: How a Botanical Bastard Grew to Global Dominance*. Chapel Hill & London: The University of North Carolina Press.

Weis, Tony. 2007. *The Global Food Economy: The Battle for the Future of Farming*. London, New York, Halifax and Winnipeg: Zed Books & Fernwood Publishing.

Weis, Tony. 2010. "The Accelerating biophysical contradictions of industrial capitalist agriculture." *Journal of Agrarian Change* 10 (3):315–341. DOI: 10.1111/j.1471-0366.2010.00273.x.

Weis, Tony. 2013. *The Ecological Hoofprint: The Global Burden of Industrial Livestock*. New York & London: Zed Books.

Werner, M. (2019). Placing the state in the contemporary food regime: uneven regulatory development in the Dominican Republic. *The Journal of Peasant Studies*, 48(1), 137–158.

Werner, Marion. 2022. "Geographies of production III: Global production in/through nature." *Progress in Human Geography* 46 (1):234–244.

Wesz Junior, Valdemar João, Fabiano Escher, and Tomaz Mefano Fares. 2021. "Why and how is China reordering the food regime? The Brazil-China soy-meat complex and COFCO's global strategy in the Southern Cone." *The Journal of Peasant Studies*:1–29. DOI: 10.1080/03066150.2021.1986012.

White, Ben. 2015. "Great transformations writ small: The power of ethnography." *Development and Change* 46 (6):1392–1400. DOI: https://doi.org/10.1111/dech.12203.

White, Ben, Saturnino M. Borras Jr, Ruth Hall, Ian Scoones, and Wendy Wolford. 2012. "The new enclosures: critical perspectives on corporate land deals." *The Journal of Peasant Studies* 39 (3–4):619–647. DOI: 10.1080/03066150.2012.691879.

Whitehead, Judith. 2013. "Accumulation through dispossession and accumulation through growth." *Gramsci: Space, Nature, Politics*:279–300.

Whitehead, Judith. 2015. "Au retour a gramsci: Reflections on civil society, political society and the state in South Asia." *Journal of Contemporary Asia* 45 (4):660–676. DOI: 10.1080/00472336.2015.1045725.

Winders, Bill. 2009. "The vanishing free market: The formation and spread of the British and US food regimes." *Journal of Agrarian Change* 9 (3):315–344. DOI: 10.1111/j.1471-0366.2009.00214.x.

Winders, Bill, Alison Heslin, Gloria Ross, Hannah Weksler, and Seanna Berry. 2016. "Life after the regime: market instability with the fall of the US food regime." *Agriculture and Human Values* 33 (1):73–88. DOI: 10.1007/s10460-015-9596-9.

Yenneti, Komali, Rosie Day, and Oleg Golubchikov. 2016. "Spatial justice and the land politics of renewables: Dispossessing vulnerable communities through solar energy mega-projects." *Geoforum* 76:90–99.

Index

Aadhaar   100–101, 170
accumulation strategies   31, 54, 168
activists   3, 97, 101, 172, 184
adaptability   134, 150
adivasis   123, 149, 159, 192
advanced capitalist economies   10, 77, 165, 172
Age of Capital   18, 182
agitations   11–13, 71, 75, 80, 158, 160
   recent   75, 80
   recent farmer   102
agrarian accumulation   48, 187
agrarian capitalism   43, 69, 190, 200
   global   40, 193
agrarian crisis   25, 62–64, 68, 75, 79, 111, 114, 129, 134, 199, 201
   ongoing   12, 36, 62–63, 83, 162
agrarian crisis in Punjab   172, 199
agrarian distress   48–49, 195, 200–201
agrarian economy   45, 47, 49, 70, 128, 137, 196
   stagnating   13, 62
agrarian environments   108, 167
agrarian India   13, 47–48, 50, 55, 72, 75, 87, 107, 110, 129, 172
agrarian landscape   68
   crisis-ridden   109
   drought-prone   120
agrarian populism   63, 160
agrarian questions   47–50, 167–68, 170, 173, 178, 185, 187, 189, 191, 193–94, 198–99
agrarian studies   6, 16, 26, 45–46, 49, 61, 123, 164, 166
   contemporary   2
   contemporary critical   75
   recent critical   113
agrarian transition   32, 48, 51, 55, 77, 170, 187, 190–91
   bypassed   187
   revisiting   170
agribusinesses   25, 39, 51, 69, 112, 115, 130–31, 137, 156, 159, 201
agricultural labourers   144–45, 153–54
Agricultural Produce Market Committee   103
agriculture census   183, 186

agro-chemicals   17, 80, 108
agro-food system   80, 85, 103–4, 131
agro-shops   121, 138–39
alliances   53, 171
   class-caste   187
Andhra Pradesh   71, 133, 137, 196, 200
Anthropocene   182, 191, 198
Araghi, Farshad   5, 8–9, 20, 23, 39–40, 49, 92, 111, 116, 119, 162, 164–65, 168
Arboleda, Martin   8, 16, 37, 50, 52, 85, 160, 168, 205
Asia   36, 172–73, 175, 202
authoritarian politics   192–93

Backward Class   124
Balagopal, K.   76, 169
Bangalore   120, 126, 131, 134, 137, 143, 146–47, 170, 185
Bernstein, Henry   3, 6, 11, 17, 26–28, 35–36, 40, 48, 83, 111–12, 116, 160–61, 170
Bharatiya Kisan Union   76
biofuels   133, 156, 171
biotechnology   90–91, 178, 193, 195
Bonefeld, Werner   6, 8, 11, 38, 41, 52–53, 66, 88, 160, 164, 171
Borras, Jun   2–3, 26, 29, 113, 151, 160, 162, 171, 175, 188, 194
Braudel   150, 172
Brazil   29, 182, 193, 195
Brazil-China soy-meat   202
Breman, Jan   146, 172
Brenner, Robert   10, 35, 41, 77, 86, 159, 165, 172
BRICS   5, 15, 29–30, 171, 175–76, 188
British Empire   9, 16–18
British hegemony   107

capital accumulation   2, 10–11, 13, 15–18, 22, 41–42, 83, 85–86, 88, 93–94, 106, 109–10, 190
capitalism   5–6, 35, 41, 43–45, 47, 49, 64–65, 67, 117, 119, 168, 171–72, 190, 194
   historical   65
   modern world   170
   peripheries of   198
   supply chain   168

INDEX   205

capitalist farmers   69, 78, 93
  dominant   69, 103
  emergent   54
  export-oriented   102
capitalist stagnation   82, 92, 166
capitalist state   11, 83–84, 109, 159, 162, 165, 171
capital's food regime   9, 11–13, 15, 41, 50–51, 58, 60, 62, 92, 107, 109–10, 112, 114, 159, 164–66
caste   45–46, 49, 55, 71–72, 74, 126–28, 146, 153, 156, 170, 175, 185, 187
  dominant   78, 124, 139, 144, 183
  higher   124, 147
  lower   58, 124, 147
  prevalent   139
  upper   149
  upper/middle   79
Chamarajanagar   135–36
Chatterjee, Partha   53, 67, 94, 174
China   10, 15, 28, 30–33, 85–86, 164, 167, 169–70, 175, 177, 182–83, 185, 189
China and India   10, 85, 167, 169
China and Latin America   32, 188
Circuits of capital   50, 59, 65, 166
Circular labour migration   27, 198
Civil society   51, 59, 67, 94, 159, 202
Class Analysis   4, 6, 46, 62–83
Class coalitions   69
  dominant   74, 93
Class composition   13, 53, 57, 59, 82
  complex   82
Class compromise   89, 95
Class dynamics   80, 91, 95, 170
Classes   26–28, 51–52, 59, 67–68, 70–72, 74–75, 77, 81–82, 109–10, 129–30, 142–44, 146, 148, 156, 160–61, 184–85, 195
  accumulating   20
  bourgeoisie   93
  corporate   98
  differentiated   6–7, 59
  divided   48
  dominated   38
  hegemonic   92
  landed   20
  middle   50, 172
  neo-middle   58
  particular   22

  rural   45, 68, 193
  subaltern   93, 106
  upper   72, 88
  variegated   165
classes of labour   6, 26, 89, 95
class interests   56, 69, 76, 80–81
  antagonistic   67
  contradictory   56
  dominant   70, 80, 110
class struggle   6–8, 11–13, 20, 34, 41, 55, 60, 63, 83–84, 161–62, 165
climate   2, 118, 143, 188
climate change   174, 188, 199
colonialism   18, 178
colonies   17, 19
  semi-tropical   18
  temperate settler   19
  tropical   19
colonization   111
  internal   201
commodities   17–18, 20, 39–40, 115, 144, 171
  agricultural   3, 17, 39, 74, 141
commodity frontiers   107–8, 110, 112, 115, 117–20, 128, 130, 134, 147–48, 155–56, 163, 166, 173
commodity production   64, 117
  petty   27, 175
Communist Party of India   98, 196
competition   33, 54, 99, 150, 199
  inter-capitalist   169
compromise equilibria   102, 110, 159
Congress Party   57–58, 69
contestations   15, 75–76, 86, 169
Corn Laws   18–19
corporate capital   1, 3, 24, 50, 56–57, 59, 74, 90–91, 94, 131
corporate concentration   2, 22, 59, 69
corporate food regime   3–4, 24–26, 28, 30–32, 62, 64, 66, 87, 89, 91, 114–16, 118, 160, 162, 188–89
corporate sector   131, 169
  concentrated   25
cotton   21, 135, 143, 148, 199
counter-movements   12, 26, 52, 62–84, 100, 156, 162
  global food sovereignty   63
  peasant   66, 75
COVID-19 pandemic   10, 101

credit   74, 134, 197, 200
crisis   3, 9–12, 23, 25, 41, 46, 48, 62–84, 156, 162, 165–66, 173–74
critical agrarian studies   2, 51, 113, 171, 176, 189, 199
cropping patterns   18, 40, 115, 127, 129, 153, 174
crops   112–13, 116, 118, 120–21, 126, 129–31, 135, 139, 142–45, 148–51, 154, 156, 163

dairy   151, 153, 192
deagrarianization   77
debts   139, 149, 185, 197
Deccan region   19–20
degradation   7
   environmental   23, 49, 108, 133
Democracy   53, 170, 183, 192–93, 196, 201
Development Studies   170, 184, 193–94
dialectics   64, 90, 167, 171, 189–90, 193
   capital-labour   95
disaggregating   28, 33, 35, 50
disaggregation   8, 27–28
dispossession   7, 47–48, 51, 58, 160, 168, 175, 180, 187, 196, 201–2
   accumulation by   26, 46, 113, 116, 159, 166
distress   48, 75, 80, 82, 134, 166
diversification   57, 78, 114, 133–34, 170
dominant classes   27, 38, 53–54, 68, 72, 78, 80, 86, 89, 93, 146
dominant farmers   54, 56–57, 77–78, 144–45, 151
downscaling   4, 6, 11, 34, 36, 110–11, 161, 164
droughts   75, 97, 126, 134, 141, 143, 149, 170

ecology   107, 118, 190
eco-Marxism   65, 118, 129
economy   47–48, 56–57, 59, 70, 74, 90, 93, 95, 168, 172, 175, 179, 181
   agro-industrial   68
   broader   146–47
   changed agrarian   21
   global capitalist   77
   industrial   21
   informal   48
   jobless growth   81
   labour-oriented household   146
   largest agricultural   69
   local   74
   national   36, 111
   need   48
   post-liberalisation   173
   rising   85
   rural   63
   stagnant agricultural   130
   world food   178
efficiency   86, 100, 106
elections   58, 102, 158–59
   national   98, 158
elites   56, 67, 89, 94
employment   27, 77, 146
   causal   147
   regular   146
   wage   27
Endnotes   160, 170, 177
environments   23, 25, 71, 75, 129, 167–68, 173, 177, 179, 184, 186, 188, 200–201
equilibria, unstable   38, 58, 88–89, 95–96, 106–7, 110
exploitation   7, 20, 27, 39, 117, 119, 146, 149, 155
export   18–19, 132
extraction   8, 20, 117, 168

family farms   20, 81
famines   19, 21, 97, 198
farmer-labourers   81, 143
Farmers' suicides   74, 185, 191
farming   6, 27, 75, 78, 82, 121, 142, 160, 202
   contract   103, 188, 198
farm laws struggle   80, 187
financialisation   64, 72, 81, 190, 197
first food regime   9, 14, 16–22, 25, 39, 107, 197
flex crops   118, 156, 171
Food corporation of India   99, 174, 182
food grains   18, 99–100, 106
food insecurity   87, 96
food regime analysis   4–5, 85–86, 109–10, 155, 162
food security   21, 31–32, 87–88, 96, 104, 106, 169, 173, 177, 183, 194
food security apparatus   58, 106–7
food sovereignty   7, 26, 62, 66, 80, 91, 170, 176, 186, 201
Friedmann, Harriet   2–3, 9, 15–19, 21, 23–24, 34–35, 38–39, 64–66, 112, 114, 116, 178–79

gender   27, 55, 74, 197

INDEX   207

Global South   21, 29, 58, 113, 186
global value relations   5, 8–9, 13, 37,
    39–40, 60–61, 111–12, 114, 118–19, 157, 161,
    163, 165–66
government   1, 73, 75, 88, 95, 97–98, 100–102,
    104, 131, 183, 185
Government of India   73, 174
Government of Karnataka   174, 185
Gramsci, Antonio   38, 51, 53, 63, 67–68, 95,
    172, 179, 191, 202
Green Revolution   21–22, 68–70, 74, 76, 78,
    83–84, 86, 98–99, 104–5, 107–8, 114,
    129–30, 133
Grundrisse   5, 28, 163, 188
Gunn, Richard   6, 8, 164, 179

Hanur   121, 123–24, 126–28, 136–37, 141, 144,
    146, 149, 151, 154, 196
Harriss-White, Barbara   27, 43–45, 47, 49, 54,
    69, 104, 121, 130, 181
Harvey, David   8, 65, 72, 92, 101, 103, 106, 108,
    116, 166, 181
health   80, 121, 150, 185
hegemonic   22, 24, 59, 89, 94, 172
hegemony   8–9, 11, 13, 37–38, 41, 44, 52–54,
    88, 90–91, 94, 96, 177, 179
    capitalist   63, 67
    corporate   11, 25, 89, 91
    international   91
    neoliberal   91
Hindu Nationalism   175, 183, 189
hunger   87, 101–2, 106

ideology   169, 181
    legitimising   86
    social democratic   58
immanent critique   3–4, 14, 161, 163, 166
imperialism   9, 18, 32, 68, 111, 194, 201
indebtedness   49, 197
India and China   30, 182
Indian governments   70, 75, 98, 108, 114, 129
Indian state   54, 56–57, 59, 62, 92–93, 95–96,
    129, 133, 174, 176, 180–81, 197, 200
    modern   93
    new   173
    postcolonial   20
    southern   13
institutions   15–17, 24, 171, 176, 179, 197, 201
    crumbling   92

international   19, 24, 29
public   51
scientific   36
integral state   22, 44, 51–60, 67–69, 74, 83, 91,
    159, 162
irrigation   71, 123, 126–27, 135, 142–43
    borewell   126
    canal   123

justice   181–82

Kannada   121, 127, 143
Polany, Karl   172, 175
Karnataka   76, 78–79, 112–13, 121, 124, 128,
    133–36, 146, 151, 174, 182, 185, 195–96
kharif   114, 121, 135
Kurubas   124, 126, 128, 153

labour   10–13, 15, 17–18, 26–27, 38–39, 55,
    58–59, 77, 81–82, 108–10, 117–18, 142–48,
    156, 160–63, 195
    additional   153, 155
    agricultural   27, 139, 144–47, 150
    bonded   144
    cheap   119
    domestic   157
    hired   76, 148
    non-human   157
    non-wage   20
    organizing   40
    rural   50, 187
    unpaid   20, 118
    women's   191
labourers   144–45
    hired   144, 148
    landless   82
    migrant   136–37
    rural-based   195
    wage   137, 144
labour migration   27, 146–47
labour regimes   111, 118, 144, 168
    local   173
land   26–27, 45–46, 48, 51, 65–66, 80–81, 124,
    136–37, 139–40, 142–45, 147–51, 154, 171,
    177–78, 187–89
land grabbing   46, 113, 190
land grabs   176, 179, 187, 189, 193
    cumulative   193
    violent   116

landholdings 68, 72, 76, 124, 126–27
landlordism 55, 181
landlords 45, 55
landscapes 118, 127, 136, 144, 198
Late Capitalism 8, 168
Late Victorian Holocausts 19, 176
Latin America 25, 32–33, 91, 171, 188, 193–94, 201
laws 1, 80–81, 98, 103, 200
legislation 86, 97, 163
   agricultural 1
   land acquisition 192
legitimacy 65, 67, 94, 96
Lerche, Jens 4, 27, 43–45, 47–48, 50, 68, 75, 81–82, 143, 161, 187
liberalisation 23, 45, 68, 74, 93, 104–5, 175, 180, 200
Lingayats 124, 128, 139, 141, 143, 146, 153
livelihoods 55, 62, 81–82, 89, 127, 129, 142–43, 147, 152, 154, 156, 196, 200
   degraded 75
   destabilising 25
   labour-oriented 148, 156
   mixed 27
   multifunctional agrarian 24
   peasant 25
   stressed 149
livestock 18, 70, 120, 127, 132, 151–53
livestock economy 152–54, 156
localism 111, 120, 164
logistics 31, 182
long downturn 10, 23, 31, 35, 41, 58, 77, 92, 159, 166, 172

Madhya Pradesh 70, 120, 133
Madras Presidency 121, 123, 136
maize 113–15, 119–21, 123, 128–35, 140–42, 144, 148–56, 180, 185, 197–98
markets 17, 21, 24–25, 58, 63, 66–67, 89, 91–92, 104–6, 137, 140–42, 173, 175
   administered 140
   agricultural commodity 201
   domestic 18, 104
   foodgrains 101
   formal 106
   informal 106
   integrated 19–20
   international 74
   licensed 103
   regional 144
   regulated 140
   seed 105
   world food staples 19
Marx, Karl 5, 7, 10, 34, 41, 47, 50, 74, 119–20, 160–65, 167, 188, 196, 198, 205
Marxism 6, 192, 199–200
Marxist 51, 67, 91, 98, 196
materiality 39, 120, 161, 163
McMichael, Philip 2–6, 9, 14–18, 20–26, 29–32, 36, 38–39, 50, 62–66, 74–75, 87–91, 107, 112–14, 116–18, 188–89
meatification 3, 50, 114, 156, 184
metabolic rifts 79, 182
methodological nationalism 37, 52, 68, 83, 85
   predominant 85
methods 40, 112, 120, 180
milk 151, 153–54
mobilisations 7, 57, 62, 66, 75, 78, 82, 95, 110, 158, 161
   counter-hegemonic 160
   grassroots 97
modes of existence of capital 28, 37, 92, 110
Modi 1, 59, 80, 95, 98, 100, 102, 159, 168, 190, 199
Modi government 58, 80, 101, 103, 158
Modi's authoritarian populist regime 1, 13, 59, 93, 114, 158–59
Modi's government 95, 98–100, 133
Modi's India 183–84, 197
Modi's regime 57, 70, 80, 100, 102, 133, 158–59
moneylenders 121, 149
Moore, Jason W. 20, 22, 64–65, 74, 104, 106, 108–9, 117–19, 129, 190–91, 205
multipolarity 5, 11, 28, 30, 32, 36, 188
Mysore 123, 136

Naidus 72, 139, 144, 191
National Democratic Alliance 98
neoliberal 11, 31, 40, 77, 90, 117, 129, 164
neoliberalisation 12–13, 47, 55–57, 59, 84–85, 87–111, 114, 162–63, 166, 173
neoliberalism 28, 53, 60, 62, 71, 83, 86, 88–89, 91–92, 109–10, 176, 181, 186, 190, 191, 195, 199, 201
   authoritarian 101
   embedded 177
   expedited 58, 69, 98
   roll-out 57

INDEX

neoliberal period   11, 63, 74, 84, 94, 114
neoliberal reforms   48, 56–57, 60, 66, 68, 77, 87, 114, 190
neomercantilism   31–33, 170
neoregulation   89–91, 195
New Farmers' Movements   172–73, 195
new rights agenda   57, 96, 197
NFSA   87–88, 97–98, 100, 102, 109

Open Marxism   61, 82, 88, 92, 164, 171, 196
opposition   1, 52, 69, 98, 158
oppression   27, 55
Other Backward Classes   58, 78, 124

paddy   115, 120, 135, 199
passive revolution   53, 93, 185, 191
patronage   57, 173
Pattenden, Jonathan   27, 77–78, 82, 89, 124, 144, 146, 194–95
peasants   4, 26, 52, 62, 75, 81–82, 160, 168, 174, 176, 189
periodization   14–16, 35, 62
peripheries   17, 136
Philippines   20, 36, 39, 117
Polanyi, Karl   17, 34, 63, 66–67, 75, 79, 171, 196
policies
    agricultural   104, 106, 176
    food subsidy   169
    foreign   21, 31
    mercantilist   17
    national food security   97
political ecology   26, 46, 49, 120, 169, 178, 200
political economy   45, 48, 58–59, 81–82, 93, 168–71, 178, 181, 185, 188, 190–91, 194, 197
    bovine   70, 184
    broader   128, 149
    global   3, 10, 16, 20, 30–31, 33, 151, 164, 174
political negotiations   13, 32, 110, 163
polycentrism   5, 30
populism   80, 98, 173
    authoritarian   159, 184, 199
Postcolonial India   9, 11–12, 18, 43–61, 92, 109
Postone, Moishe   14, 119
Poulantzas, Nicos   38, 91, 196
poultry   131–32, 151
poverty   1, 78, 94–95, 150, 175, 186
poverty line   87
    national   87, 106

power   29, 51, 53–55, 57–58, 93, 168, 170, 181–84, 186, 191, 195–97, 199, 202
    class/caste   52
    corporate   75
    legitimize   94
    localised   55
    political   69
power relations   38, 167
    international   38
    local   44, 54–55, 140
prices   20, 54, 71, 101, 140, 151, 196
    domestic agricultural   71
    fluctuating   141
    world-market   90
primitive accumulation   94–95, 159–60, 167, 175, 178, 180, 198
private sector   57–58, 103, 105, 130
productivity   108, 120, 186
    agricultural   123
    increased   55
profitability   10, 77–78, 92, 142, 151, 159
propertied classes   53
    provincial   76, 78, 80–81, 169, 185
protectionism   93, 164
protests   1, 75, 78, 81–82, 158, 173, 199
public distribution system   69, 98, 174, 190
Punjab   1, 19, 70–71, 105, 107, 120, 148, 172, 199

ragi   135, 141–42, 148, 150, 153–54
rainfed land   126, 141, 148, 150, 154
reforms   93, 102, 182, 186, 191
regulations   24, 34, 90
    national   9, 14, 21
rentierism   173
repression   7, 158–60
    authoritarian   189
    violent   159
reproduction   22, 27, 65, 82, 148
    daily   26
    long-term   71
    material   77
    social   11, 81, 108, 149, 179, 190–91
resistance   43, 62–63, 68, 79, 83, 90, 171, 177, 193, 201
resources   56, 72, 150, 160, 167
    agricultural   116
rice   21–22, 98, 104–8, 114–15, 129, 135, 142, 148, 194, 200
rice-wheat   104–6, 108, 129

Right-to-Food   12, 57, 85–109, 163
risks   14, 16, 95, 197
ruling classes   51, 94
   domestic   21–22
Rural India   27, 44, 46, 49, 55, 180, 185, 188, 195, 198, 200–201
   contemporary   112, 158, 160

second food regime   9, 17, 20–24, 36, 41, 55, 60, 87, 117, 164, 196
seeds   74, 104–5, 139–40, 145
semi-arid   123, 133–34
smallholders   2, 24–25, 27, 39, 62–63, 74–75, 79, 91
social movements   15, 52, 66, 79, 107, 173, 176, 192–94
socioecological fixes   65, 84, 118, 177, 188, 194
South Asia   43, 172, 181–82, 187, 190, 192, 196–97, 199, 202
South Asian Studies   43, 67, 172, 197
South India   79, 110, 112–13, 119, 156, 163, 169, 176–77, 191, 195, 197, 200
soybeans   70, 120
   financialised   177
   transgenic   36, 201
spatial fix   65, 108, 116, 118, 133, 181
spatiality   29, 90, 191
stagnation   10, 18, 41, 48, 63, 70, 75, 77, 83, 133
   agricultural   49
   prolonged   10
   widespread agrarian   50
state intervention   17, 100, 103, 164, 167
state-owned enterprises   31–32
state policies   17, 22, 95
state regulation   90, 103–4
subalterns   67–68, 172, 184
   rural   89
Subaltern Studies   53, 67
subsidies   17, 69, 103, 117
sugarcane   135, 143
support prices   115
   minimum   69, 99, 102
surplus populations   170, 200
   latent   81

relative   10
sustainable agriculture   46, 80, 172, 184

Tamil Nadu   45, 74, 121, 123, 133, 135, 140, 149, 151, 172, 177
technology   21–22, 135, 177, 200
   agricultural   47
   new   22, 104
   seed   131
third food regime   15–16, 23, 25, 29, 36, 172, 195, 197
trade   17, 19, 21, 76, 194
   agricultural   90
   commodity futures   197
   grain   32
   informal   70
transnational agrarian movements   26, 177
transnational corporations   24, 31, 89, 171

unemployment   77, 170
United Progressive Alliance   58, 98
unpaid work   20, 39, 117, 119, 155, 163, 173

value-form   6–8, 14, 34, 38, 61, 66, 85, 92, 156, 161, 164
value relations   6, 42, 164–65
   expanding global   157
   historical   5, 40, 92, 164
   lobal   39, 111
   political face of global   8, 111
Vasavi, A. R.   43, 46, 49, 74, 77, 149, 201
Vía Campesina   3, 6, 26, 83–84, 176
   transnational movement   62
village studies   44–45, 54
violence   116, 158–60, 198

wage labour   20, 77, 120, 143, 147, 149, 155
Warman, Arturo   150–51, 154, 202
wastelands   124, 137, 150, 169
wheat   18–19, 21–22, 98, 104–8, 114–15, 129, 187, 195
work   39, 44–46, 64, 69, 72, 80–81, 88, 90, 117–18, 136–37, 145–46, 148–49, 151–53

www.ingramcontent.com/pod-product-compliance
Lightning Source LLC
Chambersburg PA
CBHW070620030426
42337CB00020B/3870